Illustrator CS Most Wanted
Techniques and Effects

Matt Kloskowski

friendsof

DESIGNER TO DESIGNER™

an Apress® company

Illustrator CS Most Wanted: Techniques and Effects

Distributed to the book trade in the United States by Springer-Verlag New York, Inc., 175 Fifth Avenue, New York, NY 10010 and outside the United States by Springer-Verlag GmbH & Co. KG, Tiergartenstr. 17, 69112 Heidelberg, Germany.

In the United States: phone 1-800-SPRINGER, e-mail orders@springer-ny.com, or visit http://www.springer-ny.com. Outside the United States: fax +49 6221 345229, e-mail orders@springer.de, or visit http://www.springer.de.

For information on translations, please contact Apress directly at 2560 Ninth Street, Suite 219, Berkeley, CA 94710. Phone 510-549-5930, fax 510-549-5939, e-mail info@apress.com, or visit http://www.apress.com.

The source code for this book is freely available to readers at http://www.friendsofed.com in the Downloads section.

Credits

Lead Editor
Gavin Wray

Production Manager
Kari Brooks

Technical Reviewer
Michael Hamm

Production Editor
Laura Cheu

Editorial Board
Steve Anglin, Dan Appleman, Gary Cornell, Tony Davis, John Franklin, Chris Mills, Steve Rycroft, Dominic Shakeshaft, Jim Sumser, Karen Watterson, Gavin Wray, John Zukowski

Compositor
Dina Quan

Proofreader
Elizabeth Berry

Indexer
Michael Brinkman

Project Manager
Nate McFadden

Artist
Kinetic Publishing Services, LLC

Copy Manager
Nicole LeClerc

Cover Designer
Kurt Krames

Copy Editor
Mark Nigara

Manufacturing Manager
Tom Debolski

Contents at a Glance

Contents

Chapter 4: Trendy Effects **91**

Chapter 5: 3D Effects **123**

Chapter 6: Adding Depth and Dimension **147**

Chapter 7: Illustrator Animation Techniques **171**

Foreword

When I started my design career, I was introduced to a number of applications and tools that would make my life easier. The one that caught my eye, as well as the eyes of many other designers, was Adobe Photoshop. At the time, I believed this software powerhouse could do anything I wanted it to. Of course, hiding in the shadow of that wild program was a curious thing called Adobe Illustrator.

Looks and sounds too technical, I thought. What could it possibly offer me that Photoshop could not? Besides, the learning curve looked daunting and I really didn't have the time. And so, for about five years I ignored the world's most popular vector application. With each new release, I'd launch the program, make the same quick, on-the-spot judgment I'd always made of it and make a quick exit. What couldn't be done in Photoshop just couldn't be done, I thought.

Aside from an increase in the Photoshop "frustration factor," what ultimately changed my attitude towards Illustrator was the artwork I was seeing in the illustration and design annuals that crossed my desk. Clean, crisp, smooth lines that made for some astounding and outstanding images. Under the "medium-used" attribution shown alongside a piece, I'd see Adobe Illustrator or 100% vector.

I dusted off my user's manual and read it from front to back, trying out the tools in Illustrator. At the same time, I also bought a massive, Illustrator know-it-all reference book. While both the manual and this book were useful for explaining the basic ins and outs of Illustrator, the books left out all the cool stuff. So here I was, self-taught with all the facts but none of the techniques. How do I make a swanky glow for my artwork? How can I make my text look all *Matrix*-like? And just how do I begin to wrap my mind around the Mesh tool?!

In-depth, step-by-step books such as the one you're holding in your hands now weren't exactly filling the shelves at my local bookstore. And if a book did get my attention, the techniques were just slightly more useful than what I'd found in the manual. In other words, these books were useful for learning but useless in the real world. That said, I'd find books that discussed the things I wanted to do but never thoroughly explained how to do them. Imagine making your way through the explanation and discovering that the author had skipped a few steps to get to the finished results. Perhaps the author couldn't bear letting us in on ALL of their tricks.

This book, *Illustrator CS Most Wanted: Techniques and Effects,* is a bit different. It not only shows you the effects but also explains, in depth, how to get from a blank Artboard to vector lusciousness quickly and effectively.

About the Author

Matt Kloskowski is a writer, instructor, illustrator, and graphic designer based out of Tampa, FL. As well as being an Adobe Certified Expert, he holds certifications in Macromedia Flash, is a Microsoft Certified Solutions Developer (MCSD), and is an expert in dynamic- and database-driven website development. He is a 1995 graduate of the University of South Florida with majors in computer information systems and marketing. Matt hosts both an Illustrator (www.ExtremeIllustrator.com) and Photoshop (www.ExtremePhotoshop.com) website where he provides tutorials on all aspects of using the two programs. Matt's tutorials have been used in over 15 schools throughout the United States and have been translated into seven languages. He also writes a weekly column for the National Association of Photoshop Professionals (NAPP) and *Mac Design* magazine's website. In his spare time Matt enjoys jogging, golfing, playing video games, and spending time with his wife Diana and two toddler sons Ryan and Justin in their Tampa home.

About the Technical Reviewer

Michael Hamm is a freelance designer and illustrator living in Houston, Texas. He started www.ErgoDraw.com in 2001 as a way to teach others about Adobe Illustrator and digital illustration through a series of in-depth tutorials. He is a 1996 graduate of the Art Institute of Houston. Michael also teaches a number of illustration classes to students worldwide at Sessions.edu Online School of Design and, on occasion, enters the real-word classroom for instruction as well. You can reach Michael at his website http://looktwo.com.

Acknowledgments

This is the part of the book where I get to thank everyone who has helped me along my journey as a writer, instructor, illustrator, and graphic artist. I've seen many acknowledgment pages before and always thought it was a cliché when an author writes about how there isn't enough room to thank all of those involved. The funny thing is that after writing this book, I no longer think it's a cliché—in fact, they're all right. This is such a large undertaking and there is no way to give thanks to all of those who deserve it in such a short space. However, I'll try my best.

First off, I'd like to thank the technical editor for this book, Michael Hamm. He is a very talented illustrator and has kept me honest through this entire process. Although this was my first experience writing a book, I can't imagine having anyone else review my work. He has truly contributed a huge amount to the quality of this book. I'd also like to thank the editor from friends of ED, Gavin Wray, for believing in this book (and for living in the UK so I could have someone to instant message at 5 a.m. with my ideas).

Next, I'd like to thank those who have directly or indirectly inspired and helped me throughout the writing of this book and my career, specifically Roger Kohler, Scott Kelby, Robin Barna (my high school English teacher), and Bill Moore (my college writing professor). I'd also like to thank Stewart Sandler (www.fontdiner.com) and Brad Nelson (www.braineaters.com) for contributing some of the fonts used in this book and allowing them to be included on the download website so you can follow along. In addition, thanks to Kevin Ames (www.amesphoto.com) for contributing the photograph used in the photo vectorization project.

Also, thanks to my friends at NAPP, Jeff Kelby and Stacy Behan—you've given me great opportunities and been a pleasure to work with.

To my family, I can't begin to express my appreciation enough. Mom and Dad, you've always been an inspiration and encouraged me to do whatever I wanted to in life. Your guidance continues to be something that I depend on constantly. You are two of the finest people I know and I could not ask for better parents. To my older brother and sister and your spouses, Ed and Kerry, Kristine and Scott—you've been siblings that I've always looked up to and respected. Thanks for giving me something to strive for.

As for my sons Ryan and Justin, thank you for making me remember two of the most important things in my life—both of you. In other words, thanks for doing your best to divert me from getting any work done. Those forced breaks were often the most necessary things, and they always helped keep things in perspective for me.

And finally, to my beautiful wife Diana. Words cannot express the love, respect, and appreciation that I feel for having you in my life. Writing this book has been a dream come true for me, one that I would not have been able to realize without your help and guidance. You are truly the most wonderful mother and wife I could have ever hoped to find. The work you have put toward helping me write this book can never be repaid.

Introduction

If you're reading this, you most likely have some idea about what Adobe Illustrator CS is and what this program is capable of, but you may not know just how accessible it is to you. The following chapters will show you just that. From beginner techniques to advanced effects, this book will show you how and why Illustrator can be such an addictive tool. It rewards your comprehension by offering you faster and easier methods of achieving your final goals with your artwork. It fosters your creativity by presenting you with one of the richest toolsets any artist can ask for. The best part is that you can learn all of this while working through real-world projects that are geared toward teaching you some of the most wanted effects requested by aspiring illustrators. And, you can do it at your own pace. This book was written in a nonlinear fashion. This means that you can jump from Chapter 1 to Chapter 9 if you find an effect that you just can't wait to get to. Also, all the source files can be found in the Downloads section at www.friendsofed.com. I've provided some artwork to start with so that you can work from the same original file that I used. In addition, every finished Illustrator source file is included in case you need help getting to the end. Heck, there are even some free fonts so you can follow along and use the same font that the exercise uses to complete the effect.

So what are you waiting for? Sit down at your keyboard and turn to an exercise. Then get ready to delve into one of the greatest illustration programs that exist today. Soon you'll be creating artwork that's worth bragging about to your friends and family. Have fun!

Chapter 1

DRAWING AND PAINTBRUSH EFFECTS

Drawing tools are at the very heart of Adobe Illustrator. Without sophisticated drawing tools, Illustrator would differ little from Adobe Photoshop.

In this chapter, you'll learn essential techniques and effects that you need to take drawing in Illustrator to the next level. You'll learn how to work with Illustrator's drawing and painting tools so you can let Illustrator help you perfect your paths and paintbrushes, leaving you with more time for the creative aspect of illustration. Those already familiar with Illustrator's Pen tool will benefit most from this topic, as I don't cover the basics of drawing a path. Instead, you'll delve into more advanced path operations such as stroking, compound, joining, and averaging paths. You'll learn to add, manipulate, and delete anchor points. Finally, you'll learn how to create your own custom brushes to aid you in your designs or brushes that will eventually become the design.

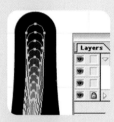

Using template layers in Illustrator

Illustrator's template layers can be a great asset when it comes to re-creating line art or tracing an already rasterized image to make it vector based. If you're already familiar with layers, then using a template layer will seem very intuitive to you. Also, with the tips you'll learn in this exercise, you'll be ready to start vectorizing your artwork in no time.

1. You'll need to complete a few tasks before you even open Illustrator. You'll need to scan a clean version of your artwork. Some guidelines for this process include scanning at a large resolution (you can always reduce it later) and trying to scan as clean a copy as possible. If you've drawn something by hand, make sure that any eraser marks have been removed and make an attempt to straighten any folds that may appear on your artwork. After you've scanned the piece, save the file in a format that Illustrator can read. TIF files work great for this process, but other formats such as GIF and JPEG will do as well.

2. Next, open Illustrator. You're going to place your scanned artwork into a new file. Choose File ➤ New. Select RGB Color as the Color Mode and click OK.

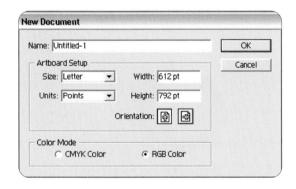

3. Choose File ➤ Place.

4. Check Template and choose a scanned artwork file that you've created. If you don't have a scanned file to work with, use `Chapter_01_myScannedArtwork.tif` from this chapter's source files. Finally, click Place.

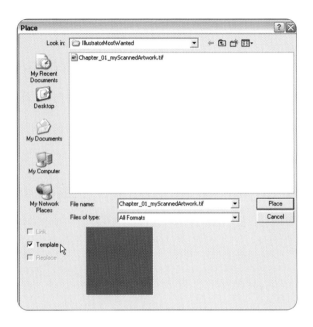

5. Illustrator has now imported your scanned artwork and generated an entirely new layer as a template layer. By default, this template layer will not print, is locked, and is dimmed to 50% opacity to make tracing easier for you.

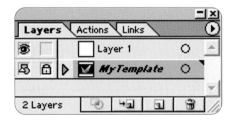

Before moving on, keep in mind that you aren't limited to Illustrator's default template settings. You can change them by performing the following steps.

6. Double-click the template layer. Alternatively, you could open the Layers palette's options menu by clicking the small arrow inside the circle at the upper-right corner of the palette and selecting Options for *(your file name)*.

7. Illustrator will bring up the Layer Options dialog box. Notice that you can change several settings, such as the name of the template layer and the color of the layer that Illustrator uses to represent it in the Layers palette, and you can choose to lock/unlock, show/hide, and print/not print the layer. Also, remember that Illustrator automatically dims this layer to 50% opacity. You can change that percentage here too, depending on your personal preference.

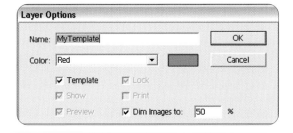

> You don't always have to follow the File ➤ Place method of creating a template layer. You can just as easily create one by displaying the layer options as described in step 6 for any layer. Then, just check the Template *check box and your regular layer will become a template layer just like that.*

OK, now that your artwork is in Illustrator, you're ready to trace, right? The answer is maybe. If you're happy with the artwork, then get right to it and start tracing. The Pen tool is the most accurate tool for this task, and it will be the primary drawing tool you use throughout this book. However, you may notice now (or during the tracing process) that your scanned artwork isn't quite working for your tracing needs. You have two options at this point. You can move into your favorite image-editing program (such as Photoshop or Fireworks), open your scanned file, and make modifications to it that will make it easier or more accurate for you to trace. Unfortunately, Illustrator doesn't offer a jumping point directly into Photoshop (or Fireworks, for that matter), so you'll need to manually start up Photoshop and open your file for modification. When you're done, save the file and re-import your artwork into Illustrator. Alternatively, you can make some simple changes right here in Illustrator. Since the subject of this book is Illustrator, I bet you can guess which method I'll cover here.

8. Once you've decided to modify your template, you first need to convert it to a regular layer. Do this by double-clicking the layer and unchecking Template in the Layer Options dialog box. Click OK and you're now free to edit that layer however you see fit.

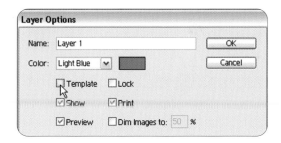

> You can also click the menu arrow with the template layer highlighted. You'll see a small check mark next to the word Template. *Clear the* Template *check box and your template layer will become a regular layer.*

9. You can now use a few Illustrator filters to help correct your image. If you choose Filter ➤ Color, you'll see several useful effects for helping out your artwork.

A few of the effects are outlined here:

- Adjust Colors: This option is fairly self-explanatory. With this filter, you can adjust the colors of your artwork to bring out certain details.

- Convert to Grayscale: This option converts the image to black, white, and shades of gray. It's very useful when you want to remove all color from your template.

- Invert Colors: This option creates inverse color values of your selected image.

- Saturate: This filter lightens or darkens the colors in your selected image. This is useful when you need to bring out detailed and colored areas so you can trace them more easily.

The Filter ➤ Sharpen ➤ Unsharp Mask option is also useful when you need to develop some contrast in any pencil artwork that you've scanned.

Keep in mind that any filters you apply to your artwork are permanent changes to the layer. They aren't live effects, so the only way to revert back to your original is to re-import the original file.

Now seems a good time to explain the difference between the Filter and Effect menus. Basically, whenever you apply a filter to your artwork, you're making a permanent change. You can't modify or remove this change unless you use the Undo function within Illustrator. However, once you close your Illustrator document or exhaust the number of undos you can revert to, you will no longer be able to change the settings applied by the filter. Effects, on the other hand, are **live**. This means that you can modify or delete the changes applied by an effect at any time by using the Appearance palette. So, the eternal question arises: Why use a filter when you can use an effect? The answer is you don't. Unless you wish to use one of the few (and I mean *few*) filters that only exist in the Filter menu, there's no reason to use a filter. Use an effect instead.

10. Once you're done, simply double-click the layer again and check the Template check box. This will convert your layer back into a template and set you up for tracing once again.

Now that you're set up for tracing, just select your Pen tool and start drawing your lines. Here's one more quick tip for you. If you've used the Pen tool before, you know that you have a stroke and a fill associated with every object you draw. So, what happens if you're tracing your artwork and you realize that you forgot to clear out your fill color for that shape? Now the fill color will start getting in the way of what you're tracing. Sure, you can clear out the fill for that object, but what happens after you've traced your entire piece of artwork and filled your objects accordingly, and you realize that you forgot to trace a small portion of the original that's hidden underneath a filled object? Now you have to go in and remove the fill for that object. Tired of the hypothetical questions yet? Hopefully, you can see that this is leading to an essential technique: Illustrator has an option called Outline.

11. To use the Outline setting, simply choose View ➤ Outline. This will remove all of the strokes and fills associated with your objects and leave you with a thin black outline where your paths exist. To return

to the default Preview mode, simply choose View ➤ Preview. In the following reference image, I've taken a screen capture of a bottle cap image that you'll create later in this chapter. The image on the left is the full colored bottle cap in Preview mode. The one on the right is the same image in Outline mode.

Alternatively, you can use the keyboard shortcut CTRL/CMD+Y.

Creating a gear wheel

If any effect falls into the "Most Wanted" category, this one does. I've seen this effect requested countless times in online forums, and I've received many messages asking me to create a tutorial on it. You'll find logos, websites, magazine ads, and brochures centered on this very shape. I've always wondered why the gear/cog shape is so sought after. Could it be that the shape itself signifies innovation and hard work—a message that many companies hope to get across? Or is it just plain cool to look at? Whatever the reason, your wish is my command. The next effect will not only teach you how to create this shape, but also give you a few ideas on how to use it in a design.

1. Create a new RGB Illustrator document.
2. Select the Ellipse tool from the Shapes flyout menu.

3. Click the Artboard once. This will bring up a dialog box asking you what size you would like your ellipse. Enter 300 pt (points) for both Width and Height.

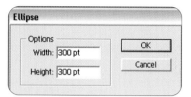

Points may be a new term for some of you. By default, Illustrator uses points as its unit of measurement. If you've used bitmap programs such as Photoshop in the past or you have a web-related background, you may be used to using pixels. If so, keep in mind that the pixel unit of measurement will yield the same result as points. However, if it truly bothers you to use points, you can simply choose Edit ➤ Preferences ➤ Units & Display Performance. *In the* General *drop-down menu, change* Points *to* Pixels.

4. Next, select the Polygon tool.
5. Click the Artboard and enter 28 pt for the Radius and 6 for the number of Sides.

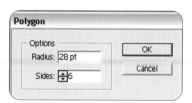

6. Make sure your Align palette is visible (Window ➤ Align).
7. Now select both of the objects using the Selection tool.

8. Set the fill color to None and the stroke color to black.

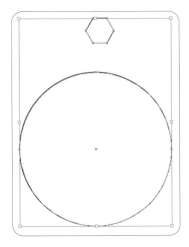

9. Select the Horizontal Align Center and the Vertical Align Center options to align the two objects.

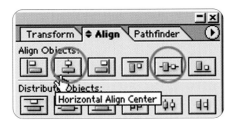

10. Select the small polygon object. Copy it (*Ctrl/Cmd+C*) and paste it in front (*Ctrl/Cmd+F*) of the circle.

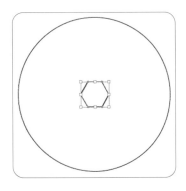

11. With the small polygon still selected, hold down the *Shift* key and press the up arrow key 15 times.

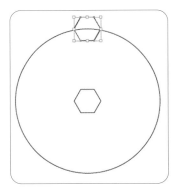

12. Select the other small polygon. Hold down the *Shift* key and press the down arrow key 15 times.

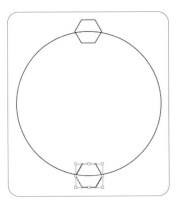

13. Next, select just the two polygons.

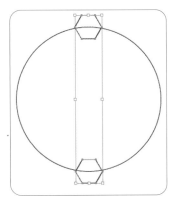

14. Choose Object ➤ Transform ➤ Rotate. Enter 30 in the Angle field.

15. Click the Copy button.

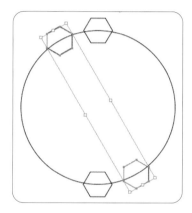

16. Create four more rotated copies of your polygons by choosing Object ➤ Transform ➤ Transform Again (or *CTRL/CMD+D*), so that you have a total of 12 small polygons around the large circle.

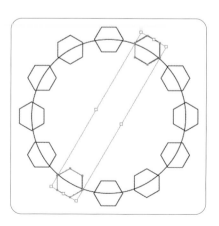

17. Next, select only the 300✕300 pt circle that you created back in step 3.

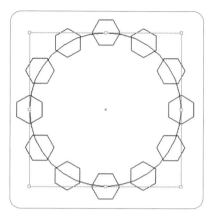

18. Choose Object ➤ Transform ➤ Scale. Select Uniform and enter a value of -60 for the Scale percentage.

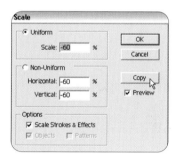

19. Click the Copy button.

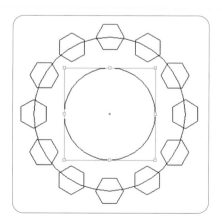

20. Now select all of your shapes by choosing Select ➤ All (*CTRL/CMD+A*).

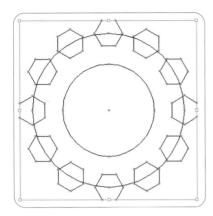

21. Make sure your Pathfinder palette is visible by choosing Window ➤ Pathfinder (or *SHIFT+F9*).

22. In the Pathfinder palette, hold down the *ALT/OPTION* key and select the Subtract from shape area option.

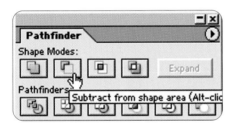

You'll notice that the ALT/OPTION key prefaces most of the Pathfinder operations you'll see in this book. The reason for this is that holding the ALT/OPTION key while you choose your Pathfinder effect will result in a new path being created. If you choose not to hold down the ALT/OPTION key, a compound path will be created instead and your original paths will still be intact. The choice is yours. Each method has its benefits and drawbacks when you work with Illustrator. As you work more with the Pathfinder effects, you'll settle in to the method that suits your workflow best.

23. Cool, huh? Instant gear. Select the gear shape and double-click the Fill selection box in the toolbox to change the fill color and to bring up the Color Picker. Set the fill color to R:5 G:92 B:122 by typing the numeric values into the corresponding text boxes. Click OK and then set the stroke color to None.

The gear should look pretty familiar by now. Next, let's add a few extra elements to spice it up a bit.

24. Select the Ellipse tool from the Shapes flyout menu.

25. Click in your Artboard and create another circle. Enter 160 pt for both width and height.

26. Set the fill color to None and set the stroke color to R:99 G:219 B:29.

27. Display the Stroke palette with Window ➤ Stroke.

28. Change the stroke Weight setting to 7 pt.

29. Select all of the shapes (Select ➤ All).

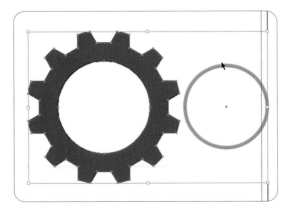

30. In the Align palette, click both the Horizontal Align Center and Vertical Align Center buttons to align all of the shapes appropriately. Your new circle shape should now be nicely aligned in the middle of the other shape.

31. Now, choose the Ellipse tool again and click the Artboard to create another ellipse. Enter 20 for the width and 150 for the height.

32. Change the fill color to None and the stroke color to R:99 G:219 B:29.

33. Change the stroke Weight setting to 4 pt.

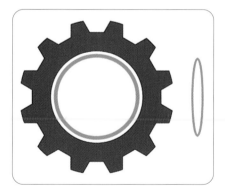

34. Once again, align this oval with the other shapes using the Horizontal Align Center and Vertical Align Center buttons in the Align palette.

35. Select the oval shape and choose Object ➤ Transform ➤ Rotate.

36. Enter 45 degrees for the Angle measurement and click the Copy button.

37. Create two more rotated copies of your oval with Object ➤ Transform ➤ Transform Again (*CTRL*/*CMD*+*D*), so you have a total of four oval shapes rotated around the center of the gear shape.

OK, it's looking good so far. Now let's add a few more elements and some text to finish it.

38. Select the Rectangle tool from the Shapes flyout menu.

39. Click the Artboard and enter 300 pt for the width and 10 pt for the height.

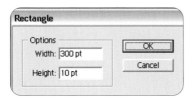

40. Make the fill color R:5 G:92 B:122 and set the stroke color to None.

41. Align this shape horizontally with the others by clicking the Horizontal Align Center button in the Align palette. Then move it into position right below the gear shape.

42. Select the rectangle with the Selection tool, choose Edit ➤ Copy, and then choose Edit ➤ Paste In Front.

43. Move this new rectangle shape down by using the arrow keys, and position it as shown in this image:

44. Create some text to fit between the rectangle shapes.

45. Finally, use the Free Transform tool (E) to modify/position the text between the two rectangles and you're done.

Creating a bottle cap

Before you get started on this project, I need to explain a few things. This illustration requires many duplicated shapes, and it can get somewhat confusing. To make this project a little easier, think of the following bottle cap illustration as having two parts, a top and a bottom, represented as a black and a gray shape, respectively:

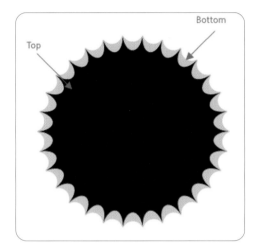

The use of these simple colors should serve to clarify the duplication process. First, let's start with the bottom shape.

1. Create a new RGB Illustrator document.

2. Select the Ellipse tool from the Shapes flyout menu.

3. Click once in the Artboard area. Enter 250 pt for both the width and height.

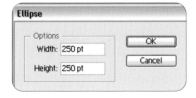

4. In this exercise, you're going to work in Outline mode, so it doesn't matter what the fill and stroke colors are right now. Go ahead and switch to Outline view (View ➤ Outline).

5. Next, create a smaller circle in a similar fashion. Click the Artboard and enter 27 pt for both the width and height.

6. Select both of the shapes.

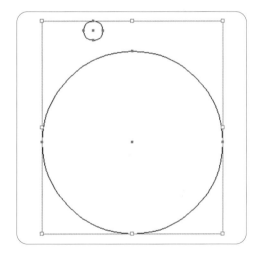

7. Use the Align palette to align the shapes both vertically and horizontally by clicking the appropriate buttons.

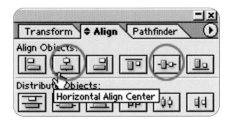

8. Select the small circle in the middle. Copy it and then select Edit ➤ Paste In Front.

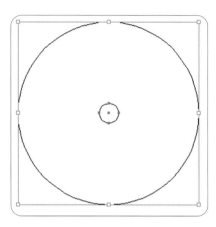

9. With the new copy still selected, hold down SHIFT and press the up arrow key 13 times.

10. Now select the other small circle. Hold down SHIFT again and press the down arrow key 13 times. This will place the circles an equal distance from each other.

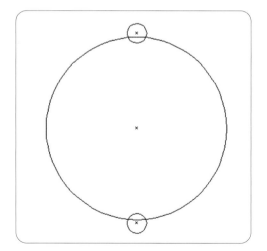

11. Select both small circles.

> You may have difficulty selecting both circles without selecting the larger circle too. The best way to do this is to click the expand layers arrow just to the left of the layer thumbnail image. You can then view all of the paths associated with this layer. Next, click the small meatball-shaped circle (see the following Note for more information) to the right of each path layer to select that path. Then SHIFT-click another layer to select it as well.

> So what's a **meatball**? "Meatball" is one of those technical terms for the small circle next to the name of the layer in the Layers palette. It may sound like an odd term, but I swear I first heard this term from Adobe's own employees at a recent conference. Ever since then, I've heard it over and over again—it seems that it's on its way to becoming an industry standard term, if you can believe that.

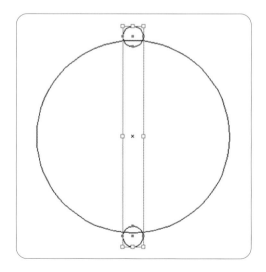

12. Choose Object ➤ Transform ➤ Rotate.

13. Enter 12 degrees for the Angle measurement and click the Copy button.

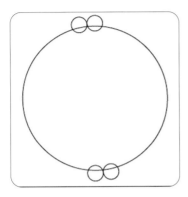

14. Create 13 more rotated copies of your circles by choosing Object ➤ Transform ➤ Transform Again (or use the shortcut *CTRL/CMD+D*), so you have a total of 30 circle shapes rotated around the larger circle.

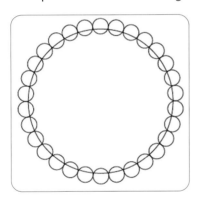

15. Select all of the shapes on the Artboard (Select ➤ All).

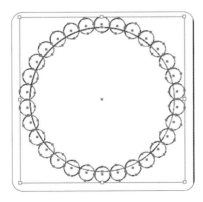

16. In the Pathfinder palette, hold down *ALT/OPTION* and click the Subtract from shape area button.

17. OK, you're done with the bottom of the bottle cap illustration. Go ahead and lock the layer and hide it for now, since you won't be using it yet.

Next, let's start the top of the bottle cap. The process is very similar to the bottom part, so I'm going to run through it rather quickly. The only difference is that the smaller shape that will get rotated around the circle is going to be an oval instead of a circle.

18. Create a new layer.

19. Select the Ellipse tool and create another large circle that's the same size as the one you created in the first part (250 pt in width and height).

20. Again using the Ellipse tool, create an oval shape. Set the width to 27 pt and the height to 50 pt.

21. Select both shapes and align them both horizontally and vertically.

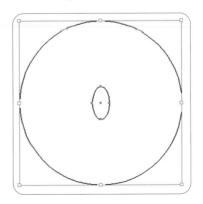

22. Select the small oval in the center. Copy and paste it on top.

23. With one oval selected, hold the *SHIFT* key and press the up arrow key 13 times. Do the same for the other oval, but press the down arrow key instead.

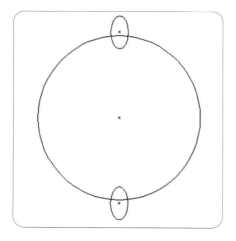

24. Select both small ovals.

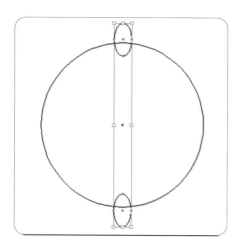

25. Choose Object ➤ Transform ➤ Rotate.

26. Enter 12 degrees for the Angle measurement and click the Copy button.

27. Create 13 more rotated copies of your circles by choosing Object ➤ Transform ➤ Transform Again (*CTRL*/*CMD+D*), so you have a total of 30 oval shapes rotated around the larger circle.

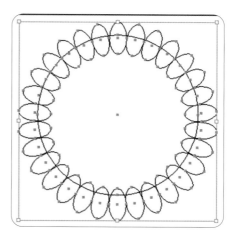

28. Select all of the shapes on this layer. (Note that you should have hidden and locked the other layer in the previous part. As a result, when you choose Select ➤ All, those shapes won't be selected.)

29. In the Pathfinder palette, hold down the *ALT*/*OPTION* key and click the Subtract from shape area button.

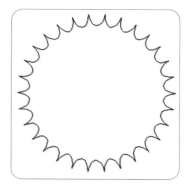

OK, now you have the top part. The rest is easy from here. You're going to add a few highlights and some depth techniques to finish it off.

30. Exit the Outline view mode by choosing View ➤ Preview.

31. Unlock the first layer you created and make it visible again.

32. Select the bottom shape and set the fill color to white and the stroke color to a medium gray. I used R:119 G:119 B:119 in the example.

33. Select the top shape, and set the fill color to red (R: 255 G:0 B:0) and the stroke color to None.

34. Select both shapes and align them horizontally and vertically.

35. Now select only the top red shape, choose Effect ➤ Stylize ➤ Inner Glow, and enter the following settings. Be sure to click the color swatch next to the Mode drop-down menu once and change the color to black. Also, check Preview so you can view your changes as you make them.

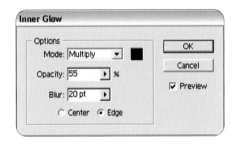

36. Your bottle cap should now look somewhat similar to this:

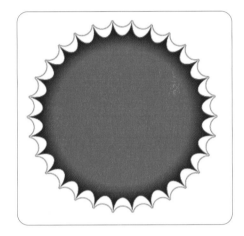

37. Now select the bottom shape. Add an inner glow to this shape with the same settings shown in the following dialog box. Be sure to select the Center radio button.

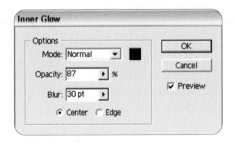

38. Your image should now look like this:

39. With the bottom shape still selected, choose Effect ➤ Stylize ➤ Drop Shadow and use the following settings:

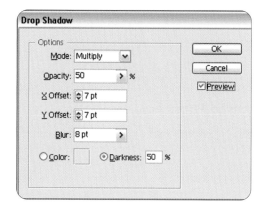

40. OK, you're almost there. Next, you're going to create a highlight and shadow. Create a new layer above the other two. Select the Ellipse tool and click the Artboard to create another circle. Enter 200 pt for the width and height.

41. Set the fill color to white and the stroke color to black.

> You can just press the D key to set your fill and stroke colors to the default settings, which are white and black, respectively.

42. Using the Ellipse tool, create another oval shape on top of the one you just created. Enter 170 for the width and 201 for the height. If it helps, change the fill color of this oval to another color so you can differentiate between the two (my example uses purple with a black stroke).

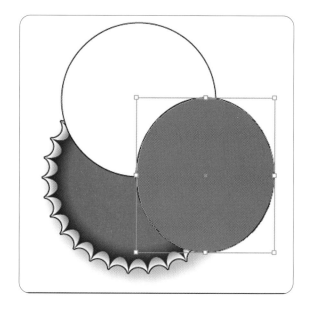

43. Select all, and align all of the shapes horizontally and vertically using the Align palette.

44. Select the purple oval and choose Object ➤ Transform ➤ Rotate. Enter -45 degrees for the Angle measurement and click OK.

45. Select both the purple oval shape and the white circle shape just below it (created in step 40).

46. Using the Pathfinder palette, hold down the *ALT/OPTION* key and click the Subtract from shape area button. You should now have an image similar to this:

47. If you click the expand arrow for this layer, notice that the previous step created a Group sublayer. Groups allow related objects to be treated as a single unit. Most Pathfinder commands automatically group separate shapes together after they're run. If you click the arrow to show the contents of the group, you'll see two paths:

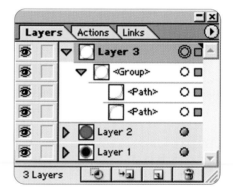

48. Select the top-left path by targeting the meatball icon for this path within the grouped sublayer. Set the fill color to white (refer to this as the highlight) and set the stroke color to None. Select the bottom-right path in the same way and make its fill color black (this will be the shadow), and set the stroke color to None.

49. Make sure the Transparency palette is visible by choosing Window ➤ Transparency.

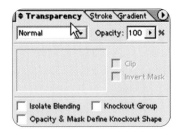

The preceding screenshot displays the full options for the Transparency palette. You can turn the display of full options on and off by selecting Show Options/Hide Options *in the Transparency palette options menu.*

50. With the shadow path (bottom right) selected, change the blending mode of the shape to Multiply. Set the Opacity percentage to 50.

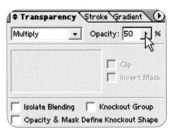

51. Now select the highlight (top left) path and set the Opacity percentage to 50.

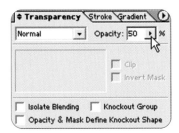

52. Finally, to add some text to the bottle cap, create a new layer *below* the highlights layer and type the word Illustrator. A bold sans-serif typeface, such as Helvetica or Arial, set at 30 pt works well here. Then with the word "Illustrator" selected, choose Effects ➤ Warp ➤ Arc. Select Horizontal and modify the Bend setting until it matches the curve of the bottle cap.

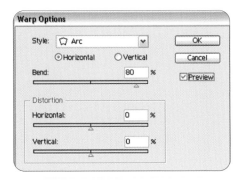

Drawing and calligraphic brush effects

Just because illustration has become almost totally digital doesn't mean you have to lose that hand-drawn feel to your work. The following effect will show you some ways to make your artwork digital but still retain some of the realistic and loose hand-drawn effects of working with paper, pencil, and pen.

1. Create a new Illustrator document.

2. Choose File ➤ Place. Before accepting the defaults and clicking the Place button, check Template. Choose the artwork file that you would like to convert to the calligraphic effect. (If you prefer, you can use the hand-drawn sketch Chapter_01_ CalligraphicBrushTemplate.tif in the source files for this chapter.) Finally, click Place.

3. Select the Pen tool. Set the fill to None and the stroke color to black.

4. Create a new layer on top of your template layer. Begin to draw lines and curves along the contours and outlines of your image where you would like to apply various brush styles. There's no need to worry about the stroke weight and other factors. Also, don't worry about fill colors yet. Just concentrate on the outlines here.

If you have an electronic drawing tablet (Wacom makes a great one; visit www.wacom.com for more information), this would be a great time to use it. You could skip down to step 9 and create your brush first, and then draw the outlines with the brush and your graphic pen and tablet.

5. This effect is very painterly, so it's not necessary to close off all of your paths. If you're drawing a path and don't want to close it off, you can press the CTRL/CMD key and click anywhere on the Artboard. You'll then be ready to start another path.

You can also press the ENTER/RETURN key when you want to end a path. The difference between using that method and the CTRL/CMD key method is that by pressing ENTER/RETURN, your path will still be active and selected. When you press CTRL/CMD and click the Artboard, your path isn't selected.

6. When you're done with the outlines, create a new layer below the Outlines layer and call it Fills. This layer will hold the objects for your solid fill colors.

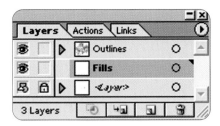

7. Lock the Outlines layer.

8. Now begin to draw the shapes that you'd eventually like to fill with a color. At this point, you can set the fill to None and use a 1 pt stroke weight to get your basic shapes in place. This is a very loose drawing, so there's no need to follow every line perfectly with a fill. The following image has the outlines dimmed so you can see the general fill shapes that have been drawn.

Now that you're done with the basic outlines and shapes that will compose the image, you need to create a calligraphic brush. Illustrator ships with a set of calligraphic brushes that are very useful, but you can also create your own. If you want to use Illustrator's brush sets, choose Window ➤ Brush Libraries ➤ Calligraphic. To create your own, just follow along with the next steps.

9. Open the Brushes palette (Window ➤ Brushes).

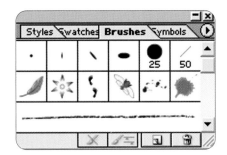

10. Click the small arrow at the top right to open the Brushes palette options menu and select New Brush.

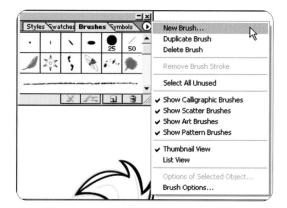

11. Select New Calligraphic Brush.

12. Enter the following settings:

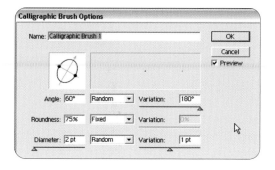

By changing the settings, you create a brush that will simulate a calligraphic pen. Many illustrators and cartoonists use this type of pen, and it produces an immediately recognizable style. Look around you during the course of your day. You'll undoubtedly see examples of this calligraphic style on TV, in magazines, and on the Web. The next step is to apply this brush to your outlines so you can try to bring some of this style into your drawing.

13. Click the Outlines layer meatball to target the Outlines layer.

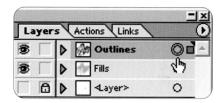

14. Notice that all of the outlines are selected. This is an example of why you put the outlines on their own layer. It makes it very simple to select them separately.

15. Click your new brush in the Brushes palette to apply it to the selected lines.

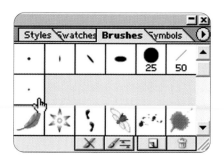

16. This step is optional. You may want to go through and select individual lines, and increase or decrease the stroke weight, or apply a different brush to them. In the following image, you can see that I've done just that. Simply click an individual line to select it, and then *SHIFT*-click additional lines to select multiple lines at once.

You may want to lock any other shapes' layers that you created when doing work like this. In fact, locking layers that you're not using is a good habit to get into when you use Illustrator. This is because in Illustrator—unlike in Photoshop—you can target objects to be selected just by clicking them. In Photoshop, everything is layer based; you always know exactly what object you're going to be working on because you must click its accompanying layer to modify it. This isn't the case in Illustrator.

Now that the outlines are taken care of, the rest is simple. Pick some colors that you would like to use for the skin tones, hair, highlights, and shadows, and add them to your Swatches palette. The easiest way to do this is to double-click the Fill selection box in the toolbox to change the fill color. This brings up the Color Picker. Set the fill color to your desired color, click OK, and then drag the Fill selection box to the Swatches palette.

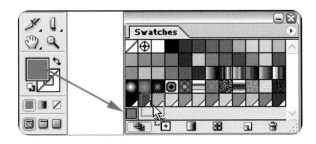

17. Select each shape and set the stroke color to None.

18. Select each shape, change the fill to an appropriate color, and you're done.

- ■ Hair color: R:239 G:187 B:69
- ■ Skin/face color: R:255 G:219 B:189
- ■ Eye color: R:113 G:215 B:255

Creating a spiral cord with a custom paintbrush

In the previous exercise, you created a brush to accentuate your lines and shapes. In essence, you used a brush to accentuate the overall illustration and effect. In this exercise, the brush you'll create will actually be the effect. And along the way, you'll learn about using a grid, using snap settings, and deleting anchor points—essential techniques that can really you help out when drawing in Illustrator.

1. Create a new RGB Illustrator file.

2. In this file you're going to create a pattern brush, the key word being *pattern*. You don't want to create every single section in the spiral cord, do you? Of course not! That's why you're just going to create a small part of it and assign that object as a pattern brush. But, since you're working with patterns, everything must be perfectly aligned and symmetrical.

To aid in this task, you're going to use Illustrator's grids, so choose View ➤ Show Grid. Your Artboard should have a pattern similar to this:

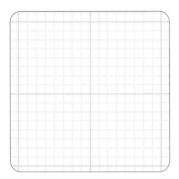

> *The keyboard shortcut for this is CTRL/CMD+". This is a good one to learn so you can toggle back and forth quickly.*

3. Next, choose View ➤ Snap To Grid. Selecting this helps when you're drawing, as it forces your anchor points into position where the grid lines intersect.

4. Select the Zoom tool and click an area in the center of your Artboard four times.

> *Alternatively, you can press CTRL/CMD and the + sign. If you want even more control, you can type your exact percentage in the text box at the bottom-left corner of your Illustrator window.*

5. Set the fill color to None and the stroke color to black. Set the stroke weight to 7 pt.

6. Select the Pen tool and begin drawing. First, click a grid point once and drag one grid square to the right.

7. Place the second point three squares up and one square to the right of the first point, and then drag up one grid square.

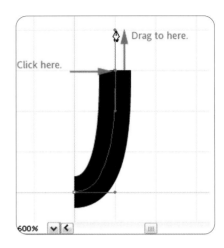

8. Select this path and choose Object ➤ Transform ➤ Reflect. Select the Vertical radio button and click Copy.

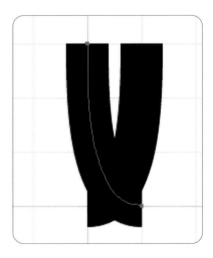

9. With the copy selected, choose Object ➤ Arrange ➤ Send Backward (*CTRL/CMD+[*).

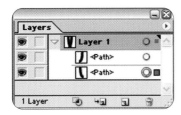

10. If you've followed along, when you choose the Selection tool you should need to press the right arrow key only once to position the duplicate in the correct place.

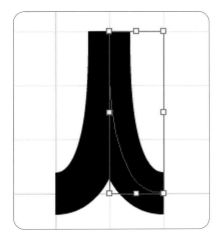

11. Next, create a circle using the Ellipse tool that's 7 pt in width and height. Set the fill color to black and the stroke color to None. Place this circle under the other two objects by choosing Object ➤ Arrange ➤ Send to Back (*Shift+Ctrl/Cmd+[*).

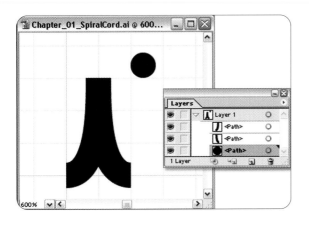

12. Turn off Snap To Grid and turn on Smart Guides. Using Smart Guides (*Ctrl/Cmd+R*), align the center point of the circle to the top points of the two paths.

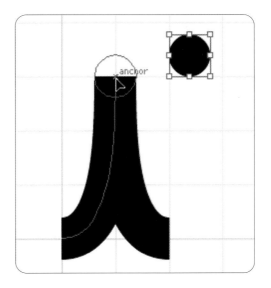

This is the basic shape for the cord. The next group of steps will walk you through creating a highlight to put on the cord.

13. Zoom in to about 1000%.

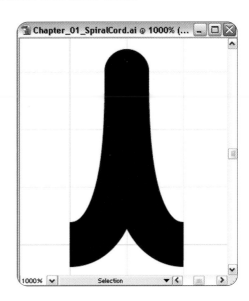

14. Make a copy of the left path. Lock the current layer and create a new one above it called BLEND. Use the Paste In Front command to paste the copy on the new layer.

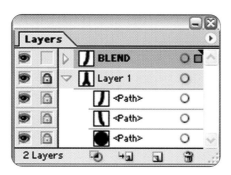

15. Change the fill color of the duplicate to a temporary contrasting color (I used orange in this example) and set the stroke weight to 3 pt.

16. Select the Add Anchor Point tool and add a point on the path near the point at the bottom, as shown here:

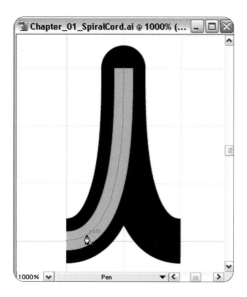

17. Use the Delete Anchor Point tool to remove the lower-left endpoint. This produces a shortened path that will serve as a highlight.

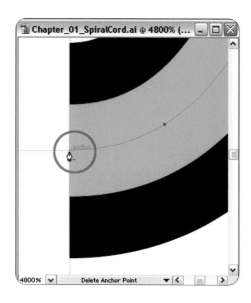

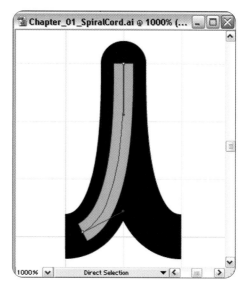

18. With the path selected, set the stroke cap to Round in the Stroke palette.

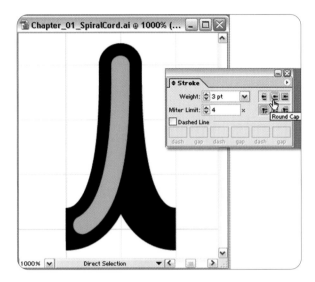

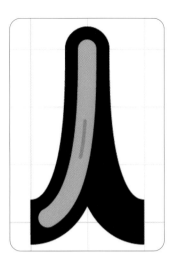

19. Next, lock the sublayer within BLEND.

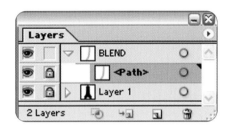

Having Smart Guides turned on will help you with the process of matching the lines up.

21. Unlock the sublayer below this new path and select both strokes. Choose Object ➤ Path ➤ Outline Stroke to convert the strokes to regular objects.

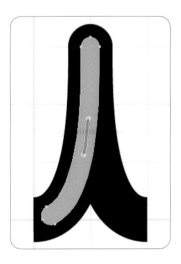

20. Select the Pen tool. Choose a light gray as the stroke color (R:153 G:153 B:153) and set the stroke weight to 0.5 pt. Draw a new line approximately in the center of the original stroke that matches the curve. This line should be only about one-third of the length of the original and should have its stroke cap set to Round.

22. Next, change the color of the thicker bottom object to black (the same color as the objects in the layer below).

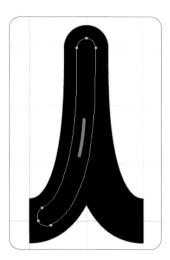

Now let's blend the two objects together to create a smooth highlight.

23. Choose Object ➤ Blend ➤ Blend Options or double-click the Blend tool icon in the toolbox. Choose Specified Steps from the Spacing drop-down menu and enter a value of 8.

24. Select both objects and choose Object ➤ Blend ➤ Make (*CTRL/CMD+ALT/OPTION+B*). This creates a smooth transition between the two objects.

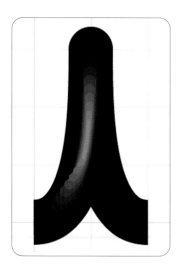

25. You'll notice that this process created a Blend sublayer. Select this sublayer, choose Object ➤ Expand, and click OK.

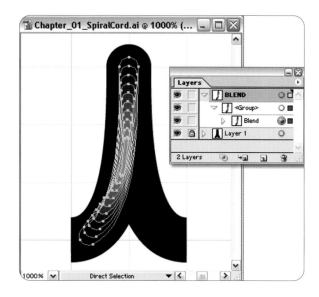

26. Lock the BLEND layer and unlock the layer below it. Select all objects (*CTRL/CMD+A*) on this layer and choose Object ➤ Path ➤ Outline Stroke to make the first paths you drew into regular objects.

27. Unlock the BLEND layer. Choose Select ➤ All and group everything together (*CTRL/CMD+G*). Don't deselect yet.

28. Make your Brushes palette visible (*F5*). Click the small menu arrow in the top left of the palette and choose New Brush from the Brushes palette options menu.

29. Select New Pattern Brush and click OK.

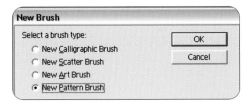

30. Accept the default settings in the next dialog box by clicking OK.

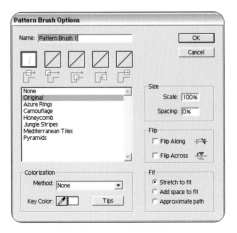

31. Your spiral cord brush is now created. To use this brush, zoom out so you can see the entire Artboard, and then create a path that you would like to apply the spiral cord brush to.

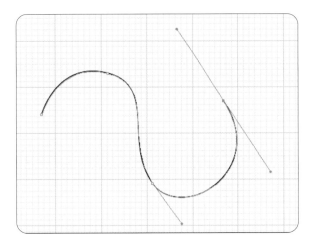

32. With the path selected, set the fill color to None and the stroke color to black.

33. Click the spiral cord brush in the Brushes palette to apply it to the path.

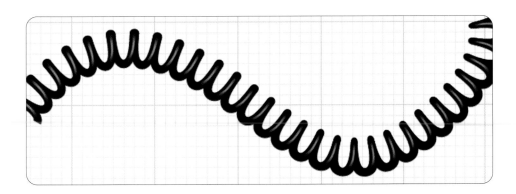

34. Alternatively, you can double-click the brush in the Brushes palette to display the Pattern Brush Options dialog box. Once there, change the Colorization Method setting to Tints and click OK to accept the changes. Set the stroke color to R:22 G:114 B:165. Now the spiral brush will be blue.

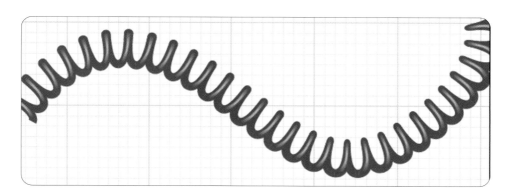

This is a very powerful effect in Illustrator, and I hope you followed along. Creating pattern brushes can save you time and allow you to produce effects that may not otherwise be possible.

Here are a few more tips for using pattern brushes:

- Try to keep any curves in your path wide. Using sharp curves or corners may cause your pattern brushes to become slightly distorted. There are ways to create corner tiles and end tiles for your pattern brushes (see Drawing ➤ Creating brushes in the Illustrator help files). But, in the case of your spiral cord, these methods wouldn't help much.

- You can adjust the stroke weight just as you can with other paths. However, the results can be somewhat unexpected. I encourage you to experiment with this, though.

Hand-drawn effects using the Scribble effect

In this exercise, you'll learn how to add a relaxed, hand-drawn style to your artwork using Illustrator CS's new **Scribble** effect. If you're not a fine artist, have no fear. This tool will help you along and allow you to add a fine-art, hand-drawn feel to your artwork in just minutes.

1. Create a new RGB Illustrator document.

2. Go to Window ➤ Brush Libraries ➤ Food_Fruits and Vegetables. You're going to use a built-in Illustrator brush for this technique, but you can just as easily use any artwork that you've created already.

3. Drag the Apple Color brush to your Artboard.

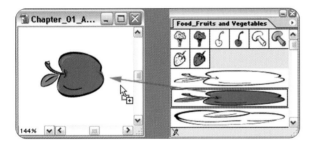

4. Select the apple and go to Object ➤ Transform ➤ Rotate. Enter -90 for the Angle setting.

5. With the apple still selected, go to Object ➤ Transform ➤ Scale. Select Uniform and enter 400 in the Scale field.

Now that you have your object in place, you're going to create the illustration in layers. Sure, you could just select each color and apply the Scribble effect to it and produce something like this:

However, this tends to portray a very childlike drawing effect. If that's the look you're going for, then great—follow one of the upcoming steps for each color and you're done. But if you'd like a more artistic look, then follow along and create multiple layers of Scribble effects to build the illustration's fine-art look.

6. You're going to start from the bottom and work your way up. Make sure your Appearance palette is visible (Window ➤ Appearance).

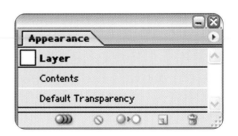

The Appearance palette works like the Layers palette in many ways. You can add many effects to your artwork (strokes, fills, effects, transformations, and distortions) through the Appearance palette alone. Those effects are then live, and you can edit them at any time without doing permanent damage to your artwork. As in the Layers palette, you can move the Appearance attributes up and down and change their stacking order. For a great text effect that will familiarize you with the Appearance palette, see the exercise in Chapter 2 titled "Text Effects: Creating Multiple Stroke Text."

7. Click the expand layers arrow, just to the left of the apple layer's thumbnail in the Layers palette, to display a Group sublayer. Expand this sublayer to reveal yet another Group sublayer. Finally, expand that Group layer to reveal the majority of the artwork used to create the apple.

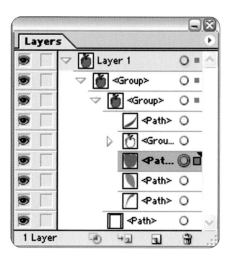

8. Select the red shape sublayer that makes up the majority of the apple's fill. Since you're working with a group, you'll need to either use the Direct Selection tool for this or target the sublayer within the Layers palette.

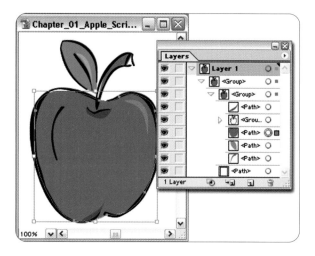

9. After you select the red shape, notice the change in the Appearance palette. Take particular note of the Fill layer. Select the Fill layer and change the color to R:255 G:0 B:0.

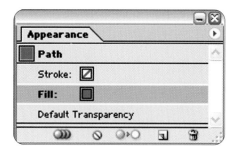

10. With the Fill layer still selected, choose Effects ➤ Stylize ➤ Scribble and enter the following settings:

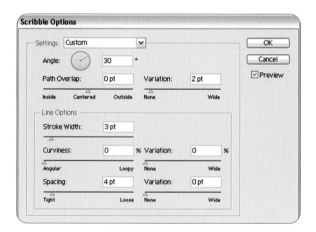

11. Your apple should now look similar to this image:

12. Next, create the middle layer of the Scribble effect. Select the Fill layer in the Appearance palette that you just modified and click the Duplicate Selected Item button at the bottom of the Appearance palette to duplicate this layer.

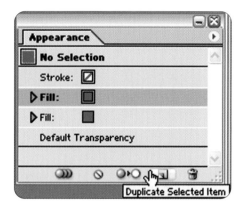

13. Select the new Fill layer and change the color to R:255 G:128 B:118.

14. Double-click the Scribble effect for that Fill layer and modify the settings as shown in the following screenshot. You may need to first click the small arrow to the left of the layer to expand its contents.

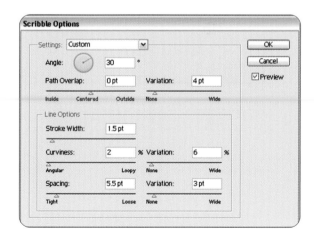

15. The second Scribble effect should leave you with something like this:

16. Repeat steps 10 through 12 to create another Appearance palette layer. This time, set the fill color to R:226 G:20 B:20.

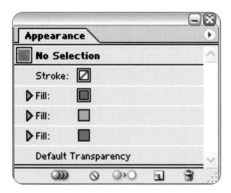

17. Again, modify the Scribble settings for this new Fill layer to match those in the following screenshot:

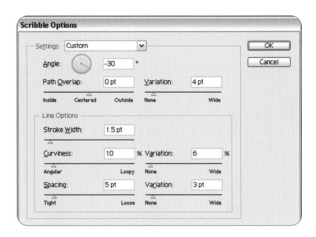

18. Finally, add a Scribble effect to the green leaf at the top of the apple. Select Moiré from the Settings drop-down menu.

19. Your apple should now look similar to this:

Advanced path techniques: TechTV logo

This effect is near and dear to my heart. I'm a TechTV addict. For those of you who don't know what TechTV is, it's a cable TV channel (broadcast from San Francisco) devoted to technology (www.techtv.com). My particular favorite is a show called *The Screensavers*. But that's neither here nor there—how does this fit in with Illustrator? The channel's logo, of course! I saw this logo and realized that it was a prime candidate for an Illustrator technique. It's so simple to re-create, yet the techniques used are some of the most advanced path commands that exist in Illustrator. Once you learn to use them, they'll not only open an entirely new world of creative potential for you, but also save you time because you're letting Illustrator do all of the difficult work for you. In fact, these techniques require about 30 seconds of drawing—the rest is selecting, deleting, and joining paths.

1. Create a new RGB Illustrator document. Set your fill color to None and your stroke color to black. Since you won't be working with any filled objects until the end of the exercise, this will make things easier as you create new paths.

2. Select the Ellipse tool. Click the Artboard and create a new circle by entering 100 pt for the width and height.

3. Now copy the circle and paste it in front (*CTRL/CMD+F*). Hold down the *SHIFT* key and press the right arrow key 11 times, nudging the new circle shape to the right.

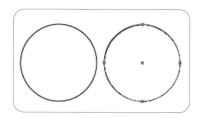

4. Select both circles and duplicate them using the Copy and Paste In Front commands. Now nudge the two circles down by pressing the down arrow key 11 times.

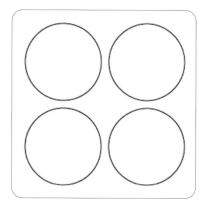

5. Next, select the Direct Selection tool (*A*).

6. Drag an area around the top-left circle similar to the following screenshot. The goal is to marquee-select the anchor points on the top and left of the upper-left circle.

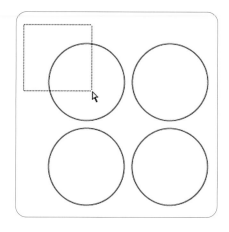

Once you release, your circle should look similar to this:

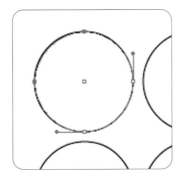

7. Notice the filled square anchor points and the hollow anchor points. Well, the filled ones are those currently selected. You need to remove these, so press the *DELETE* key.

8. Now do the same for the bottom-right circle. Your image should now look like this:

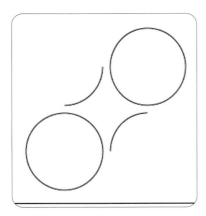

9. Select the two path segments that you just created.

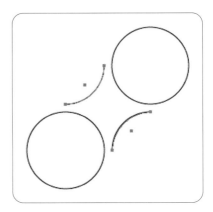

10. Choose Object ➤ Path ➤ Add Anchor Points. Notice how this adds an anchor point in the middle of each segment.

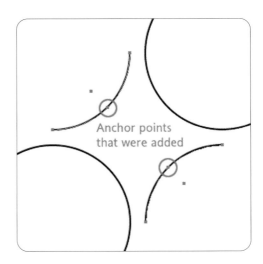

Anchor points that were added

11. Select the middle anchor point on the top-left segment with the Direct Selection tool. Nudge the anchor point down and to the right by pressing the down arrow key three times and the right arrow key three times.

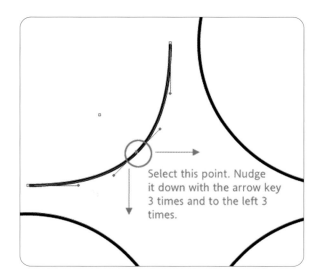

Select this point. Nudge it down with the arrow key 3 times and to the left 3 times.

12. Do the same for the other segment, but nudge it up and to the left three times each.

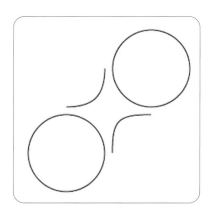

13. Next, you need to move the two rounded segments inward slightly. Using the Selection tool (V), select the top-left path segment. Alternatively, you can use the Layers palette to select the path by clicking the small meatball icon next to the path.

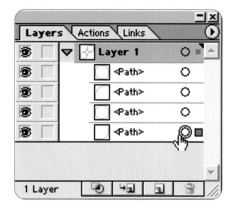

14. Press the down arrow key nine times. Then press the right arrow key nine times.

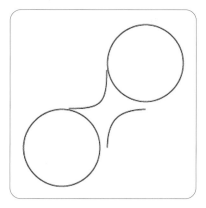

15. Do the same for the other segment, but move it up and to the left instead.

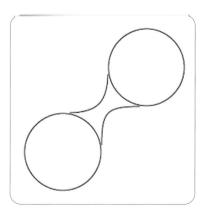

16. Next, select the portion of the other circles that are between your two segments by clicking with the Direct Selection tool.

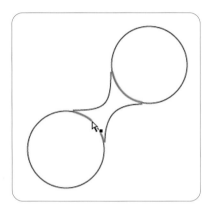

17. Delete that portion of the path by pressing the *DELETE* key, and do the same for the other circle. You need only draw a small selection marquee around a portion of this particular segment to select it.

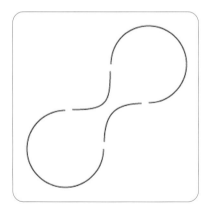

18. Using the Direct Selection tool, select two of the anchor points on each end of one of the gaps.

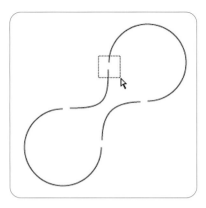

19. Choose Object ➤ Path ➤ Average and select Both in the Axis area.

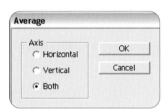

20. Choose Object ➤ Path ➤ Join and select the Smooth option:

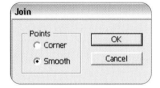

Instead of going through the menu each time you need to average and join paths, you can always use the keyboard shortcut SHIFT+CTRL/CMD+ALT/ OPTION+J. This shortcut performs the Average command as well as the Join command.

21. You should now have something that resembles this screenshot:

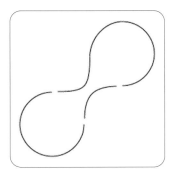

22. Repeat this process for the three remaining gaps. (Be sure to use the shortcut *Shift+Ctrl/Cmd+Alt/Option+J*.) You should have something like this when you're done:

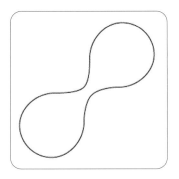

23. Next, set the fill color of this new object to red (R:255 G:0 B:0) and the stroke color to None.

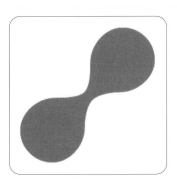

24. Create three more 100×100 circles, fill them with black, and position them in a similar way to this image:

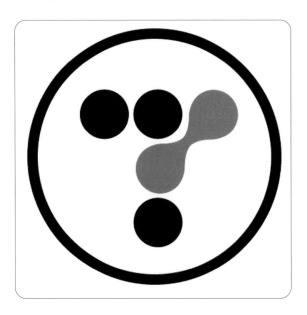

That's it. Go TechTV and *The Screensavers*!

Summary

Wow! It feels like the first chapter flew by. Hopefully, you're finding out that Illustrator is indeed a wonderful tool. I know you've covered a lot in this chapter's exercises and your head may be spinning with information right now, but I encourage you to look back through these techniques if there's anything you didn't grasp the first time. Drawing techniques and path operations are certainly vital concepts to understand within Illustrator. This chapter provided you with a good foundation in some of the tools you can use to make these tasks easier.

OST
NTB

Chapter 2
TEXT EFFECTS

The written word is very powerful. Because of this, almost every illustration you create will have some form of text in it. Why? Because text is a highly effective way to communicate a message. Unless you're a very gifted designer (very possible) or have a very flexible client (highly unlikely), you won't be creating illustrations without text. A company's name, product name, dates, times, the company slogan, these are all things that you may need to use in your illustrations. Even larger amounts of text for menus, magazine ads, and websites can be created in Illustrator. Although other programs such as Quark, InDesign, and Dreamweaver may all be better suited for those tasks, Illustrator offers you many options with which to create text. To make it even more appealing, Adobe has totally rewritten the text engine in Illustrator CS from the ground up. Illustrator, Photoshop, and InDesign now share the same text engine. So let's tackle the next chapter: Text effects.

Creating multistroked text

This is perhaps one of the most popular text effects in Illustrator. Putting a stroke around your text is one thing; many paint programs can accomplish this task easily. But adding multiple strokes around text can lead to problems. Often, you'll start to lose the integrity of the original typeface that you selected. But by using the Appearance palette in Illustrator, you can retain the original integrity of the type and easily add multiple strokes to achieve various text effects. The best part is that you can save it as a style and apply it to other objects with just one click.

1. Create a new RGB Illustrator document.

2. Select the Type tool and enter the text that you would like to use for this effect. I used the Arial Black font and typed MOST WANTED at 90 pts.

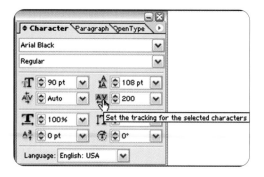

3. Choose Window ➤ Type ➤ Character. This will bring up the Character palette.

4. You'll want to make sure that your letters aren't too close together for this effect (a 10 pt width is adequate). If you're happy with the spacing then move on to the next step. If you would like to increase the spacing, simply change the tracking value in the Character palette. I increased the tracking to 200 for this effect.

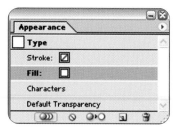

5. Now make sure your Appearance palette (*Shift*+*F6*) is visible.

6. Select the text with the Selection tool.

7. Open the Appearance palette's options menu by clicking in the small circle in the upper-right corner of the palette. Select Add New Fill.

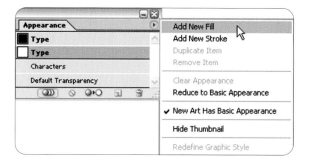

> From this point forward you'll be working with the Appearance palette for this effect. You won't make any modifications to the actual layers in the Layers palette.

8. Select the Fill attribute in the Appearance palette and change the color to white. At this point you may not be able to see the type but rest assured that it's still there.

9. Remember, the Appearance palette works in a similar way to the Layers palette. You can drag Appearance palette attributes above and below each other in the same way you would layers. Go ahead and drag the Stroke attribute below the Fill attribute. Be sure the Stroke attribute is targeted by clicking it.

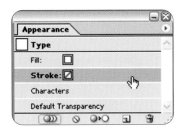

10. Set the stroke color to black.

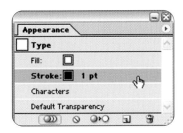

11. Make the Stroke palette visible by choosing Window ➤ Stroke or by double-clicking the Stroke attribute. Set the stroke weight to 4 pts.

12. Next, with the type selected, open the Appearance palette's options menu again and select Add New Stroke.

13. Set the stroke color to R:14 G:155 B:125 and the stroke weight to 10 pts.

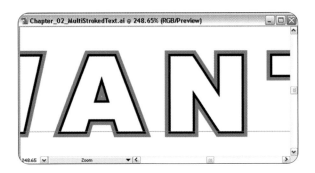

14. Drag this stroke over the Duplicate Selected Item icon at the bottom of the Appearance palette. Alternatively, you can select the Stroke attribute and click the same button.

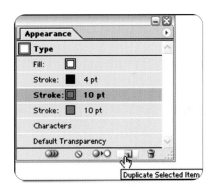

15. Select this bottom stroke item and change the color to black and the stroke weight to 13 pts.

Great, the effect is now complete. Remember, the sky is the limit on this effect. You can add as many strokes as you like. You also don't need to keep your text editable. In the following example, I set my type and used Illustrator's **Create Outlines** feature (Type ➤ Create Outlines or *CTRL/CMD+SHIFT+O*) to reduce the type to basic paths. You'll look at the Create Outlines command again later in this chapter. However, it basi-

cally allows you to edit your type with selection tools and gives you more control over the outline of the letters. I then selected each letter and repositioned them to give a slightly sloppy look. Finally, I added the same type of stroke settings as you used in this exercise. I've included the outlined type in this chapter's source files (Chapter_02_RetroText.ai) in case you would like to dissect it.

44

Now, what happens if you want to apply this effect to multiple words? Wouldn't it be nice if there was a way to create a new word and have these settings instantly applied without having to add all of those strokes each time? Well, you're in luck, there is. Just follow along with these last few steps.

16. At the top of your Appearance palette you should see a small square swatch (although you may not be able to see it unless you have good eyes), which is a representative thumbnail of all the strokes and fills so far in your type.

17. Drag this swatch over to the Graphic Styles palette (Window ➤ Graphic Styles or *SHIFT+F5*). Be sure to click only the small square swatch area when you drag. Also, once your new style is in the Graphic Styles palette, double-click its thumbnail to give it a meaningful name such as MultiStroked Type.

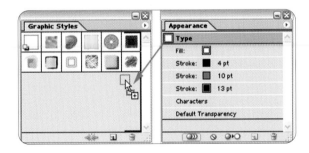

That's it. Your style is created and ready to be your best friend. And believe me, the first time you need to reapply it to multiple objects, it *will* be just that.

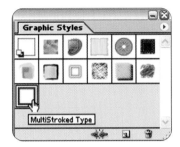

Matrix text

1. Create a new RGB Illustrator document.

2. Select the Rectangle tool. Click the Artboard to create a new rectangle and enter these settings:

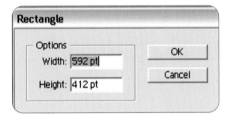

3. Set the fill color to black and the stroke to None. Lock this layer and name it BACKGROUND.

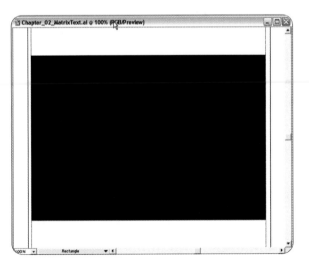

4. Create the text that you would like to use for this exercise. If available, use Times New Roman for the font face. This example shows THE MATRIX. I created two layers for this effect, one for each word: "THE" and "MATRIX."

5. Set the fill color to a bright green (R:0 G:255 B:0) and the stroke to None for both text layers.

6. Make your Character palette visible by choosing Window ➤ Type ➤ Character (CTRL/CMD T). Select the "THE" word layer and change your settings to look similar to these:

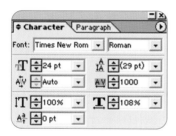

7. Do the same for the MATRIX layer, but use these settings instead:

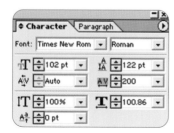

8. Next, select the MATRIX layer and choose Type ➤ Create Outlines (CTRL/CMD+SHIFT+O). I've dimmed the fill color of the MATRIX word so you can see the effect this command has.

9. With the text still selected, choose Object ➤ Ungroup (CTRL/CMD+SHIFT+G). Your Layers palette should now look similar to the following image. Note that the layers are expanded to show sublayers.

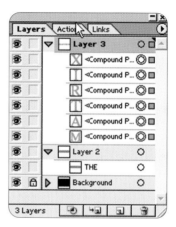

10. Now you can start modifying your text. Select the Rectangle tool from the shape menu in the toolbox.

11. Lock all text layers/sublayers except for the M layer.

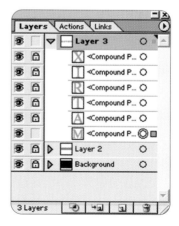

12. Draw a rectangle over the portion of the letter that you would like to cut. Set the fill and stroke settings for this rectangle to None.

I've switched to Outline view (View ➤ Outline) to make it easier for you to see what I'm drawing. Also, it may be easier for you to select objects this way as you follow along. However, a mixture of switching between the two modes will most likely work best. When you wish to return to the Normal view just choose View ➤ Preview (CTRL/CMD+Y).

13. Using the Layers palette, target and select the rectangle and the letter shape M.

14. Open your Pathfinder palette (Window ➤ Pathfinder).

15. Hold down the ALT/OPTION key and select the Divide button.

16. You'll notice this produces a group in your Layers palette. Click the small arrow next to the group to expand its contents.

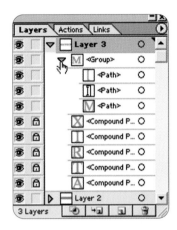

Clicking each path layer reveals that the Pathfinder operation created three paths. The first is the portion of the M that wasn't covered by the rectangle, the second is the portion that was, and the third is your rectangle with that M shape punched out of it.

17. Next, hide the punched-out rectangle shape.

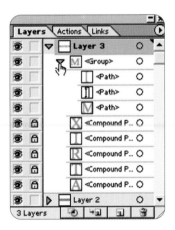

18. Using the Layers palette, target and select the right portion of the M layer by clicking its meatball icon. Note that I've switched back to Preview mode in this reference image.

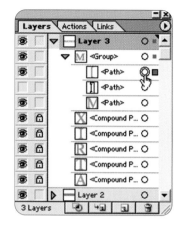

19. Choose Object ➤ Transform ➤ Rotate. Enter 180 degrees and click OK.

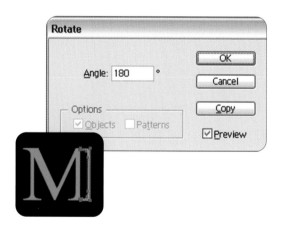

20. Drag that path over to the left side of the M and position it, as shown here:

21. Using the Free Transform tool (E), enlarge this shape as I've done here:

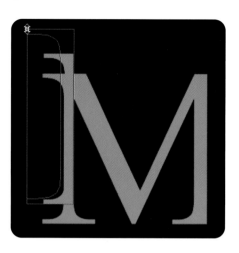

22. Create another rectangle around the bottom portion of this shape.

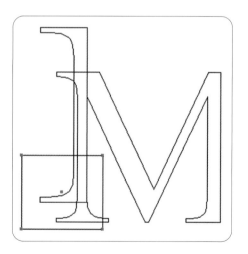

23. Using the Layers palette, select the new rectangle and the disconnected shape that you just enlarged.

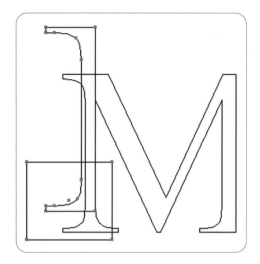

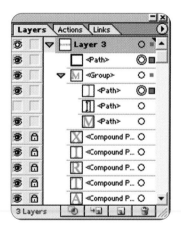

24. Hold down the *ALT/OPTION* key and select the Subtract from Shape Area button in the Pathfinder palette.

25. Nudge the new shape over slightly with the right-arrow key until it appears to be in place.

26. Finally, to complete the M, create one more rectangle.

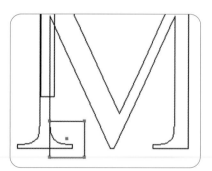

27. Again, set the fill and stroke settings to None for this shape.

28. Using the Layers palette, target the M path and the new rectangle path.

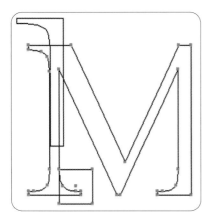

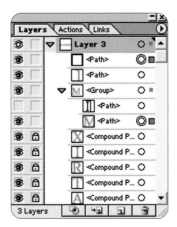

29. Hold down the *ALT/OPTION* key and select the Subtract from Shape Area button in the Pathfinder palette.

The following two images show what your M should look like in both Outline view and in Preview mode:

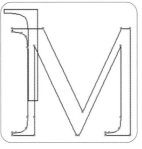 

30. To clean things up, select the two layers that make up your M shape and choose Object ➤ Group. Since the exercise requires many layers as you move along, doing this will help avoid a cluttered Layers palette. Also, this is good practice for general housekeeping in your files.

31. Repeat the previous process for each letter. Here are a few tips:

- Be sure to unlock the layer of the letter you're working on. However, it's a good idea to keep the other layers locked to avoid accidentally selecting them.

- Every time you create a rectangle shape to use as a knockout for your letters, be sure that you set the fill and stroke settings to None.

- Since the Pathfinder operations will always create a group when applied, you need to select and target each shape with the Layers palette or the open-arrow Direct Selection tool. If you use the Selection tool you'll select the entire group. You could avoid this by ungrouping each group but that can get messy. If you do, just be sure to group everything back together before moving on to the next letter.

- The A, T, and X are all created in a similar way. The I requires no changes. The R, however, will require that you create two rectangles. The only difference is that when you reach step 13 and select the rectangle and R letter, you'll need to select both rectangles.

The following are screen examples of each letter and the shapes that I drew to break them apart. In addition, I've provided some tips on how to move each shape into place after you execute the Pathfinder effect.

32. The A letter. Create one rectangle and delete this area from the A.

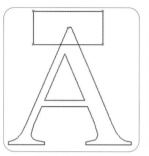 

33. The T letter. Create one rectangle. Nudge the left half of the T down slightly and nudge the right half up slightly.

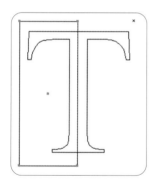 

34. The R letter. Create two rectangles. Delete this area from the R shape.

 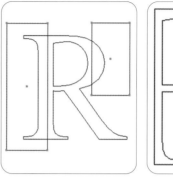

35. The X letter. Create one rectangle. Nudge the top half to the right.

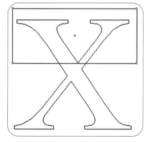 

36. When you're done with the letters, select the Line Segment tool.

37. Set the fill color to None and the stroke color to R:0 G:255 B:0.

38. Draw lines between the letters and in the areas indicated by the reference images. This may take some fine-tuning to get them into place perfectly. Use the Zoom tool to zoom in and drag them or use the arrow keys to position them perfectly.

39. Use a 1 pt stroke for the line under the THE word.

40. Use a 2 pt stroke for the rest of the lines within the MATRIX word.

Text warping

Illustrator's warping effects offer many options when creating text. They are dynamic live effects that allow you to warp your text and change the settings of that warp at any time without retyping the text. But you aren't limited to just warping text. As you've seen so far in the chapter, text can have fills, strokes, and other effects applied to it. The warp effects not only allow you to warp the text you create but the effects you've added to it, too.

1. Create a new RGB Illustrator document.

2. Using the Type tool, enter some type that you would like to apply this effect to. I've used a font called Comix Heavy (see note on this font later). It's best to keep it simple for now.

This is a screenshot of my Character palette if you have the font and want to follow along closely.

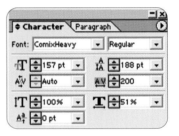

I've found that thick fonts work best for this effect, because you'll be applying multiple strokes to it. Also, because this effect involves warping and distorting the text, I thought a fun font would be suitable. The Comix Heavy font is available at many websites for free or for a nominal fee. A search on www.google.com for "Comix Heavy" should help. Also, in the download files, I've included an outlined copy (by choosing Type ➤ Create Outlines) of the text that I'm using for this effect so you can follow along. The file name is Chapter_02_WarpText_Start.ai.

3. Select your text layer.

4. Open the Appearance palette (Window ➤ Appearance) and select Add New Fill from the options menu.

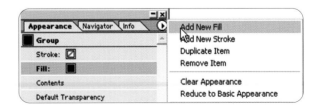

5. Create a gradient similar to the following image. If you're using the source file (Chapter_02_WarpText.ai) for this chapter, the gradient will already be included in the Swatches palette.

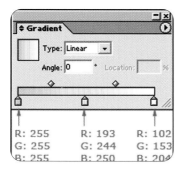

6. In the Appearance palette, select or target the Fill attribute by clicking it.

7. Click your gradient in the Gradient palette or the Swatches palette to apply it to the Fill attribute.

8. Select the Gradient tool (*G*). Drag the tool down to the height of your text to position the gradient, as shown here:

9. Select your type layer. Click the Fill attribute. Choose Effects ➤ Stylize ➤ Drop Shadow and enter the following settings:

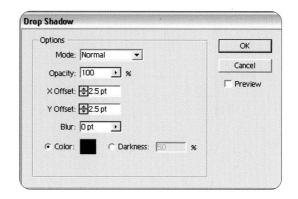

Your image should look similar to this:

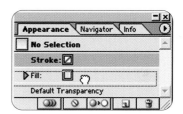

10. In the Appearance palette, drag the Stroke attribute below the Fill attribute.

11. Your Appearance palette should now look like this:

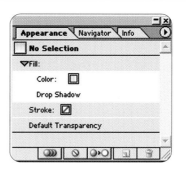

12. Select your text and click the Stroke attribute. Change the color to R:0 G:90 B:155. Change the stroke weight to 18 pts.

> You may notice that I'm always instructing you to select your text attribute. The text must be selected before you make modifications to the Appearance palette or your changes will not affect it.

13. Duplicate that Stroke attribute and change the color to white. Enter 25 for the stroke weight. Your Appearance palette should now look like this:

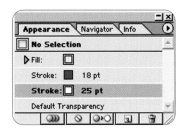

14. Once again duplicate that Stroke attribute and change the color to black. Enter 28 for the stroke weight.

15. With this new Stroke attribute selected, choose Effects ➤ Stylize ➤ Outer Glow and enter the following settings:

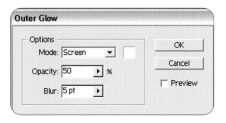

16. Again with the white Stroke attribute selected, choose Effects ➤ Stylize ➤ Drop Shadow and enter these settings:

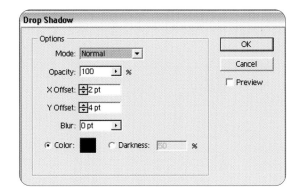

17. Your Appearance palette should now look like this in its fully expanded state:

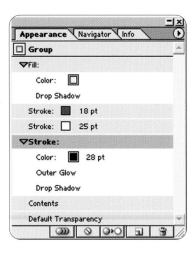

18. Next click at the very top item of the Appearance palette where it reads Type or Group (this depends on whether you're using your own live type or using the grouped type in the source file).

19. Choose Effects ➤ Warp ➤ Arc and enter these settings:

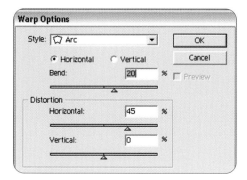

20. Great! Now your text is basically done. At this point you could make this a style so you can quickly apply it for future projects.

All that's left to do is make some background elements to place the text on. For this example, I created two rectangles. I filled them with different color gradients and applied a white stroke and then a black stroke around them. Then, I applied the same warp effect on each of them that I applied on the text so that they match up. I positioned them in place and added a small drop shadow to the top (blue) rectangle. The source file is Chapter_02_WarpText.ai and includes these effects. Here is the finished product:

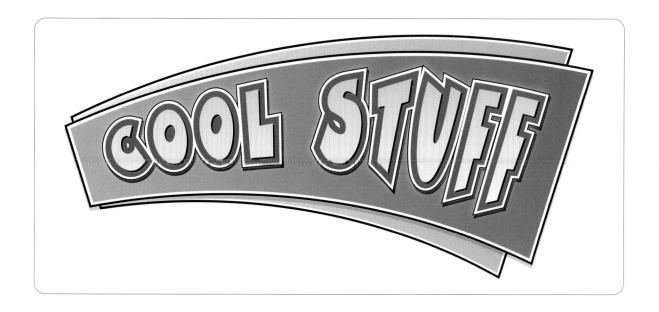

Shiny aqua blue text

You're in for a special treat with this effect. This text effect was originally created by your friendly neighborhood technical editor Michael Hamm (www.ergodraw .com). He's not only the technical editor of this book, but a talented illustrator, too. Although it's somewhat lengthy, it's well worth every step. This effect is somewhat different from the previous effects, in that it will not remain editable and, unfortunately, you cannot turn it into a style. However, it's an advanced effect and will teach you such concepts as creating highlights, and using opacity masks and gradients to make your type stand out.

1. Create a new RGB Illustrator document.

2. Select the Type tool and create the text that you would like to use for this effect. The name of my home state seems like a good candidate. Because this exercise will require a number of different layers, rename the initial one BASE. Set the Type at 200 pts, the fill color to R:102 G:153 B:204, and the stroke to None.

Thick script or sans-serif fonts tend to work best for this effect. Also, keep in mind that later, you're going to be modifying each letter individually. This means that the longer the word you create the more steps you're going to have to go through. So, for learning purposes, I suggest starting with a smaller word.

3. Select the type and choose Type ➤ Create Outlines (*CTRL/CMD+SHIFT+O*). You may want to duplicate the type and hide it before you create the outlines so you can revert back to it later if needed.

Creating outlines allows your type to be edited in many more ways than live type. However, you lose the ability to edit the text itself. This is the reason I suggested to make a copy of the type before you convert it to outlines.

4. Create a new layer above BASE and call it HIGHLIGHTS.

5. Select the type and press *CTRL/CMD+C* and lock the BASE layer. Select the new HIGHLIGHTS layer and choose Edit ➤ Paste In Front (*CTRL/CMD+F*).

6. Select the type in the new HIGHLIGHTS layer.

7. Choose Object ➤ Path ➤ Offset Path and enter the following settings:

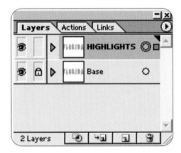

At this point you shouldn't notice much of a difference in the appearance of your type. However, if you expand the HIGHLIGHTS layer, you should see that a group has been created for you. In this group are the shapes of the original type objects and the inset shapes that the Offset operation produced.

8. You should now be left with two layers for each letter. One is the original shape for each letter and the other is the offset shape that should be slightly inset or smaller. Select all of the inset letter shapes, set the fill color to white, and the stroke to None.

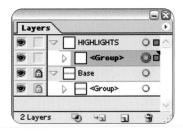

9. Delete the original blue text shapes from the HIGHLIGHTS layer, leaving only the white shapes.

10. Select the grouped layer that the Offset operation produced and choose Object ➤ Ungroup.

11. Next do a Select All (*CTRL/CMD+A*) and choose Object ➤ Compound Path ➤ Make. (Remember, your BASE layer should be locked so doing a Select All will not select anything on that layer).

12. Select the inset paths, then do a Copy and Paste in Front (*CTRL/CMD+F*). Change the fill color of the copied path to red (R:255 G:0 B:0) and keep the copy selected.

13. Nudge the copied path down twice using the down arrow, then nudge it to the right twice with the right-arrow key.

14. Make your Pathfinder palette visible (Window ➤ Pathfinder) and select the red and white inset paths. Hold down the *ALT/OPTION* key and press the Subtract from Shape Area button in the Pathfinder palette.

15. Open the Transparency palette (Window ➤ Transparency).

16. With the HIGHLIGHTS layer still selected, change the blending mode to Overlay and the opacity to 80%.

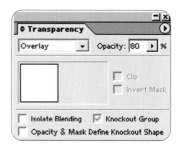

17. You should now see something like this:

> If your HIGHLIGHTS layer doesn't look like the previous screenshot you may not have applied the Compound Path operation to them as stated in step 11.

18. Lock the HIGHLIGHTS layer and unlock the BASE layer. Select the type object and copy it. Lock the BASE layer again.

19. Create a new layer above the BASE layer but below the HIGHLIGHTS layer. Name this layer OPACITY.

20. Paste your type object in front (*CTRL/CMD+F*) to keep everything aligned properly.

21. Fill the copied layer with an icy blue color (R:204 G:255 B:255). Don't deselect the OPACITY layer yet.

22. Hold down the Scissor tool icon in the toolbox to make the flyout menu appear. Select the Knife tool from the flyout menu.

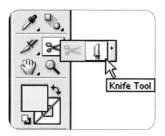

23. Drag a wavy line across your type objects, as shown in this screenshot. This will cut the path in half.

24. Before you deselect the object, choose Object ➤ Ungroup. This will separate the upper and lower cut portions of the type object.

25. Delete the lower halves of the type objects so you can only see the BASE layer object showing through.

26. Select the Rectangle tool and draw a rectangle so that it encompasses the bottom and sides of the icy blue type object. Fill the rectangle with a black to white linear gradient (black on top, white on bottom), as shown here:

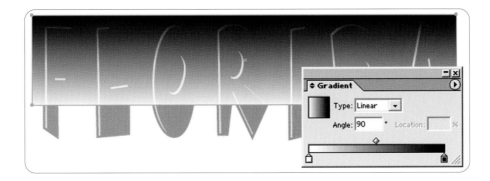

You're going to use this gradient as an opacity mask. This means that the portions of the mask that are black will reveal the artwork below it. The areas that are white will hide the artwork below and any shade of gray in between will have varying degrees of opacity.

27. Select all of the objects on the OPACITY layer (the icy blue object and the rectangle gradient box).

28. Choose Make Opacity Mask from the Transparency palette's options menu.

29. With the objects on the OPACITY layer still selected, set the Opacity setting to 65%.

30. Lock the OPACITY layer. Once again, unlock the BASE layer. Select the type object, copy it, then lock the BASE layer again.

31. Create a new layer below the BASE layer and call it OUTLINES. Use the Paste In Front command and paste your copy on to this layer.

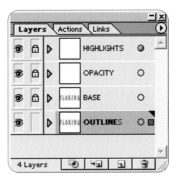

32. Fill this type object with yet another blue (R:51 G:153 B:204).

33. With the object selected, press *SHIFT+X* to swap the fill with the stroke. Now set the stroke weight for this object to 15 pts (this number may differ when using other fonts).

34. With the OUTLINES layer still selected, add a drop shadow by selecting Effect ➤ Stylize ➤ Drop Shadow and using the following settings:

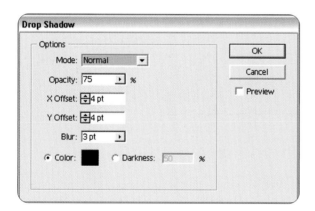

35. Your image should now look like this:

36. OK, you're almost done. Select the BASE layer type object (unlock it, if necessary) and apply the following linear gradient (if you're using the source file for this chapter, the gradient will already be in the Swatches palette). The white part of the gradient should start at the bottom of the type object.

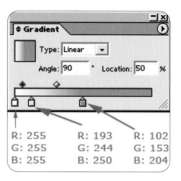

37. Finally, add a glow to the BASE type object by choosing Effects ➤ Stylize ➤ Outer Glow and entering the following settings:

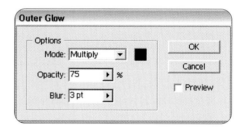

That's it. You did it! I know it was a long one but I believe the effect is well worth the time spent. Let's give a round of applause to Michael Hamm for conjuring up this behemoth of a type effect.

Type on a path

This effect definitely falls into the Most Wanted category. Aside from editable type itself, type along a path is one of the most powerful type effects available. This effect will walk you through the basics of creating type on a path (which isn't terribly difficult). However, you'll also delve into some other effects you can achieve with type along a path and how to modify that type once you have input it.

1. Open the Chapter_02_TextOnPath.ai file. I've given you a head start and created a small logo.

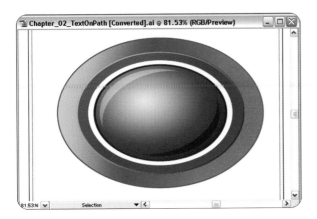

You'll notice that the logo is lacking something—text! To change this, you're going to add text that wraps along the red oval's path. This is what the final illustration will look like:

2. First, you need to create a path to which you'll attach the text. In this illustration, the outermost blue oval will do just fine.

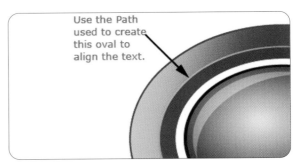

Use the Path used to create this oval to align the text.

3. Select the inner oval layer and copy it to the clipboard.

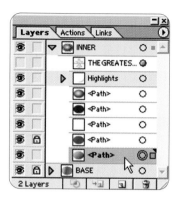

4. Lock the BASE and INNER layers. Create a new layer above the INNER layer called TEXT.

5. Using the Paste In Front command (*CTRL/CMD+F*) to keep things aligned, paste the oval on to the TEXT layer.

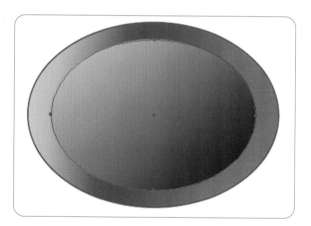

> It will appear as if this new oval is covering up the center of the logo. This is fine. When you attach type to the oval's path, the actual fill and stroke settings within the oval will disappear.

6. Hold down the Type tool icon and select the Path Type tool from the flyout menu.

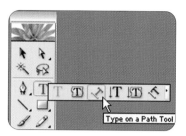

7. OK, now you're ready to attach the type. With the Path Type tool active, click the oval path and enter your text. I used 32 pt Arial Black type with the fill color set to white and the stroke set to None.

8. If your image looks similar to mine then the type probably isn't centered along the path, which is as it should be initially. To change this, select the type layer with the Selection tool if it isn't already selected. You'll notice an I-Beam cursor in front of the text.

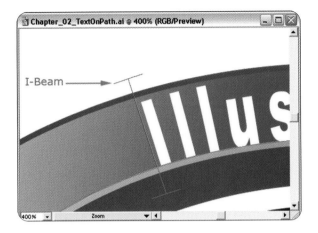

9. With the Selection tool, drag the I-Beam around the outer rim of your bounding box and position your text in place.

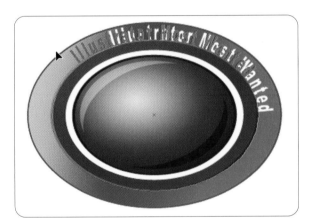

10. Now you need to add text along the bottom. Unlock the INNER layer and duplicate the same oval shape that you used for the previous text. Re-lock the INNER layer. Using the Paste In Front command, paste the oval into the TEXT layer. Lock the existing text that you created in step 7. Your Layers palette should now look like this:

11. Select the Path Type tool once again. Click the bottom of the oval path to attach type to it and enter the rest of your text. I used the same Character palette settings as in step 7. You should notice that the text begins at the point on the path at which you click.

Looks good, right? If you've followed along then it probably isn't ready yet. Most likely, your text is upside down. But the changes you need to make are simple.

12. Select your type with the Selection tool. Drag the I-Beam cursor around the outer edge just as you did previously. Notice how the text follows your cursor around the outside edge of the oval? But, if you start to drag your cursor inside the oval, you'll see that the text now wraps around inside the oval and is right-side up. Go ahead and drag your text so it appears like the screenshot here:

13. Next, make the Character palette visible (Window ➤ Character) and ensure that you have all character options visible by clicking the small arrows to the left of the word Character.

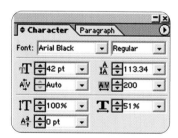

14. Unlock the first text layer that you created and select it with the Selection tool or by targeting the meatball in the Layers palette.

15. Click the up arrow in the Baseline Shift text box until your text appears similar to mine. This will raise the text off the baseline path (the oval) that you used to attach the text to. Click the arrow until your text is neatly centered vertically in the red area.

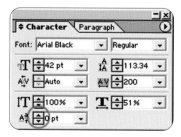

If you've used a different font or font size than I did, you may need to adjust the size of the text so it fits in place.

16. Feel free to adjust the tracking as well at this point, if you would like to modify the spacing between the letters.

See Using Type ➤ Selecting Type Attributes *in the Illustrator Help file for detailed explanations on what Baseline, Shift, and Tracking mean.*

17. Now do the same for the bottom text layer. However, click the down-arrow key in the Baseline Shift option to move your text downward into place. You may need to use the Selection tool and the I-Beam handle while doing this to move your text back into place. I also adjusted the Tracking setting for this layer to 400 to spread the type out.

18. Once the text is in place, add a drop shadow effect to make it stand out more. Do this by selecting each text layer (select one text layer and hold down the *SHIFT* key to select the other) and choose Effect ➤ Stylize ➤ Drop Shadow. Enter the settings shown here:

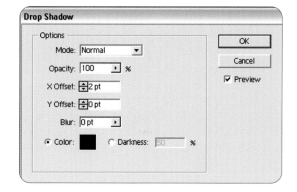

19. Of course, you can add some text in the middle of the image to complete the effect. The "The Greatest Book On Earth" text was first created with the Type tool and then modified with the warp effects.

Modifying a restaurant menu: new CS features

What? Modifying a restaurant menu? That sounds like a project, and the projects are supposed to be at the end of the book. Well, think of this exercise as a miniproject. At the start of this chapter I mentioned that Adobe has completely rewritten the text engine for Illustrator CS. In fact, all of the CS products (Illustrator, Photoshop, InDesign) now share the same text engine. With this new text engine, Adobe has added several new features to Illustrator. The best way that I could think to show you these features is to show them in action.

Using custom character styles

1. Choose File ➤ New from Template.

2. Navigate to your Illustrator CS installation folder, then choose Templates ➤ Restaurant. Choose `Restaurant 2 Menu.ait` and click the New button. This opens a new file based on a template included with Illustrator CS.

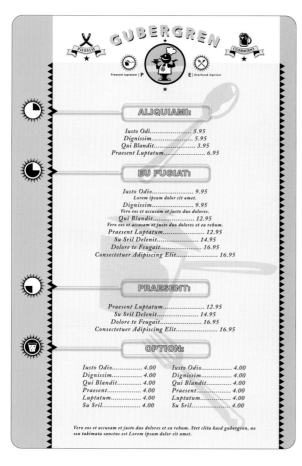

Examine the layout of this template. For this exercise, you're going to work with the four category names. First, you'll create a new character style and then you'll apply that style to the four category names with just one click.

3. Make the Character Styles palette visible (Window ➤ Type ➤ Character Styles).

4. Select New Character Style from the Character Styles palette's options menu. Name this style Category Text.

5. The new style now appears in the Character Styles palette. Double-click the new style to edit its properties.

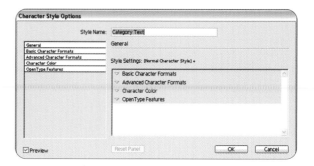

6. Select Basic Character Formats from the left option list and change your settings to match those shown in the following figure. I've chosen Arial Black as my font but you can choose your own if you would like. You're going to apply a stroke to this font in the next step so it's best to choose a thick font.

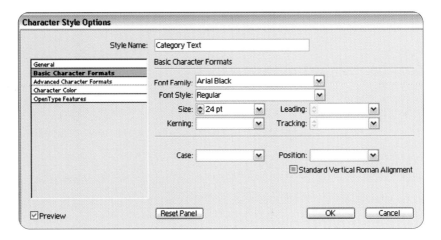

7. Now select the Character Color item from the option list on the left. Change your settings to those shown here:

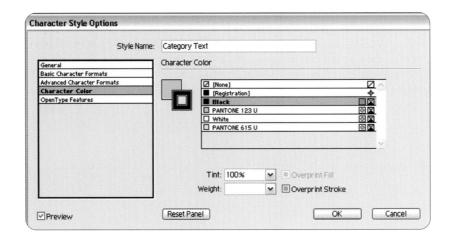

8. Click OK to close the Character Styles dialog box.

9. Now that the style is created you can apply it to any new type that you create or, in this case, any existing type.

10. Select all of the category layers by selecting one and *SHIFT*-clicking on the others to select them all at once. Alternatively, you can select them in the Layers palette by *SHIFT*-clicking them as well.

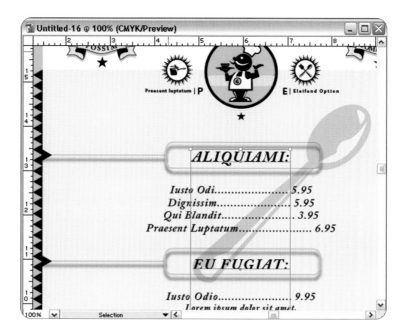

11. Now simply click the Category Text item in the Character Styles palette and your new style will be applied to all of the selected text layers.

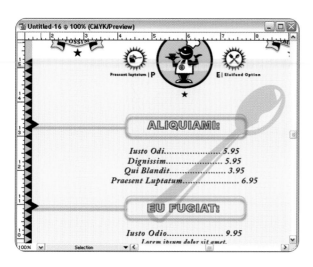

Great, your new character style is now applied to the selected text layers. But what if you want to change the Character Style settings? Do you need to go back and select the text objects and reapply it? Of course not! Changing the original Character Style settings will automatically update any text that the style has been applied to. Just follow these steps:

12. Double-click the Category Text style to open the Character Style Options dialog box. Click the Character Color option.

13. Click the Foreground Fill swatch and change the color to white. Also be sure that the Preview check box is selected so you can view your changes behind the dialog box.

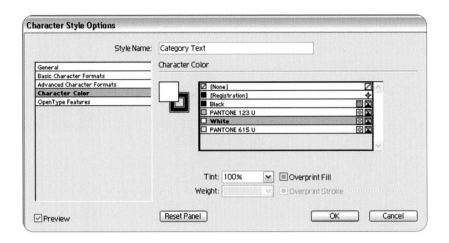

14. Your changes to the Character Style options should update the text that it was originally applied to. Click OK. You've now updated all four text layers without selecting any of them.

Paragraph styles

Paragraph styles are similar to character styles. However, as the name suggests, you can set certain paragraph-level settings using this feature. Some of these settings include the following:

- Tabs
- Indents and spacing
- Hyphenation
- Justification

In this part of the exercise, you're going to learn one of the new text features in Illustrator as well as explore the use of paragraph styles.

1. Choose File ➤ New from Template.

2. Navigate to your Illustrator CS installation folder, then navigate to Templates ➤ Restaurant.

3. Choose `Restaurant 1 Menu Inside.ait` and click the New button. This will open a new file based on a template that is included with Illustrator CS.

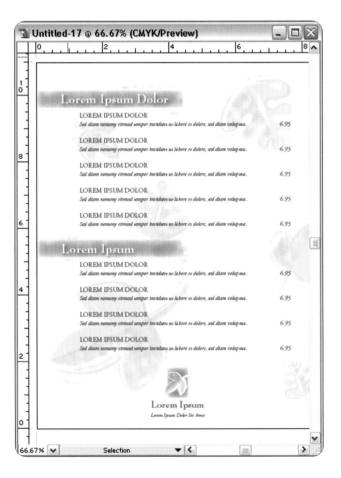

Examine the layout of this template. Notice that every menu item is named Lorem Ipsum Dolor. Underneath the menu item is gibberish text, Sed diam nonumy eirmod tempor invidunt ut labore et dolore, sed diam voluptua, followed by the price ($6.95 in this case). For this exercise, you're going to create a paragraph style that you'll apply to all of the paragraphs on this menu. This style will contain a custom tab leader that will fill in the space between the item descriptions and the price.

4. Make the Paragraph Styles palette visible by choosing Window ➤ Type ➤ Paragraph Styles.

5. This time, before you create a new style, select the top menu item text group (just below the first heading) using the Selection tool.

6. Select New Paragraph Style in the Paragraph Styles palette options menu. Name this style Description Text.

Selecting the text group before you created a new paragraph style informs Illustrator that you would like to keep the existing text group settings intact. However, if you change any settings then Illustrator will override them using the new paragraph style.

7. The new style will now appear in the Paragraph Styles palette.

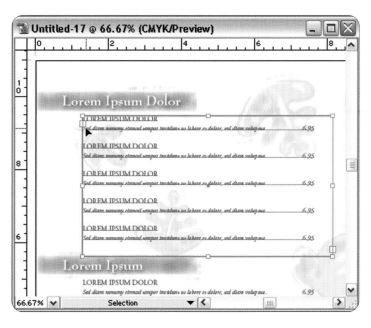

8. Double-click the new style to edit its properties.

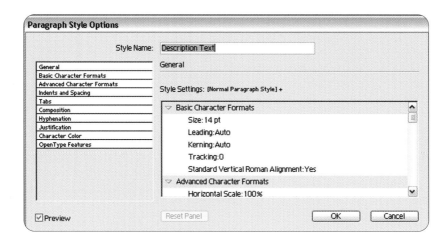

9. Select Tabs from the left option list and change your settings to match those shown in the following image. Take particular note of the 6 that was entered in the X text box and the period typed into the Leader text box. As you type the 6 into the X text box notice a small arrow appear on top of the 6-inch pt on the ruler. Click OK.

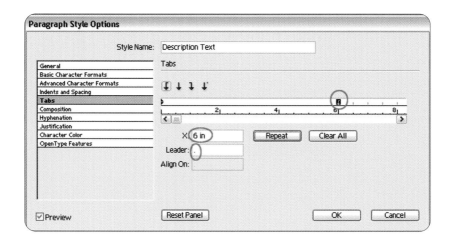

A leader is a character that fills the space created by tabbing. Leaders are often used in a table of contents to draw the reader's eye from the chapter name across to the page number.

10. Select the three blocks of text in this menu by *SHIFT*-clicking on each text block or by targeting their meatball icons in the Layers palette.

11. Click on the Description Text paragraph style and watch as periods are inserted between the description text and the price.

Summary

Text effects are some of the most popular effects in graphic design and illustration. The possibilities are limitless. Although this chapter is just the tip of the iceberg when it comes to type effects in Illustrator, it should have given you a good foundation to build from. Techniques such as adding multiple strokes to your type, reducing type to outlines, and using opacity masks are invaluable and will likely be used in many of your text-based illustrations. Look at the world around you. Text effects are everywhere. Study them and think about how they were created and why certain effects look good or bad. This process will not only allow you to have better control over your type in Illustrator, but it will empower you to create your own text effects as well.

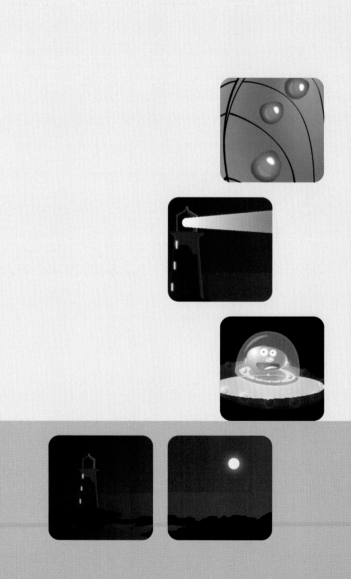

Chapter 3

BLENDING

The Blend tool is one of Illustrator's oldest tools. Even though Adobe has blurred many of the lines between Photoshop and Illustrator over the years, they have kept some of them very distinct. The Blend tool is one of those distinct differences. The sophistication and timesaving techniques that the Blend tool offers Illustrator users cannot be measured. In this chapter, I hope to show you some essential techniques for using the Blend tool and how to make this an indispensable part of your workflow.

Basic blending—fading light effects

This effect is a great starting place for exploring the capabilities of the Blend tool. An illustration has been created for you to follow along with. Once opened, you'll notice that it's missing something—lights.

1. Open Chapter_03_Lighthouse.ai. This file contains a nighttime lighthouse scene. Your task is going to be to add some lights to the lighthouse.

2. Create a new layer on top of the LAND layer named SPOTLIGHT.

3. Select the Ellipse tool and create a circle in the light tower of the lighthouse as displayed in this reference image. Set the fill color to R:255 G:255 B:227 and the stroke to None.

4. With the circle still selected, choose Object ➤ Transform ➤ Scale.

5. Select Uniform and enter 400% for the Amount setting. Choose Copy.

6. This will create a new circle that is considerably larger than the first. Drag this new circle off to the right.

7. Choose Object ➤ Blend ➤ Blend Options. Match your settings to this reference image.

8. Select the two white circles.

9. Choose Object ➤ Blend ➤ Make (CTRL/CMD+ALT/OPTION+B). Illustrator will blend the area between the two circles with its own interpretation based on the settings that you entered in step 7.

> *If you find that Illustrator hasn't added enough steps or has used too many steps you can always modify the Blend settings. Blends are live effects and can be edited at any time by choosing* Object ➤ Blend ➤ Blend Options *or by double-clicking the Blend tool in the* Tools *palette. Once you click* OK *in the Blend Options dialog box, your blend will be recalculated automatically.*

Very cool but your light is missing something, right? Most spotlights fade as the light gets further away from the source. This means that you'll need to change the opacity of one side of the blend to achieve the fading effect. So do you have to backtrack and create the blend all over again? Of course not. Illustrator will allow you to make changes to either side of the blend dynamically. It will then automatically redraw the blend based on your changes.

10. Select the larger circle at the top of your Blend layers in the Layers palette. The best way to do this is to target the path in the Layers palette by clicking it. Alternatively you could use the Direct Selection tool (*A*) as well.

11. Open the Transparency palette (Window ➤ Transparency). Enter 0% for the Opacity setting.

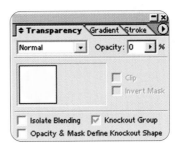

12. After you make this change, Illustrator will recalculate your blend and it should appear as if the spotlight fades as it gets further away from the lighthouse source.

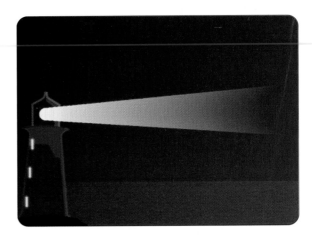

OK, here is a special treat. Now that you know how to create the spotlight, adding some reflections on the water for the moon should be a breeze. However, you can also apply any of the effects from the Effects menu to your blends as well. This makes for some very interesting techniques.

13. Next, you're going to add some reflection from the moon on the water. Create a new layer named Water Reflection. Create two circle shapes, similar to the way that you did previously in this exercise.

14. Set the opacity of the large oval to 0%. Choose Object ➤ Blend ➤ Make (*CTRL/CMD+ALT/OPTION+B*) as you did earlier.

15. Expand the arrow on the new Blend layer so you can see the blend paths and spine. The spine is a path that the blend objects align themselves to. By default, the spine is a straight line but you'll meet this topic again in the next exercise and learn how to modify it. Select the larger oval path by clicking the meatball next to the word Path.

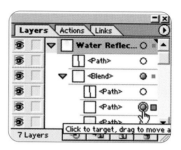

16. Choose Effect ➤ Distort & Transform ➤ Scribble & Tweak and enter the following settings, and then click OK.

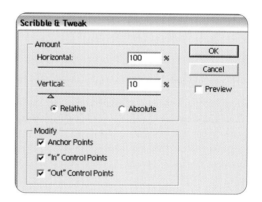

17. Your image should now look similar to the following figure:

18. To finish off the effect, select the entire Water Reflection layer. Using the Transparency palette, change the Blending mode from Normal to Soft Light.

Blending objects along a path

In the previous exercise you created two objects and blended them together. Illustrator did all of the work of interpolating how the "in-between" objects fit together. However, it also arranged them in a straight line. This straight line is called a spine. The default spine has one point for each object in the blend. Since you only used two objects, there were only two points.

If you connect those two points together you would get a straight line. You can see this by opening the Blend layer that was created when you added the spotlight. Alternatively, viewing the illustration in Outline mode will give you a good representation as well. You'll notice the two circle objects you created but you'll also see a third path as well. This path is the spine. The spine behaves much like a regular path. You can add, delete, and move the anchor points that comprise the spine. You can also modify the handles just as you can a regular path. In this exercise you'll learn how to create a custom path to apply to a blend by replacing the original spine.

1. Open Chapter_03_Spaceship.ai. This file contains a space scene with an alien spaceship flying away from the earth. However, it seems to be missing something. Perhaps a motion trail behind the spacecraft would add a little movement to the illustration.

This effect is much like the spotlight effect. You're going to draw two shapes and blend them together. Then you'll drop the opacity of one shape so it appears as if the blend is fading away. But you're going to take it a step further this time. You're going to draw a new curved path and replace your blend's straight path spine with the curved path.

2. Take note of the layers in this file. The top layer contains the spacecraft SPACECRAFT, the middle layer MOTIONTRAIL will contain the motion trail that you're about to draw, and the bottom layer BACKGROUND contains the space scene background.

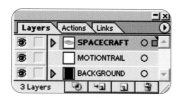

3. Lock the top (SPACECRAFT) and bottom (BACKGROUND) layer and select the middle layer (MOTIONTRAIL).

4. Select the Ellipse tool. Draw a large oval behind the spacecraft. This oval should be entirely hidden by the spacecraft. However, a reference image is included here to give you an idea of the size of this oval.

5. Set the fill color of this oval to a light yellow (R:255 G:255 B:102). Set the stroke to None.

6. Next, draw a small oval on top of the earth. Use the same fill and stroke settings as the previous oval.

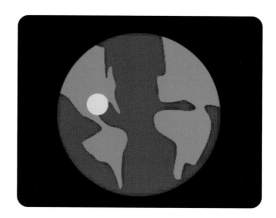

7. Select the two ovals and choose Object ➤ Blend ➤ Blend Options. Enter settings similar to this reference image.

8. Choose Object ➤ Blend ➤ Make (CTRL/CMD+ALT/ OPTION+B). You should now have a smooth blend between the two oval shapes.

9. Now, much like the spotlight effect, select the small oval and change the opacity settings to 0% in the Transparency palette.

Notice how the blend follows a straight path much like the spotlight effect. If you expand the arrow next to the blend layer in the Layers palette you'll notice a straight path in a layer on top of the two oval objects that you've blended together. This is the spine. You're now going to draw a curved path to replace that spine.

10. Select the Pen tool. Create a new layer. Draw a curved path similar to the reference image here. Press *ENTER/RETURN* to close the path.

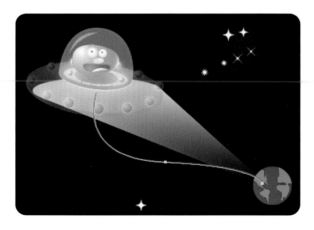

11. Select the curved path that you just drew. Hold down the *SHIFT* key and select the blend that you created in step 8.

12. Choose Object ➤ Blend ➤ Replace Spine. Your blend should now follow along the curved path that you created in step 10.

Remember, this new spine is merely a path and subject to all the rules and regulations of a path. You can add, delete, and modify anchor points just as you would a regular path. You can select the entire path and move it wherever you like and the blend will follow. In this instance, I wanted to modify the path so the curve was reversed.

13. The best way to do this is to lock the blended objects so you don't accidentally select one of them instead.

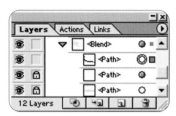

14. Select the Path sublayer in the Blend group (the spine).

15. Select the Convert Anchor Point tool from the Pen flyout menu.

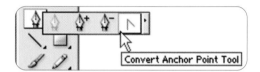

16. Click the middle point in the curved path and begin dragging. Drag this point up and to the right.

17. Release your mouse button and your blend will instantly redraw itself.

Simulating reality with blends—create a water droplet

So far, the previous two exercises have used the Blend tool to create the entire effect. In this exercise, you're going to learn how to use blends to add to an effect that will help simulate reality.

1. Open Chapter_03_LeafStart.ai. This file contains a leaf that was modeled using the Mesh tool. Don't worry, you'll see this leaf again in Chapter 6 so you can learn how to create it.

2. Next, create a new layer named WATERDROP. You need to draw a water droplet shape. You can use the Pen tool to create this or you could draw an ellipse and use one of the Warp tools in the Tools palette (*SHIFT+R*) to create this shape. Either way the shape needs to be somewhat of a blob. Water drops aren't perfectly round so keep that in mind when creating this shape. You'll notice that there is an extra layer in the source file named WATER-DROP. I have predrawn a shape for you if you would like to use this instead.

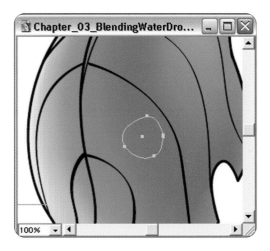

3. Using the Gradient palette, create a radial gradient similar to this reference image.

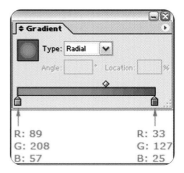

4. Select the water-drop shape. Fill it with the radial gradient that you created in step 3.

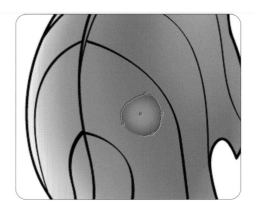

5. Select the water-drop shape again. Copy it and do a Paste In Front (*CTRL*/*CMD+F*). The bottom copy will now become the shadow. Set the fill color to black and the stroke to None.

6. Select the shadow object. Nudge the object down and to the left by using the arrow keys.

7. Using the Transparency palette (Window ➤ Transparency), change the Blending mode of the shadow to Multiply and set the opacity percentage to 40%.

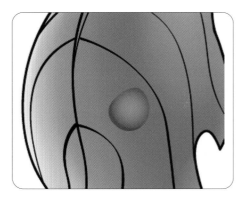

Now you have the base of the water drop in place. Next you need to add some highlights. Before moving on, it's probably best to lock the base WATERDROP layer and shadow. This will make it easier to create and select objects on top of it.

8. Next, zoom in on the water-drop object.

9. Draw a small highlight similar to this reference image. Set the fill color to white and the stroke to None.

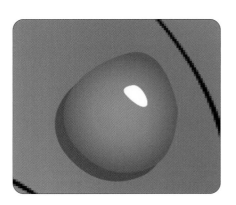

10. Select the highlight and choose Object ➤ Path ➤ Offset. Enter the following settings and click OK.

11. Change the fill color of the new offset shape (which should be underneath the smaller highlight shape) to R:69 G:192 B:50.

12. Your Layers palette should now look like the following reference image:

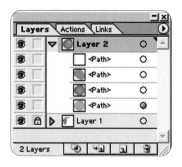

13. Select both the small highlight shape and the offset path behind it.

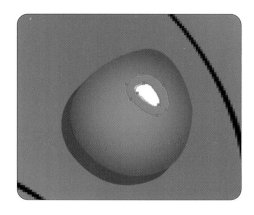

14. Choose Object ➤ Blend ➤ Blend Options. Enter the following settings:

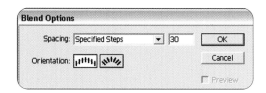

15. Choose Object ➤ Blend ➤ Make (*CTRL/CMD+ALT/ OPTION+B*).

You have now created an artificial highlight. Notice how quick and easy this was in comparison to creating a custom gradient. Also, when using a gradient, you're limited to two options—Radial and Linear. Neither of those methods will create a gradient that follows along the shape of the paths. Alternatively, you could use the Mesh tool but that is even more time consuming and may be overkill for your purposes. The next step is to create another highlight shape in a similar way. Except this time you'll use slightly different colors.

16. If you haven't already, zoom in on the water drop. Using the Pen tool, create a shape similar to this reference image. Set the fill color to R:68 G:226 B:68. Set the stroke to None.

19. Select both paths and choose Object ➤ Blend ➤ Make (*CTRL/CMD+ALT/OPTION+B*).

17. Select the new shape and choose Object ➤ Path ➤ Offset. Enter the following settings and click OK:

18. Select the new Offset path and change the fill color to R:25 G:178 B:25. Set the stroke to None.

You may have noticed that I didn't ask you to change the Blend options. Illustrator will remember the previous settings you used so there was no need to reenter them.

Here is the final image. I've added a few more water drops and spread them around.

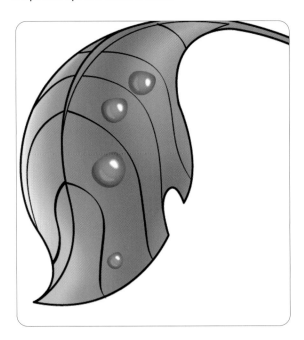

Using the Blend tool to create contoured gradients

This exercise is about using the Blend tool to simulate gradients. Why not just create a gradient you ask? Because a gradient will not conform to the contours of a nonlinear or noncircular shape. This is best described with an example image.

In the previous images, you'll notice that if the shapes are perfectly straight or round a gradient will work fine. However, once a gradient is applied to a more complex shape, things start to head south. Enter the Blend tool. By using the Blend tool you can simulate gradients that follow the contours of these more complex shapes. Once this is achieved, you'll start to unlock the true power of the Blend tool and why it has become an indispensable part of Illustrator.

1. Open `Chapter_03_FlowerStem.ai`. This file contains an illustration with a flower on a sunny day. However, the flower has no stem. It's just floating out there so you need to add something to hold it up.

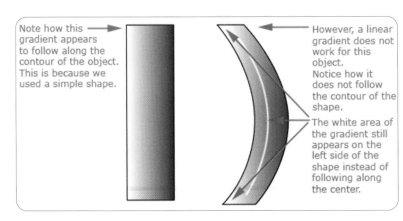

Note how this gradient appears to follow along the contour of the object. This is because we used a simple shape.

However, a linear gradient does not work for this object.
Notice how it does not follow the contour of the shape.

The white area of the gradient still appears on the left side of the shape instead of following along the center.

2. If you examine the Layers palette, you'll notice a layer named FLOWER, a layer named STEM, and a layer named BACKGROUND. The FLOWER layer and the BACKGROUND layer have been locked, because you don't need to modify them.

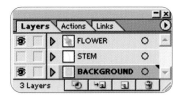

3. Create a new path with the Pen tool on the STEM layer. Nothing elaborate—just a line that's curved enough to make the stem look real. For reference images, I've removed the background layer to make the paths easier to see.

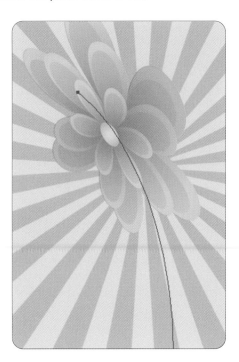

4. Click the *ENTER/RETURN* key to end the path. Set the fill color of this path to None and the stroke color to R:186 G:204 B:55. Set the stroke weight to 1 pt. Name this path LEFT.

5. Duplicate the path using the Copy and Paste In Front commands. Select the duplicate and nudge it to the right using the arrow keys. Name this layer CENTER and set the stroke color to R:51 G:204 B:51.

6. Duplicate the CENTER layer. Nudge it to the right again. This path will be the right edge of the stem so be sure to place it according to how wide you would like the stem to be. Name this layer RIGHT and set the stroke color to R:0 G:153 B:0.

8. Choose Object ➤ Blend ➤ Make (*CTRL/CMD+ ALT/OPTION+B*). Like magic, your flower stem should now appear in all of its glory. It's as if you created a custom gradient and applied it to your stem shape. In essence, you did, but you used the Blend tool instead.

OK, all of the components needed for your blend are in place. Now it's a simple matter of blending from the LEFT path to the CENTER path. Then, the CENTER path to the RIGHT path.

7. Select all three paths (LEFT, CENTER, RIGHT). Choose Object ➤ Blend ➤ Blend Options and change your settings to be similar to this reference image.

This step is optional and has nothing to do with the Blend tool but I feel it's necessary to complete the effect. Your stem needs a highlight.

9. Select the CENTER path layer. Duplicate this path using Copy and Paste In Front. This operation should place the path outside of the Blend group so that it will not affect the blend.

10. Set the stroke color of this path to white and the fill color to None. Set the stroke weight to 3 pts. This will be your highlight.

11. With the path still selected, choose Effect ➤ Blur ➤ Gaussian Blur. Enter 3 pixels for the Radius value.

12. There you have it, instant highlight.

Summary

If you haven't yet realized, Illustrator's Blend tool is simply unrivaled. Although it may seem difficult to use at first, I hope this chapter has shown you that the Blend tool isn't a mysterious feature that only experts know. In fact, the core set of features and options associated with this tool are actually minimal. That's the beauty of it—the exercises in this chapter required little drawing and most were comprised of simple shapes and paths. But the results you achieved by using the Blend tool would have been very difficult and time consuming had you created them another way. My advice to you at this point is to practice. Study reality and look at objects in the world around you. Whenever you're confronted with a difficult illustration, stop and think for a moment how a blend may help. This tool is a turning point for many illustrators. Once I started to think of my illustrations in terms of blends my skills increased exponentially. I hope this will be the case for you as well.

Press Me

Chapter 4

TRENDY EFFECTS

Trends

"Trendy" is defined as being very fashionable and up to date. Although typically associated with the fashion industry, trends can be seen throughout graphic design and illustration. Once an effect is deemed popular, more designers will tend to use it in their artwork—much like a new style of denim jeans. Clients begin to see these trends in use and start asking their designers to create them as well. Before you know it an effect or design style is deemed "trendy." But alas, much like the fashion industry, a trend will eventually fade. By the very nature of its definition, a trend must be up to date. Since things constantly change as time goes on, a trend must also fade or take on another form. In this chapter, I hope to demonstrate some trendy effects that exist now. Some are slightly older than others. However, as of the writing of this book, they are all still in use and some even getting more popular as time goes on. Trends such as the aqua style are new effects that haven't been reborn from another era, but rather created as a new style developed in recent years. Others such as the poster type and pop art effects are styles that existed several decades ago and are now becoming popular again (if you see any correlation here between graphic design and fashion you're not alone). Whatever the trend, the main goal of this chapter remains the same—to teach you some of the most wanted trendy effects and inspire you to use Illustrator to merge these techniques with your own style.

Starburst effect

This effect has been around for quite a while. If you pay attention to the advertising you see every day, you'll most likely see this effect used on a billboard or in package design. It works great for illustrations that you would like to apply a dynamic "jumping-out-of-the-page" effect to. Many times you'll see a starburst effect behind some type of product to make it look like lights are behind it, thereby displaying the product in all of its glory.

1. Open the source file named Chapter4_StarBurst Effect_Start.ai. This file contains a nice sunset scene in which you'll add your starburst. If you examine the layers you'll see layers named SKY, GROUND, and SUN.

2. Create a new layer above the rest. Name it STARBURST. Also, be sure the other layers are locked.

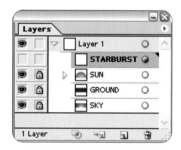

3. Select the Polygon tool. Click the Artboard to display the Polygon dialog box and enter the following settings to create a triangle. Click OK.

4. Set the triangle's fill color to white and the stroke to None.

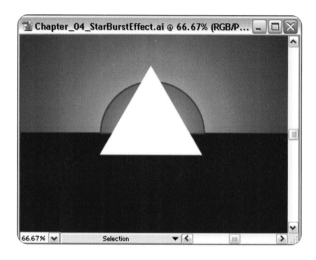

5. Choose Object ➤ Transform ➤ Scale. Enter the following settings and click OK.

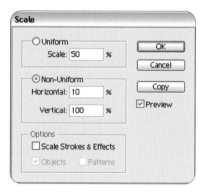

6. Choose Object ➤ Transform ➤ Rotate. Enter 180 degrees for the Angle settings and click OK. Drag this object so the bottom point just touches the horizon line in the center of the sun.

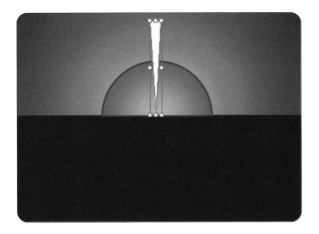

8. You should now have an image similar to this.

The basic effect is now in place. However, please take note that this is a live effect. If you select the starburst shape and examine the Appearance palette you'll see a Transform attribute that can be modified at any time. You'll also notice only the first starburst ray is selectable.

7. Next, choose Effect ➤ Distort & Transform ➤ Transform. Enter these settings into the dialog box and click OK. Take particular note of the copies and reference point locator settings. The reference point locator is the small bounding box icon just above the Random check box. This will allow you to scale an object relative to a handle on the object's bounding box.

9. Finally, to finish the effect off, you need to fade the starburst into the background, as the light gets further away from the center.

10. Create a new layer above the others. Select the Ellipse tool and click the Artboard area. Enter 450 pts for the width and height settings. This will create a circle that is the same size as the starburst shape.

11. Turn on Smart Guides (*CTRL/CMD+U*). Align the new circle precisely over the existing starburst shape.

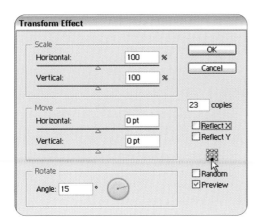

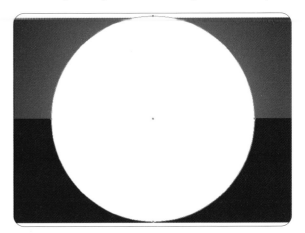

12. Fill the circle with a radial gradient similar to this. Set the stroke to None.

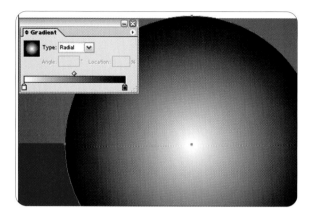

13. Pres *CTRL/CMD+A* to select all objects (the gradient circle and the starburst triangle shapes).

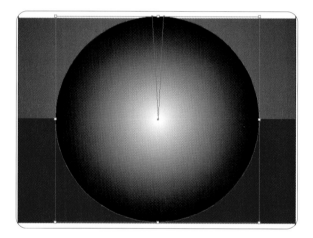

14. Open the Transparency palette (*SHIFT+F10*). Select Make Opacity Mask from the Transparency palette's flyout menu.

15. Next, select the Free Transform tool (*E*). While holding down *SHIFT+ALT/OPTION*, drag the outer handle of the triangle shape upward to enlarge it. This will expand the Starburst shape so it encompasses the entire illustration.

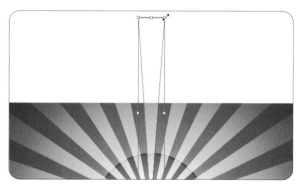

16. Finally, select the starburst shape and change the Blending mode to Soft Light in the Transparency palette. Set the opacity to 75%.

This completes the steps for this exercise. However, I encourage you to enhance or modify any of the settings outlined. One option would be to substitute the Soft Light Blending mode in step 16 with the Overlay mode. This enhances the color of the illustration a bit—especially around the sun. Then reduce the opacity to around 50% to soften the effect. You may also want to try moving the starburst sublayer below the SUN sublayer.

Retro background patterns

Retro is back! Take a look around you. What was "in" 30 to 40 years ago is back in today. This holds especially true for graphic design and illustration. Many artists are turning to the '50s, '60s, and '70s for inspiration. This effect will walk you through creating a retro-style background pattern to apply to your illustrations so you can give them that nostalgic feel. It will also teach you essential techniques for creating patterns within Illustrator. Patterns must be perfectly symmetrical in order for them to tile seamlessly. Illustrator offers many tools that remove the guesswork when you're creating repeating patterns by allowing you to create more precise patterns.

1. Create a new RGB Illustrator document.

2. Select the Rectangle tool and click once on the Artboard. Enter 100 pts for the Width and Height settings.

3. Set the fill color to R:102 G:201 B:0 and the stroke to None. Name this layer BACKGROUND and lock it.

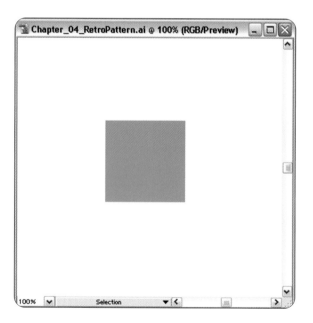

Color choice makes up a retro style image as much as the actual artwork itself. I encourage you to search for your own color combinations. Websites, old magazines, and books can all be sources of inspiration when choosing colors and patterns. About.com offers two palettes that I found particularly useful:

1950s Palette—http://desktoppub.about.com/ library/weekly/blcpatomicage.htm

1960s Palette—http://desktoppub.about.com/ library/weekly/blcpsixties.htm

Also, some color index books have preselected color combinations already included. Many times they offer the RGB and CMYK equivalents so all you need to do is type in the settings—a real timesaver.

OK, now that your base tile outline is in place you need to add some guides. You're also going to use Smart Guides in this exercise. As I mentioned previously, keep the keyboard shortcut for Smart Guides handy to minimize any frustration when using them (CTRL/CMD+U).

4. First, choose View ➤ Smart Guides (CTRL/CMD+U). Next, turn on the rulers if they aren't on already by choosing View ➤ Show Rulers (CTRL/CMD+R).

5. Create a new layer. Drag a vertical guide from the left ruler area out toward the center of the square and allow it to snap to the center point so you can separate the square vertically. You may notice this guide trying to snap to certain points because you have Smart Guides turned on. The key to making it snap to the center point is to drag your cursor over the center point of the square. This targets that square as the object in focus. Illustrator will then allow you to snap your guide to the center point.

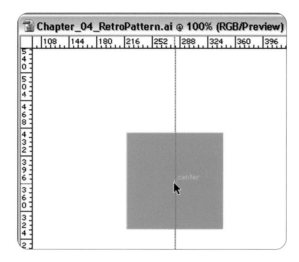

6. Drag a horizontal guide from the top ruler area in a similar way to separate the square horizontally.

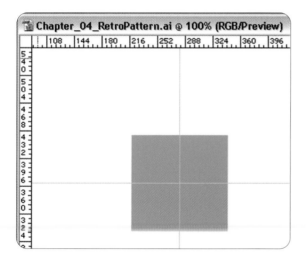

By creating guides, you've broken your square into four quadrants. This will help you visually lay out your pattern to ensure that it's symmetrical.

7. Now let's start with the top left quadrant. Create a new layer above the BACKGROUND layer. Select the Pen tool and draw an irregular rectangular shape similar to this reference image. Set the fill color of the rectangle to R:165 G:235 B:134 and

the stroke to None. This shape doesn't have to be perfect, nor should it. Wavy and uneven shapes are trademarks of the retro style.

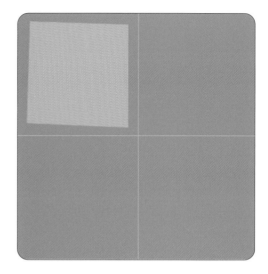

8. Again, draw another rectangle shape on top of the previous one. Change the fill color of the new shape by keeping it selected and selecting the Eyedropper tool (I). Then simply click once on the original background square to apply its fill and stroke attributes to the selected shape.

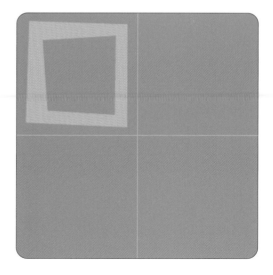

9. Finally, draw yet another rectangle shape on top of the previous one. Set the fill color to R:2 G:122 B:187 and the stroke to None.

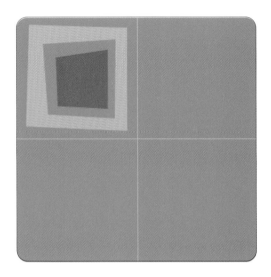

10. Now add a small stroked rectangular shape on top of the previous shape you drew. This time set the fill color to None and the stroke color to R:255 G:153 B:0.

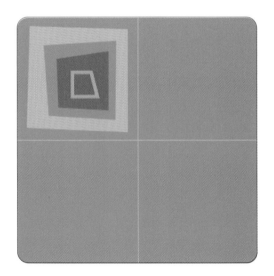

11. Select all (*CTRL/CMD+A*) of the shapes that you just drew (remember that your original BACKGROUND layer is locked so it will not be selected). Duplicate them using the Copy and Paste In Front commands. Drag this duplicated set to the bottom right quadrant.

12. Choose Object ➤ Transform ➤ Rotate and enter 180 degrees for the Angle settings.

If you haven't turned Smart Guides off yet, do so now. You may have noticed how they can become annoying if you forget to turn them off when you don't need them.

13. Repeat steps 8 and 12 for the top right and bottom left quadrants. This time, use the reference image for color settings when creating the rectangles.

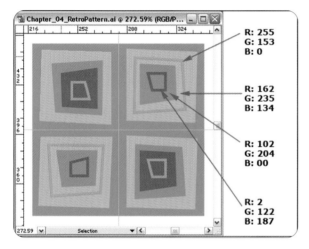

R: 255
G: 153
B: 0

R: 162
G: 235
B: 134

R: 102
G: 204
B: 00

R: 2
G: 122
B: 187

Now that you have the pattern tile created, it's time to save it as a swatch so you can apply it to shapes later on.

14. First, unlock the BACKGROUND layer.

15. Select all shapes on the Artboard (*CTRL/CMD+A*).

16. Make sure your Swatches palette is visible (Window ➤ Swatches).

17. Now, simply drag the selected objects into the Swatches palette. You'll notice a small swatch appear that indicates that your selection has been turned into a pattern swatch.

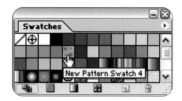

18. To see this new pattern swatch in action, draw a shape on the Artboard with the Pen tool and set the fill attribute for this shape to the swatch that you just created. Instant pattern!

You can vary the size of the tiled pattern by inserting a step between steps 16 and 17. After you do a Select All (CTRL/CMD+A), use the Free Transform tool (E) or choose Object ➤ Transform ➤ Scale and scale your tile down to the appropriate size. Then drag it into the Swatches palette for a smaller pattern.

Aqua smooth plastic buttons

What trendy effects chapter could be complete without a plastic effect exercise? Aqua plastic effects have been, and still are, one of the hottest trends in web and graphic design. Apple started it a few years back with their release of the Mac OS X operating system. After that, tutorials on how to create plastic blue X's have appeared everywhere. Tutorials on buttons, shapes, and just about everything that someone could find to add a plastic effect to followed soon after. However, most of these effects revolved around using paint programs (Photoshop, Fireworks, and so on) to create them. Many contained elaborate steps to produce the final rasterized product. This effect, however, is achieved in Illustrator. The benefit of this is that it's a vector shape. This means it remains editable and can be scaled to your heart's content—try doing that in Photoshop.

1. Create a new RGB Illustrator document.

2. Select the Rounded Rectangle tool. Click the Artboard and enter the following settings. Name this layer BASE. This will be your button shape.

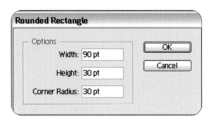

3. Fill this shape with the following linear gradient. The light blue color stop is R:138 G:219 B:255 and the dark blue color is R:0 G:51 B:153. Set the stroke to None.

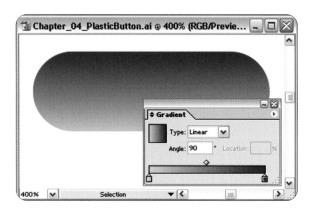

4. Copy the BASE layer shape. Lock the BASE layer and create a new layer above it named BLEND1. Paste the copy in front of the original (CTRL/CMD+F).

5. Change the fill color to R:2 G:122 B:187 and use the Transparency palette to set the opacity of this shape to 80%.

6. Select the BLEND1 layer shape. Choose Object ➤ Transform ➤ Scale. Enter the following settings and click Copy.

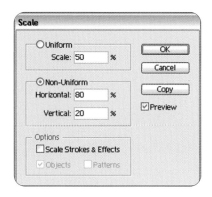

7. Change the fill color of this new shape to R:105 G:223 B:255. Drag or nudge it down toward the bottom of the BLEND1 layer shape.

8. Your Layers palette should now look like this:

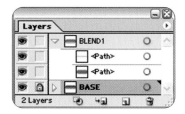

9. Select the two shapes in the BLEND1 layer. Choose Object ➤ Blend ➤ Blend Options. Change the spacing to Smooth Color and click OK. Then choose Object ➤ Blend ➤ Make (CTRL/CMD+ ALT/OPTION+B) to apply the blend. Lock the BLEND1 layer at this point.

As you've witnessed in the previous step, the Blend Options dialog box offers a Spacing *setting named* Smooth Color. *When creating a blend based on this setting, Illustrator will attempt to approximate a smooth color transition between the objects being blended. For the most part, Illustrator will create a smooth blend with this setting. However, if it doesn't, you may need to resort to the* Specified Steps *setting and experiment with larger step values.*

10. Unlock the BASE layer. Select the BASE layer shape and copy it (CTRL/CMD+C). You may need to temporarily hide the BLEND1 layer if you want to see the gradient shape. Lock the BASE layer again and create a new layer above BLEND1 called HIGHLIGHT. Paste the copied shape in front to maintain alignment on the HIGHLIGHT layer.

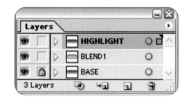

11. Select the HIGHLIGHT layer shape. Choose Object ➤ Transform ➤ Scale. Enter the following settings and click OK.

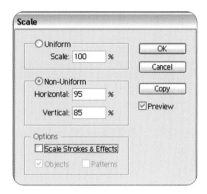

12. Set the fill color of the HIGHLIGHT layer to white and the stroke to None.

13. Create a new layer above the HIGHLIGHT layer. Select the Rectangle tool and create a rectangle that is slightly larger than the white shape you created in the previous step. Be sure this rectangle extends slightly beyond the rounded rectangle shape in all directions.

14. Fill this rectangle with the following white to black linear gradient and set the stroke to None.

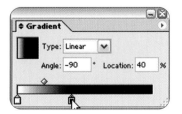

15. Your image should look like this reference image so far.

16. Choose Select ➤ All (*CTRL/CMD+A*) to select the gradient rectangle shape and the white HIGHLIGHT layer shape (Remember, the BASE and BLEND1 layers are locked so they will not be selected).

17. Be sure the Transparency palette is visible by choosing Window ➤ Transparency.

18. With the two shapes selected, choose Make Opacity Mask from the Transparency palette's fly-out menu.

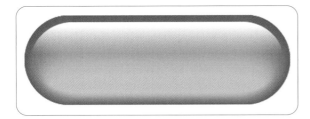

19. Nudge this new object up slightly so it's almost even with the top of the BASE layer shape.

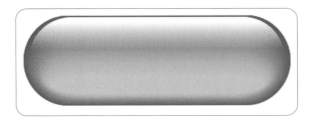

Great! The aqua plastic button is now complete. You can take this a few steps further and add a drop shadow and an inner glow to add some depth to the button.

20. Unlock the BASE layer. Select the BASE layer shape. Choose Effect ➤ Stylize ➤ Drop Shadow and enter the following settings:

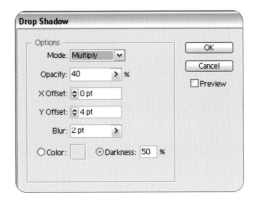

21. With the BASE layer still selected, Choose Effect ➤ Stylize ➤ Inner Glow and enter these settings.

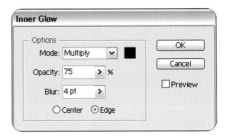

22. Add some text and you're finished. An 18 pt sans-serif font such as Myriad or Lucida Grande works well here.

Retro style poster type

When working through this exercise, it will be necessary to draw a wineglass shape. This shape will eventually be filled with text that conforms to its contours. The benefit of using the source file for this effect is that this shape is already predrawn for you. However, if you're in a particularly creative mood when you read this and would like to draw your own, by all means, do so. Other than a hidden layer showing you what the final outcome of this effect is, you'll gain nothing else from using the source file and can just as easily create a new Illustrator document.

1. Open Chapter_04_PosterType.ai from the source files. You'll notice a BACKGROUND layer that contains an outline of the wineglass and some other elements.

2. Regardless of whether you're using the source file or your own, the first step is to create a triangle shape to use as a container for your type. Create a new layer above BACKGROUND and name it CONTAINER.

3. Using the Pen tool, draw a triangle. This triangle should be the same shape as the top of the wineglass without the stem. However, don't trace the exact outline of the glass. Instead, draw the triangle just within the boundaries of the white outline. Fill this container shape with black and set the stroke to None.

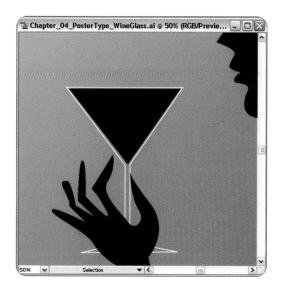

> *As you create this effect, you'll notice that the type you use will conform to the shape you draw in step 1. If you used the entire wineglass shape (stem included), your type would try to conform down that long skinny rectangle shape. You definitely don't want this to happen, which is why I've created an outline wineglass shape as well as the triangle shape within.*

You may want to save a duplicate of that shape since you may need it later for a background.

4. Create a new layer on top of the CONTAINER layer called TYPE. Now draw three wavy lines with the Pen tool as I have in the reference image. Set the fill color to None and the stroke to white. Also set the stroke weight to 3 pts.

5. Select the three lines you've just created. Choose Object ➤ Path ➤ Outline Stroke. Your strokes have now been turned into editable shapes. Don't deselect the paths yet.

6. Make sure the Pathfinder palette is visible by choosing Window ➤ Pathfinder.

7. *Shift*-select the BACKGROUND layer shape in addition to the three line shapes that should still be selected.

8. Hold down the *Alt/Option* key. Choose the Subtract from Shape Area option in the Pathfinder palette. This will subtract the line shapes from the basic background shape and leave you with four individual shapes. Note how the background now shows through where the lines were.

9. Next, choose Object ➤ Ungroup *(Shift+Ctrl/ Cmd+G)*. Your Layers palette should now look like this.

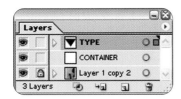

10. Select the Type tool. On the same layer as the CONTAINER shapes, create four **separate** type objects off to the side. To do so, you need to type a word, then click once on the Type tool in the toolbox and click elsewhere on the Artboard to type another word. Repeat this for the remaining two words. Don't simply type all four words within the same type container. I used a font called Keep On Truckin, set at 72 pts. This font can be downloaded for free from www.fontdiner.com (it's a great site for some nice retro style fonts).

11. *Shift*-select the four type objects. Choose Object ➤ Arrange ➤ Send To Back. This will put all of the type objects behind any other objects within that layer. Your Layers palette should look similar to this now.

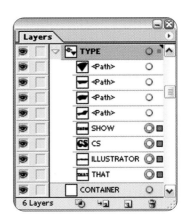

12. Select the THAT type object and *Shift*-select the top piece of the wineglass container. Choose Object ➤ Envelope Distort ➤ Make with Top Object *(Ctrl/Cmd+Alt/Option+C)*. Notice that it isn't necessary to align the word anywhere near or above the container shape.

13. Repeat this process for the remaining type objects and wineglass shapes.

Everything looks good so far but you may notice that the ILLUSTRATOR word is warped too much. You can fix this by changing the font size of some of the letters within the word. Just follow along with the next few steps.

14. Select the Envelope sublayer in the Layers palette that contains the ILLUSTRATOR word.

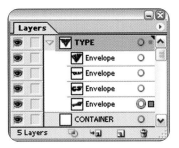

15. Choose Object ➤ Envelope Distort ➤ Edit Contents.

16. Switch to Outline view (View ➤ Outline) so you can see the text more easily. You can now edit the text as you normally would.

17. Select the first 7 letters of ILLUSTRATOR— (**ILLUSTR**).

18. Change the font size to 33 pts for those letters.

105

19. Select the A and change the font size to 30 pts.

20. Select TOR and change the font size to 48 pts.

21. Deselect the text and switch back to Preview mode (View ➤ Preview). You may notice the text is now slightly off to the left and doesn't conform to the container shape.

22. To remedy this, target the ILLUSTRATOR word's Envelope sublayer. Drag (or nudge with the arrow keys) the text to the right and slightly up to position it into place.

That's it! Your retro poster type is now created. However, the text could use a different fill color.

23. To change the color of the words, select each type object and choose Object ➤ Envelope Distort ➤ Edit Contents *(SHIFT+CTRL/CMD+V)*. You can now change the fill color as you normally would (I used R:255 G:255 B:62).

> *You can SHIFT-select each Envelope type object and choose the* Edit Contents *command all at once. This reduces the inconvenience of selecting each layer individually.*

24. When you're done with your changes simply choose Object ➤ Envelope Distort ➤ Edit Envelope. Turn the page to see the final picture.

High-tech Euro collage effects

High-tech Euro collages are typically trademarked by abstract 3D models created in programs such as Maya, 3D Studio Max, Lightwave, and Cinema. Over time, they have been referred to as "Euro" collages—I suppose if you're from Europe then they are just collages. Whatever the name, 3D abstract collages took the graphic design community by storm. While Illustrator now has a 3D tool (which I'll cover in Chapter 5), it's probably not the best place to create the key 3D elements of these objects. However, it isn't just the 3D aspect that makes these collages so popular—it's the effects and small graphic elements that go along with them. See the screenshot opposite for an idea of what I mean.

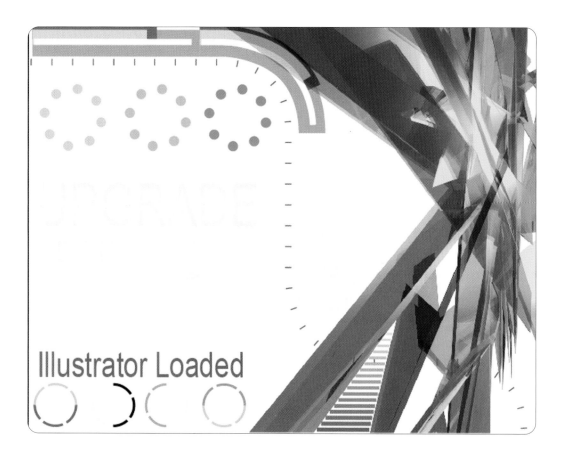

Many times, these effects are created in paint programs such as Photoshop. In this exercise, I hope to show you a better alternative to this task. In addition to saving you time, these techniques will inspire you to use Illustrator's tools to enhance your artwork. They will also demonstrate how powerful Illustrator can be with only a few simple shapes to work with.

Open `Chapter_04_CollageEffects_Start.ai`. Note that there is one layer in this file. It's named BACKGROUND and it contains an image that was rendered in a 3D program. You aren't going to modify this layer but you will be adding many components to layers on top of it.

There are six mini-effects that you're going to work through in this exercise. Each of these is one small treatment to add to the collage that will build the overall artwork up.

Effect 1: Fading bars

1. First, note that the BACKGROUND layer is locked so it doesn't get in the way. Create a new layer above BACKGROUND. Zoom in on the lower right-hand portion of the image.

2. Using the Rectangle tool, draw a rectangle between the two orange objects protruding out from the center. Fill this rectangle with R:112 G:112 B:112 and set the stroke to None.

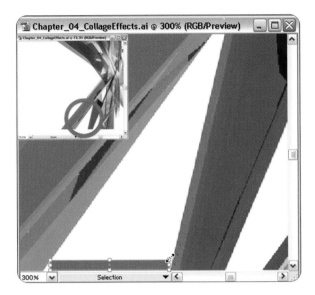

3. Draw a smaller rectangle as the reference image portrays. Set the fill color to R:242 G:242 B:242 and the stroke to None.

Effect 2: Dashed circle

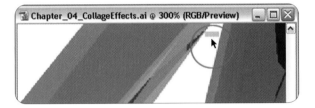

6. Create a new layer. Select the Ellipse tool and click the Artboard to draw a circle. Enter 25 pts in the Width and Height settings.

7. Set the fill color to None and the stroke color to R:200 G:200 B:200.

8. Move the circle into place as shown in the following image.

4. Choose Object ➤ Blend ➤ Blend Options and make your settings similar to this reference image.

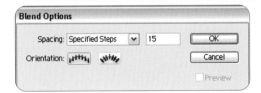

5. Select the two rectangle shapes and choose Object ➤ Blend ➤ Make.

9. With the circle selected, open the Stroke palette (Window ➤ Stroke). Enter settings similar to this reference image. Note that the Dashed Line check box is checked. You should also specify that you would like the dashes to extend 25 pts, and that you would like to leave a 5 pt gap between each one.

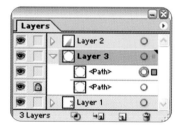

10. Next, select the circle and make a copy of it (CTRL/CMD+C). Paste this copy in front (CTRL/CMD+F) to maintain alignment. Lock the sublayer containing the bottom copy of the circle.

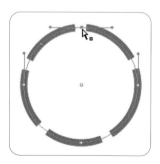

11. Change the stroke color of the top copy to R:117 G:117 B:117 and leave the fill color set to None.

12. Select the open arrow Direct Selection tool (A). Select the top anchor point on the circle and press the DELETE key.

13. Now lock this sublayer and unlock the bottom copy of the circle.

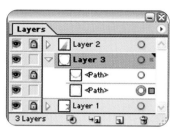

14. Using the Direct Selection tool again, select the bottom anchor point of the circle and press the DELETE key.

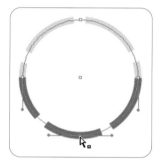

15. You should now have something that looks like this.

16. Unlock all layers and sublayers used to create this shape and make three copies. Spread the copies horizontally along the image that you can see overleaf. Also, change the colors of the copies to different shades of gray to give a slightly random look to them.

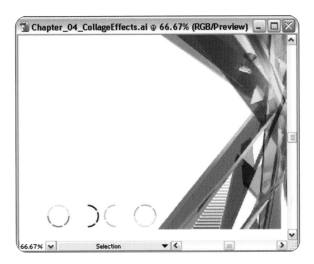

Effect 3: Dashed path

17. Create a new layer above the others. Using the Pen tool, draw a path, similar to the one shown, along the image, as I have here.

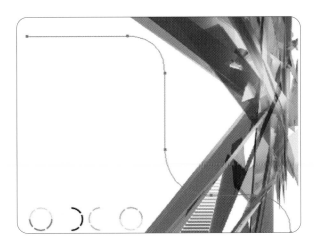

18. Set the fill color to None and the stroke to R:102 G:102 B:102. Open the Stroke palette and enter settings similar to what you see this reference image.

19. This will create a dashed line as shown here.

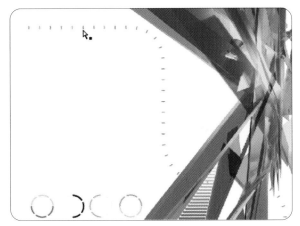

Effect 4: Jagged line brush

20. Next, lock all layers. Create a new layer. Select the Rectangle tool and click the Artboard to draw a rectangle. Enter 200 pts for the width and 30 pts for the height.

21. Set the fill color to R:114 G:114 B:114 and the stroke to None.

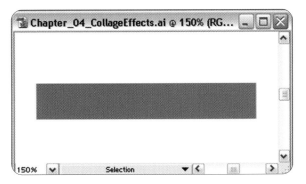

22. Zoom in on this rectangle. Draw another rectangle shape on top of the previous one using the mouse this time instead of entering the exact settings. Set the fill color to black and the stroke to None.

23. Once again, draw another rectangle. Set the fill color to R:181 G:181 B:181 and the stroke to None.

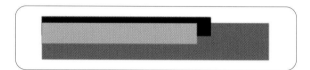

24. Finally, draw one more rectangle. Set this fill color to white and the stroke to None. Note that this isn't an exact science and I haven't provided you with exact measurements. A certain degree of randomness is appealing and necessary when creating this pattern.

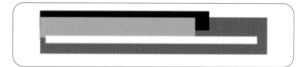

25. Select the four rectangle shapes that you just created. You're going to create a pattern brush out of this shape so be sure your Brushes palette is visible (Window ➤ Brushes).

26. Drag the selected shapes into the Brushes palette. When the New Brush dialog box displays select New Pattern Brush and click OK. The Pattern Brush Options dialog box will open next. Enter Jagged Line Brush in the Name text box and click OK to select the default options.

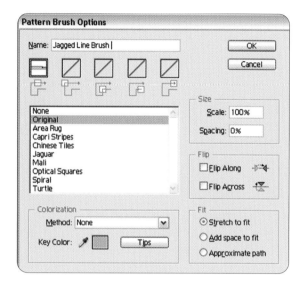

27. Using the Pen tool, draw a path similar to what you see in this reference image.

28. Set the fill color to None and the stroke to black. With the path still selected, click the new Jagged Line Brush to apply it to the path. Also, using the Transparency palette, change the opacity settings for this shape to 50%. Your image should now look like this:

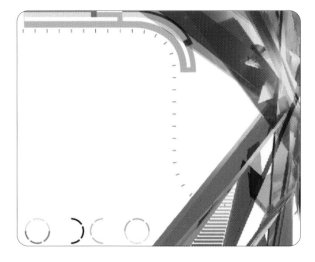

Effect 5: Circles

29. Create a new layer. Using the Ellipse tool, create a circle that is 12 pts in width and height. Set the fill color to R:115 G:190 B:30 and the stroke to None.

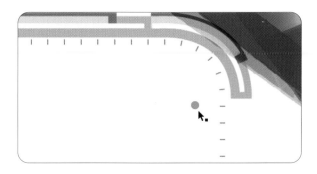

30. Select the circle shape and choose Effect ➤ Distort & Transform ➤ Transform. Enter the following settings. Again, be sure to select the correct point on the reference point locator icon located in the bottom right of the dialog box.

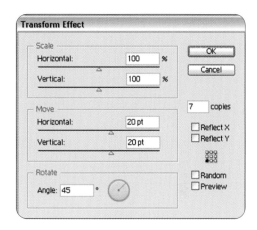

31. You should now have an object that looks like this:

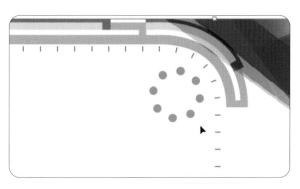

32. Create two duplicates of this object and position them according to this reference image:

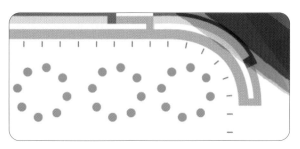

33. Change the fill colors of the two objects to R:255 G:180 B:100 (Orange) and R:211 G:211 B:211 (Gray).

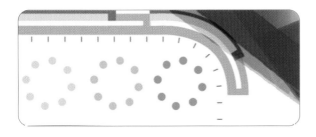

Effect 6: Text

34. The last effect isn't really an effect but it's a necessary component—Text.

35. Using the Type tool, create some strategically placed text throughout the Illustration. Technical terms such as "Uploading," "Loading Complete," and "Upgrade" always seem popular.

36. In this final image, you can see that I've varied the typeface, size, and opacity settings to finalize the effect.

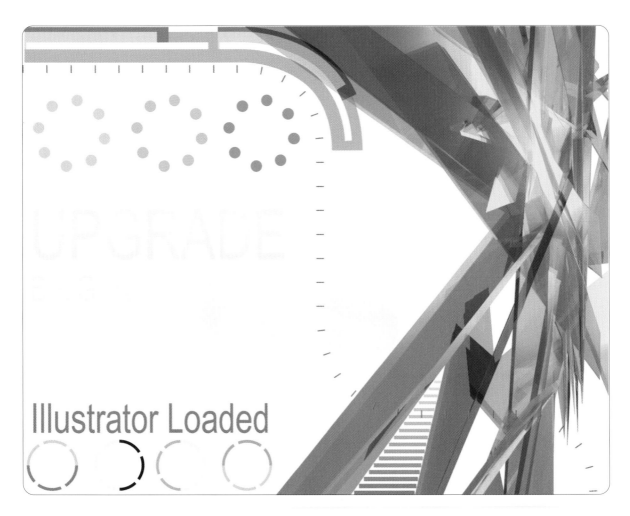

Pop art vector illustration

Pop art was a very popular artistic style that emerged in the mid 1950s and lasted well into the 1960s. This movement focused on bringing back the materials of everyday life to popular culture—hence the word "pop." Today, pop art has been somewhat revived. As with many things in our current culture, what was once out is in again. This holds true for pop art. Many illustrators are beginning to bring this style back into their work. With this in mind, you'll walk through the creation of a pop art illustration and see how Illustrator can be used in creating artwork based on this revived style.

1. Create a new RGB Illustrator document. Using the Ellipse tool, click once on the Artboard and enter 265 pts for the width and 455 pts for the height to create an oval. Name this layer BASE.

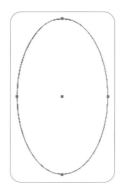

2. Open the Appearance palette (*SHIFT+F6*). Set the Fill attribute color to R:138 G:219 B:255. Drag the Stroke attribute below the Fill and set the stroke color to R:7 G:124 B:165.

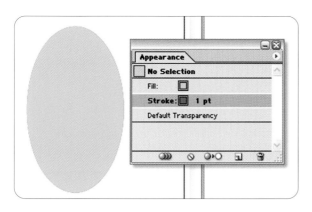

3. With the Stroke attribute selected, click the Duplicate Selected Item box at the bottom of the Appearance palette. Select the duplicate and set the color of this stroke to R:138 G:219 B:255. Using the Stroke palette, set the weight of this stroke to 33.

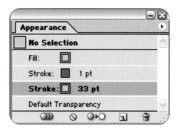

4. Repeat this process using the accompanying image as a reference. When you're done you should have a large oval that appears to contain several ovals with various strokes within.

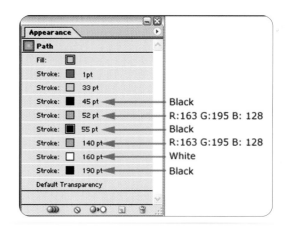

5. Choose Window ➤ Brush Libraries ➤ Borders_ Geometric1 to open a new Brush palette. Select the first Stroke attribute in the Appearance palette and click the Triangles 1.1 brush to apply it to the selected Stroke attribute.

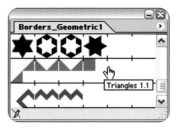

Notice that by applying this brush you've also changed the color to red. This is because the actual brush is red. This color doesn't fit with the illustration so you need to change it.

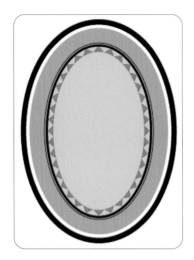

6. Next, open your Brushes palette. Notice the brush applied in the previous step is now located within this palette. Double click it to display the Pattern Brush Options dialog box. Under Colorization, change the method to Tints and click OK. When asked if you would like to apply the changes to existing brush strokes, click the Apply to Strokes button. This will allow the stroke color (in this case, dark blue) to be applied to the pattern brush.

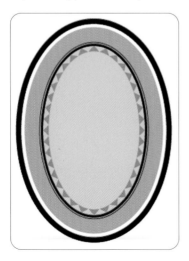

Next, you're going to add some halftone dots to start adding that pop art feel.

7. Duplicate the BASE layer and position the duplicate below the original. Rename this layer to DOTS. Lock and hide the BASE layer.

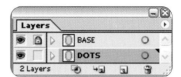

8. Select oval in the dots layer and press the *D* key to reset the Fill and Stroke settings to their defaults. Rename this sublayer ORIGINAL.

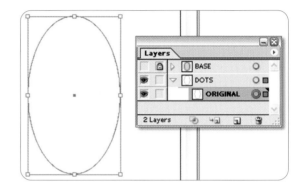

9. Select the ORIGINAL oval and choose Object ➤ Path ➤ Offset Path. Enter 150 pts for the Offset setting and click OK. Set the fill color of the resulting path to white and the stroke to None. Also, rename this sublayer to OUTER BLEND.

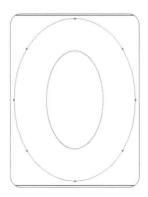

10. Select the ORIGINAL oval one more time. Once again, choose Object ➤ Path ➤ Offset Path. This time enter –50 pts in the Offset setting text box and click OK. Set the fill color of this oval to black and the stroke to None. Rename this sublayer INNER BLEND.

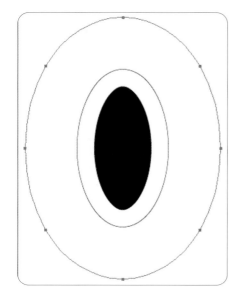

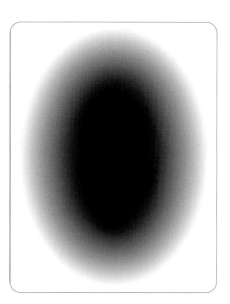

> *If you aren't happy with the gradient produced by the blend operation, you can edit the blend options by selecting the* Blend *sublayer and choosing* Object ➤ Blend ➤ Blend Options.

11. Delete the ORIGINAL sublayer because you no longer need it. Your Layers palette should now look similar to this reference image:

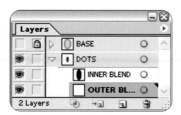

Next, you're going to blend the two ovals together to produce a black to white gradient.

12. Select the INNER BLEND and OUTER BLEND sub-layers and press *CTRL/CMD+ALT/OPTION+B* to blend them together.

Now you'll add the dots.

13. Select the Blend sublayer located within the DOTS layer. Choose Effect ➤ Sketch ➤ Halftone Pattern. Set the size to 1 and the contrast to 41. Also, be sure the Pattern Type is set to Dot and click OK.

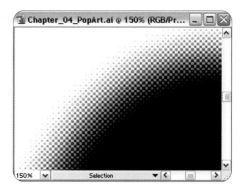

14. If you've followed along so far, go ahead and unhide the BASE layer. You should now have something similar to this reference image.

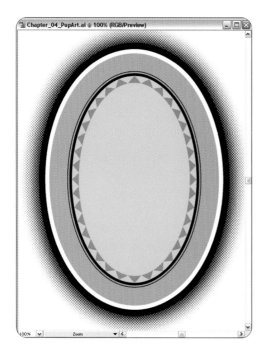

Great. The pop-art effect is now taking shape. The next group of steps will walk you through adding some retro-style clip art to the illustration. Since you're going to be opening another file, now would be a great time to save your illustration.

15. Open Chapter_04_GuyWaving.ai from the source files for this chapter. This file contains clip art of a man riding in a car and waving.

16. Do a Select All (*CTRL/CMD+A*) and copy (*CTRL/CMD+C*) this art to your clipboard. Now move back to the original illustration you've been working on. Create a new layer above BASE named CLIPART. Lock the BASE and DOTS layer at this time as well.

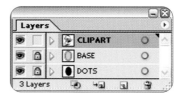

17. Paste (*CTRL/CMD+V*) the clip art into the CLIPART layer.

18. Select the clip art. Position it in place and scale it using the bounding box or Free Transform tool to match this reference image. The key here is to have most of the man and car within the blue area of the oval but leave part of his left hand protruding out.

19. Notice how certain areas of the clip art are white. You didn't notice this on the white background but it's very obvious against the oval background you're using in this illustration. This is a common issue when using clip art. To alleviate this problem, select the WAVING MAN sublayer and change the Blending mode to Multiply using the Transparency palette.

Next, you'll add some color to the clip art.

20. Create a new sublayer below the WAVING MAN sublayer. Name this sublayer COLOR.

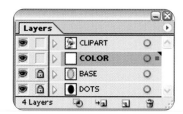

21. Using the Pen tool, trace around any skin areas of the man. This process will require three shapes—one for the head, the right hand, and the left hand. However, this doesn't have to be exact. One characteristic of the retro pop-art illustration style is that this type of colorization is very loose. When you're done, fill these shapes with R:255 G:255 B:184 and set the stroke to None.

22. Next, create a thin shadow by duplicating the WAVING MAN sublayer. Paste the duplicate on a sublayer directly below the original. Rename this sublayer SHADOW.

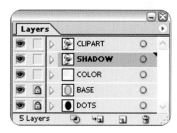

23. Select the SHADOW sublayer and change the opacity to 20% in the Transparency palette. Then use the arrow keys to nudge this duplicate down and to the left several times.

All that remains is the addition of some text to bring this illustration alive.

24. First, you need a path to align your text to. Duplicate the BASE layer once again. Position the duplicate layer below the CLIPART layer and name it TEXT.

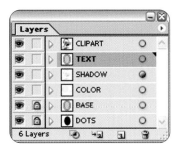

25. Select the oval shape within the TEXT layer and press *D* to reset the Fill and Stroke settings.

26. Next, select the oval and choose Object ➤ Path ➤ Offset Path. Enter 30 pts and click OK. This will produce another path slightly larger than the original. This will be the path that you'll align the text to.

27. Delete the original smaller oval path. Select the Type on a Path tool and click the oval created in the previous step to align your text to this path. Type any text you see fit here in caps. For the font, I chose a bold Chaparral Pro (ships with Illustrator CS) set at 48 pts. You may need to adjust the Baseline Shift setting up to 3 pts for this as well.

For a detailed example of how to apply text to a path refer to the Type on a Path exercise in Chapter 2.

28. Finally, add more text throughout the illustration. I've added more type at the bottom of the oval as well as some inside.

Summary

After working through this chapter you should feel as if you've sampled various trendy effects that exist today and learned how to create them in Illustrator CS. However, I encourage you to go beyond this chapter in search for trendy ideas in illustration. Inspiration exists everywhere. Magazine ads, TV, and the Web all contain many examples of trendy artwork. I urge you to attempt to study and re-create these effects in Illustrator on your own. Once you begin to see the thought process that other illustrators went through you'll begin coming up with your own ideas. At that point, you'll be well equipped to create illustrations that not only contain trendy effects, but also carry your own unique and individual style with them.

Chapter 5
3D EFFECTS

The new 3D effect

The new 3D effect in Illustrator CS is perhaps one of the biggest upgrades in the product's history. Using this tool, you can now add the illusion of depth to an otherwise flat illustration in just minutes. While many 3D effects were possible in previous versions of Illustrator, they often required a great deal of time to create. In addition, the quality of these effects was often lacking the professionalism required for commercial illustration. Third-party plug-ins were also available but none were native to Illustrator in the way that the 3D effects within CS were. These effects not only give you new creative possibilities but they are all live effects. This means that you're never "stuck" with an effect. If you see the need to change your 3D settings later, you have the same flexibility as you have with Illustrator's other live effects such as Drop Shadow or Outer Glow. In this chapter, you'll learn several techniques and tips for creating 3D illustrations within Illustrator CS. You'll be quickly introduced to the basic settings within the 3D Effects dialog boxes. You'll then move on to more advanced techniques where you'll learn to create objects you never thought possible in Illustrator.

Creating dice with the 3D tool

Creating 3D objects out of 2D drawings isn't the only task that the 3D effect tool can accomplish. It can also map custom artwork to your objects. In this exercise, you'll jump right in and use the Extrude & Bevel effect. But you aren't just going to create a 3D object—you're going to map artwork to the six sides of it and create some dice so that you're ready to roll some big money in Las Vegas (or Monopoly if that's more your style).

1. Open `Chapter_05_DiceStart.ai`. This file contains seven layers. The bottom layer (SURFACE) is a red square and each layer on top of it (ONE through SIX) corresponds to the dots on the side of a pair of dice. However, before you can begin, you must complete some prep work. In order to map artwork to a 3D object, the artwork must reside in the Symbols palette. That is going to be your first task.

> *Note that the bottom layer's (SURFACE) red square has its* Opacity *setting in the Transparency palette set to* 75%*. This is because most dice are translucent. You can actually see the sides facing away from you through the sides that are in front. When you map this artwork to the cube, you can instruct Illustrator to preserve this transparency thus adding to the realism of this effect.*

2. First, make sure your Symbols palette is visible (*SHIFT+F11*).

3. Select the SURFACE layer and *SHIFT*-select the ONE layer.

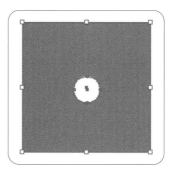

> *You may want to hide the other layers to make it easier for you to see what is selected.*

4. Click the New Symbol button at the base of the Symbols palette and enter Side 1 as the symbol name. You should now see your object as a new symbol in the Symbols palette.

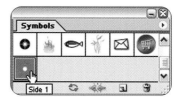

5. Next, hide layer ONE and unhide layer TWO. Select the SURFACE layer and *SHIFT*-select the TWO layer. Repeat step 4 but name this symbol Side 2.

6. Repeat this process for the remaining four sides of the die, making sure to keep the established naming convention (Side 1, Side 2) intact as you progress.

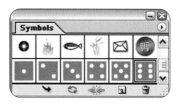

Your artwork is now created and ready to be mapped to a 3D object.

7. Lock and hide the SURFACE and ONE to SIX layers. Create a new layer on top of the others and name it DICE.

8. Select the Rectangle tool and click the Artboard once. Enter 200 pts for the width and height settings to create a square shape.

9. Set the fill color of the square to R: 255 G:0 B:0 and the stroke to None.

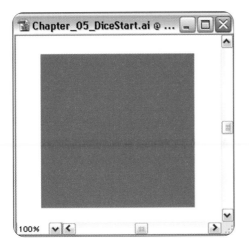

10. Select the square and choose Effect ➤ 3D ➤ Extrude & Bevel. Select the Preview check box. You only need to change two settings in this dialog box. First the Extrude Depth setting. You want the square to be extruded (length) by the same amount of its width and height setting (200 pts from step 6). So enter 200 pts for the Extrude Depth setting. Next, be sure to check the Draw Hidden Faces check box at the bottom of the dialog box. Don't click OK yet.

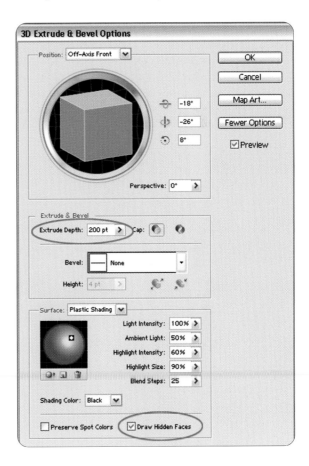

11. Click the Map Art button to bring up the Map Art dialog box. Take particular note of the Surface setting. Remember, you now have a cube that has six sides, hence the description 1 of 6 in the text box.

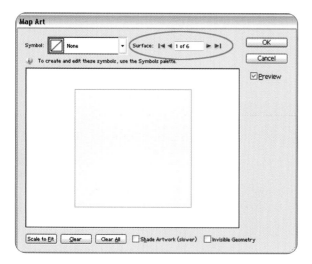

12. Next, choose the artwork that you would like to map to surface 1 from the Symbol drop-down box. Since you've already created the six sides of the die, simply click the drop-down arrow and select Side 1.

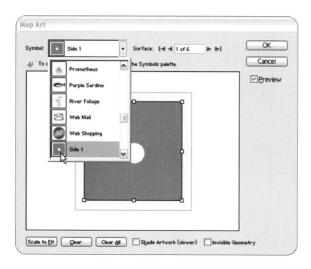

13. By looking in the Preview area you'll notice the artwork doesn't fit exactly on top of the side of the cube.

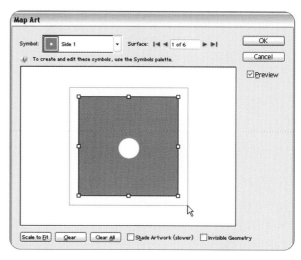

14. This is easily remedied by clicking the Scale to Fit button in the bottom left of the Map Art dialog box.

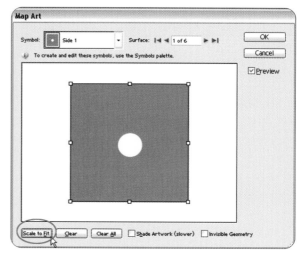

15. Next, click the Next Surface arrow button, just to the right of the text box, to move to surface 2. Select Side 2 from the Symbol drop-down menu. Once again click the Scale to Fit button.

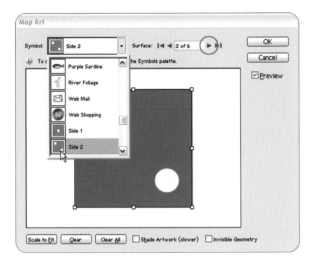

16. Repeat this process for the remaining four sides, making sure to click the Scale to Fit button each time. Once you've done this, you're still not ready to click the OK button just yet.

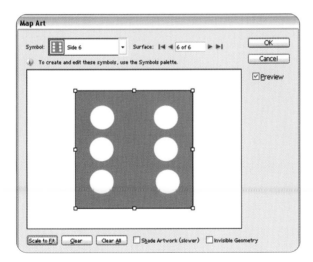

17. If you don't have the Preview check box checked, please check it at this time. The Artboard should reflect your changes and you should now have a red cube with all six sides of the dice mapped to it.

However, you may notice that the die looks flat. It's almost impossible to tell that it's actually supposed to be a cube. This is where shading comes in to play. On any 3D surface, light (or lack thereof) is what allows you to see that an object has depth. In this case, there's no light shining on this cube so it appears flat. This can easily be changed with a setting inside the Map Art dialog box. Just follow along to see how.

18. Adding depth is a three-part process. First, put on your "God" hat. Next, in a loud booming voice say, "Let there be light!" Finally, check the Shade Artwork check box and your cube will now have dimension.

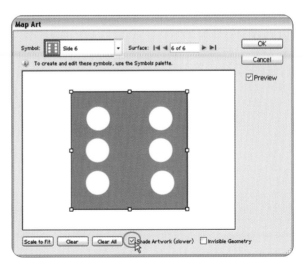

127

19. Next, check the Invisible Geometry check box, so that all the die sides show through one another, and click OK.

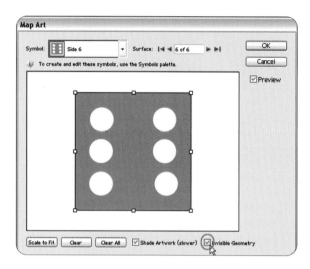

20. If you've followed along, your die should now look similar to this reference image.

In the beginning of this exercise I included a tip about setting the transparency of the red surface. Before clicking the Invisible Geometry check box, you couldn't tell that anything was transparent. By checking the Invisible Geometry check box in conjunction with the Draw Hidden Faces check box (on the 3D Extrude & Bevel dialog box), Illustrator will draw all sides of the object—even the ones that are hidden from you. If the surface has any transparent properties then you'll be able to see through to those otherwise hidden surfaces. Had you not set your object to 75% initially, and had you left it opaque, then checking the Invisible Geometry options would have done nothing.

21. Since dice always come in pairs, duplicate the dice layer and set the copy off to the side of the original. To make a quick copy, hold down your *ALT/OPTION* key and click and drag the die until a new copy appears.

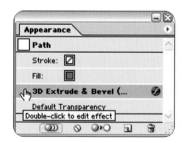

22. Select the duplicate dice object and look at the Appearance palette (*SHIFT+F6*). Remember how I explained that the 3D effects are live effects? You can go back and change them at any time. The Appearance palette will attest to this, as it will display a 3D Extrude & Bevel attribute below the Fill attribute.

23. Double-click the 3D Extrude & Bevel attribute to open the 3D Extrude & Bevel dialog box. Check the Preview check box and use your mouse to rotate the cube so it looks different from the other copy. You can also enter the settings directly into the text boxes I have circled in this reference image.

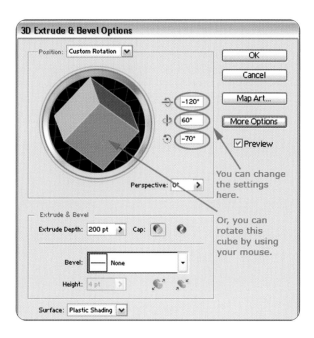

You can change the settings here.

Or, you can rotate this cube by using your mouse.

24. Finally, you should have a nice set of dice. Las Vegas, here you come!

Creating 3D text

Creating 3D text has been the topic of many Illustrator tutorials and effects in the past. Some of these effects were quite lengthy and involved reducing the type to outlines and using the Blend tool to create a 3D effect. Adding to Illustrator's previous limitations, there was no way to control the light sources so gradients needed to be used. Needless to say, this left illustrators with 3D type that was very inflexible. If changes needed to be made, then it usually meant starting over again. Now, with Illustrator CS, 3D type can be created in one step. You can control the lighting, extrusion depth, and rotation all in one dialog box. Best of all, you can edit your type with the Type tool as you normally would and any changes will be instantly reflected in the artwork.

1. Create a new RGB Illustrator document.

2. Select the Type tool and create the type that you would like to use for this effect. I used the same font you used in Chapter 4 (Keep on Truckin, which is included with the download files for this chapter) set at 72 pt. Set the stroke and fill color to None. (Note that I've set the stroke color to black in this reference image so you can see the type.)

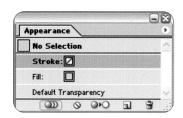

3. Select the type and open the Appearance palette (*SHIFT+F6*). Click the Appearance palette flyout menu arrow on the top right and select Add New Fill. Set the fill color to R:230 G:196 B:230.

129

4. You'll notice the previous step has also created a Stroke attribute. Drag this below the Fill attribute and set the stroke color to R:70 G:115 B:180.

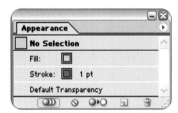

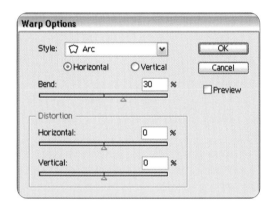

5. Next, with the type still selected, choose Effect ➤ Warp ➤ Arc. Change the Bend setting to 30% and leave the Horizontal and Vertical Distortion settings at 0%.

Yep, you guessed it. You can even add warp effects to your type and still have the 3D tool recognize them.

6. With the type still selected once again, choose Effect ➤ 3D ➤ Extrude & Bevel. Here is a reference image of the settings I used. Please take particular note of the Surface group. Be sure that you move your light source accordingly by clicking the small black square with the white circle inside of it. Click OK to apply the effect when you're finished.

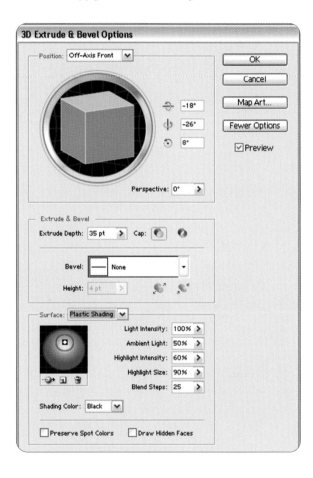

This effect isn't for those who are computer-processor challenged (that is, if you have a very old computer). I use a PC with a Pentium 1.3 GHz processor and this effect took around 15 to 20 seconds to render. Keep in mind how long it took Illustrator to render objects when there was only one. It now has an entire word to render, which will undoubtedly take more time.

7. You should now have some stylish 3D text. Keep in mind that all of the attributes of this type are still editable. You can change the font size, fill or stroke colors, as well as the warp and 3D effects at any time, and your type object will be automatically updated. I've included several examples in the source file of other effects you can achieve with the 3D tools and type.

Adding depth to a flat object

So far, you've only worked with the extruding capabilities of the 3D tool. But when you choose 3D from the effects menu you'll notice a couple of other commands as well. One of them is called Revolve. At first glance, it may look innocent enough. However, as this exercise will show you, this effect is quite powerful.

1. Open Chapter_05_RevolveStart.ai. The file contains one main layer with two sublayers. The top layer (LEAF) is a leaf that will go on top of the apple. Leave that layer hidden and locked for now. The bottom layer is an odd-looking, but vaguely familiar shape. This shape is, in fact, half of an apple and it's your starting point for this exercise.

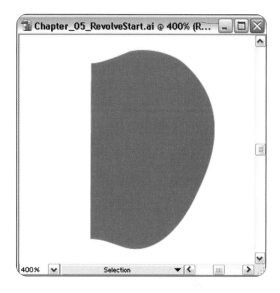

The Revolve effect can be slightly difficult to grasp. The Illustrator Help file best describes its function: "Revolving an object sweeps a path or profile in a circular direction around the global Y axis (revolve axis) to create a 3D object. Because the revolve axis is vertically fixed, the open or closed path that you revolve typically needs to depict half of the desired 3D object's profile in a vertical and front-facing position; you can then rotate the 3D object's position in the effect's dialog box."

2. I've included a reference image to help illustrate this point, because it's the key to understanding the Revolve effect. Now you'll see why you're using half an apple.

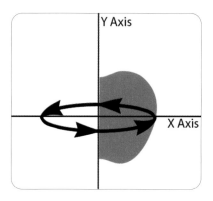

3. Now, you're ready for some 3D effects. Select the half apple shape. Choose Effect ➤ 3D ➤ Revolve. This will bring up the 3D Revolve Options dialog box.

4. First, check the Preview check box. If you examine the Artboard, you should immediately see some wonderful results.

5. However, there are a few changes you can make to further enhance the 3D qualities of your shape.

6. If it isn't already selected, click the More Options button to expand this dialog box further.

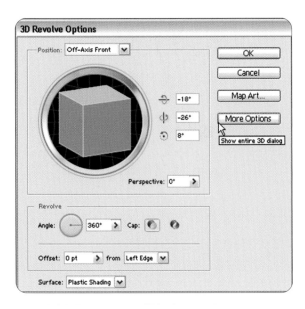

If you only see a Few Options *button instead of a* More Options *button, then you're already viewing the fully expanded dialog box.*

7. In the Surface group change the highlight intensity to 85% and the highlight size to 100%. This should produce a slightly shinier effect.

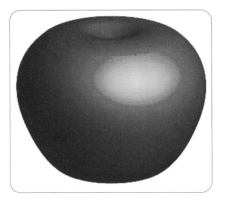

8. Next, you're going to add another light source to your object.

9. Click the New Light button below the Lighting Sphere.

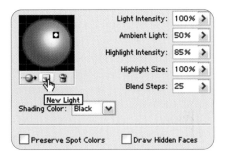

The Lighting Sphere is a key element in Illustrator's 3D Effects dialog boxes. Light controls how much of an object is represented in 3D space. By repositioning the lights, or by adding new ones, you can dramatically change the appearance of your 3D effects. I encourage you to experiment with this option as you work through this chapter.

10. Select this new light by clicking it. Click the Move Selected Light to Back of Object button shown as a sphere with an arrow running through it. Now position this light source to the lower-left area of the Lighting Sphere. This adds a nice touch and produces slight lighting that appears to come from behind the object.

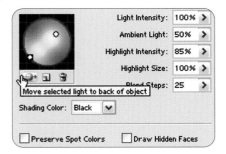

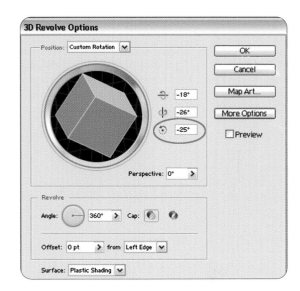

11. Click OK. You should now have something similar to this reference image:

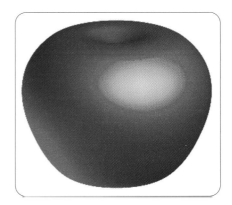

12. Next, apply the same effects to the green leaf at the top of the apple by selecting the shape and choosing Effects ➤ 3D ➤ Revolve. Accepting the default settings will work fine except for the Rotate setting. Change this value to –25 degrees. Click OK when you're done.

13. Finally, unlock and unhide the LEAF layer. Move the leaf into place so it's centered within the top of the apple.

Wireframe objects

A wireframe effect outlines the contours of an object but leaves each surface transparent. Since the tech boom in the late 1990s, wireframe effects have been extremely popular and synonymous with technology. However, creating these effects usually involved the use of a 3D modeling program. It was possible to fake this effect in Illustrator but, as with many "faked" effects, the results are usually unpredictable and don't represent top quality. Illustrator CS has changed all of that with 3D effects, though. You can now reduce any 3D object you create to a wireframed object. In this exercise, you'll learn not only how to accomplish this but how to use a popular technique for incorporating wireframe objects with other artwork.

1. Open `Chapter_05_WireframeStart.ai`. This file contains a stylized figure-eight shape that should be familiar to you from Chapter 1 in the Tech TV logo exercise.

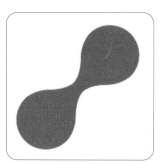

In order to use this shape, you need to make a few modifications.

2. First, select the object and choose Object ➤ Transform ➤ Rotate. Enter 45 degrees for the Angle settings and click OK.

3. Select the open arrow Direct Selection tool. Drag around the outer left half of the figure eight to select those anchor points. See the reference image for an idea of what area to select.

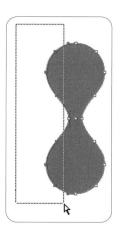

4. Press the *DELETE* key to remove the anchor points. You should now have a very odd-looking shape. Don't worry, you'll fix it.

5. Again, with the Direct Selection tool, select the top-left and bottom-left anchor points.

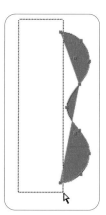

6. Join (*CTRL/CMD*+J) these two points to close off the shape. This will leave you with half of the original shape.

7. Now, you're ready for some 3D effects. Select the half figure-eight shape. Choose Effect ➤ 3D ➤ Revolve. This will bring up the 3D Revolve Options dialog box.

8. First, check the Preview check box. If it isn't already selected, click the More Options button to expand this dialog box further.

9. Make your settings appear as shown in this reference image. Don't forget to add another surface light to the bottom left of the Lighting Sphere.

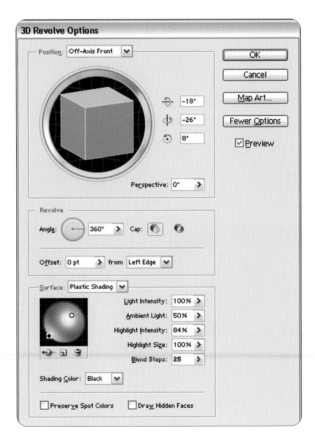

If you recall, your original shape was rotated 45 degrees to the right. In step 2 you rotated the object back to a vertical state because of the way 3D Revolve effects work. If you were to click OK now, and try to rotate the new 3D shape using the traditional Object ➤ Transform ➤ Rotate method you would get something similar to the following figure:

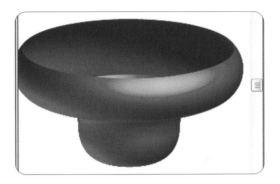

Very unpredictable isn't it? Remember, because these are live effects, you're rotating the live path on the Artboard and not the true 3D object. To maintain the object's integrity, be sure to rotate it within the 3D dialog box. This will be your next step.

10. Enter –45 degrees in the Rotate text box.

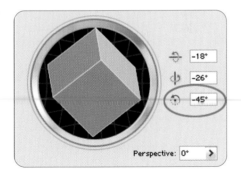

135

11. Click OK. You should now have something similar to this reference image:

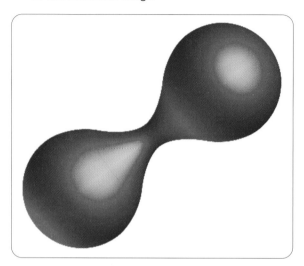

12. Name this layer SHADED.

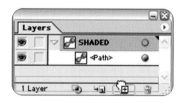

13. Make a duplicate of this layer by dragging the layer over the Create New Layer button at the bottom of the Layers palette. Name the new layer WIREFRAME.

14. Your Layers palette should now look like this (with sublayers expanded).

15. Target the Path sublayer within the WIREFRAME layer by using the Direct Selection tool or by targeting its meatball within the Layers palette. Also, make sure the Appearance palette (*SHIFT+F6*) is visible.

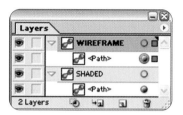

16. In the Appearance palette, you should notice a 3D Revolve attribute. Double-click this attribute to bring up the 3D Revolve dialog box for the WIREFRAME object.

17. In the Surface drop-down list, change the choice from Plastic Shading to Wireframe.

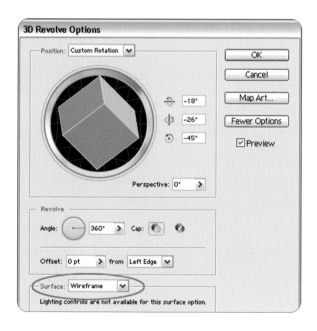

18. Click OK. You'll now have a wireframe representation of the object as well.

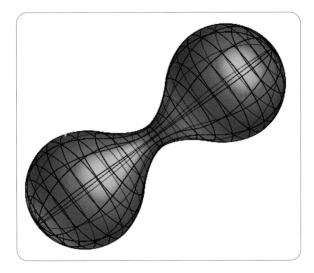

The next part of this exercise will entail merging the two objects so it looks as if the 3D shaded object is fading out and wireframe object is emerging from it or vice versa.

19. First, lock and hide the WIREFRAME layer so you don't accidentally modify it. Next, create a new sublayer within the SHADED layer but on top of the shaded object or Path sublayer. Name this layer SHADED MASK.

20. Select the Rectangle tool and on the SHADED MASK layer create a square that encompasses the entire shaded object. Fill this square with a black to white gradient as seen in this reference image. Note the angle setting of 45 degrees. Also, be sure to move each color stop accordingly. The white Color

Stop is positioned at 40% and the black Color Stop is positioned at 60% for this example. You can change these by clicking on the small white and black swatches along the bottom of the Gradient palette and modifying the Location setting.

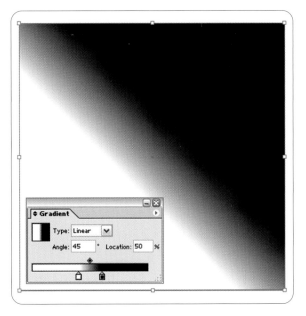

21. Duplicate the gradient square in the SHADED MASK layer by dragging it over the Create New Layer button at the bottom of the Layers palette. The new layer will appear directly above the existing one. Name this layer WIREFRAME MASK.

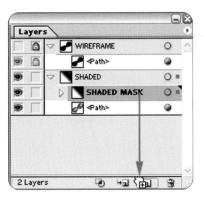

22. Now unhide and unlock the WIREFRAME layer. Drag the duplicate above the existing wireframe object. Your Layers palette should now look similar to this reference image.

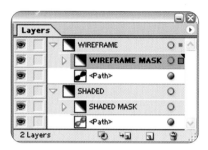

23. Select the WIREFRAME MASK layer and choose Object ➤ Transform ➤ Rotate. Enter 180 degrees for the Angle setting.

OK, you're almost done. Now all that is left to do is to create two opacity masks to blend the objects together.

24. Lock and hide the parent layer that contains the WIREFRAME and WIREFRAME MASK sublayers.

25. Choose Select ➤ All (*CTRL/CMD+A*). Then select Make Opacity Mask from the Transparency palette's flyout menu.

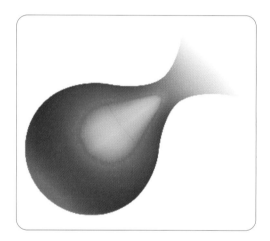

26. Lock the parent layer that contains the SHADED sublayer. Unhide and unlock the layer containing the wireframe object and gradient square.

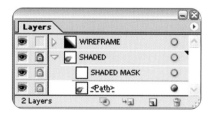

27. Choose Select ➤ All (*CTRL/CMD+A*). Then select Make Opacity Mask from the Transparency palette's flyout menu.

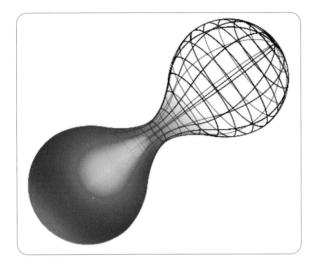

28. If everything went well it should now appear as if the wireframe and shaded 3D object morph into each other. One finishing touch would be to reduce the opacity of the WIREFRAME layer to about 40% to make the effect a little subtler.

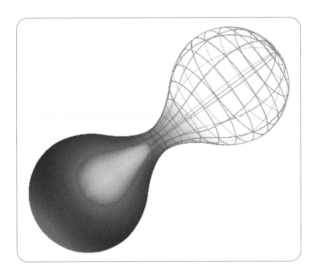

Modeling a wine bottle

This exercise will walk you through the creation of a slightly more complex 3D object—a wine bottle with a cork. Although the basic steps in creating this object remain the same as the others, I will point out a few key areas that will help to give you that extra bit of realism. Not only will you create the wine bottle but you'll make a cork to close it. Finally, you'll examine an area within the Revolve dialog box called Map Art. This is very similar to the effect that you used in the dice exercise at the beginning of this chapter. However, you'll be pleasantly surprised at how well it works for complex 3D objects as well.

1. Open Chapter_05_WineBottleStart.ai. This file contains several elements.

   ■ The wine bottle path that you'll be applying the 3D Revolve effect to.

   ■ The cork path that you'll be applying the 3D Revolve effect to (on a hidden sublayer).

   ■ A label, which will be used to wrap around the bottle, that has already been saved in the Symbols palette (also on a hidden sublayer).

You can just as easily create all of these elements yourself. There's no secret trick other than using the Pen tool to draw the wine bottle and cork. I've included them in the source file to make it easier for you to follow along and get used to the tools.

2. Examine the Layers palette and you'll notice three sublayers: BOTTLE, CORK, and LABEL. CORK is hidden for now. You'll save that part for last. LABEL is also hidden, and you'll be using it later in the exercise.

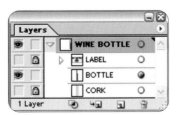

As you examine the BOTTLE sublayer shape you'll notice that it follows the previous precedent of only creating half of the shape that you wish to model. However, I would like to point out a couple of key areas that I concentrated on when creating this shape.

First, by looking at the top of the bottle you'll notice an area that protrudes out slightly. Most wine bottles have a beveled area near the cork. This protrusion will add a great deal of realism when you apply the Revolve effect.

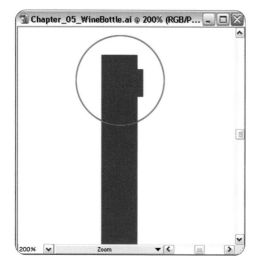

Also, notice the bottom of the bottle. Most wine bottles don't have a flat bottom. Instead, they're concave and extend up into the bottle—almost as if a portion was scooped out. This isn't something you would see by looking at the front of the bottle but if you turn it over, you would definitely notice it. Since you're creating a 3D view of the bottle, you may want to rotate the bottle in 3D space. By drawing the upward curve at the bottom, you would see the bottom of the wine bottle cave in just as you would if you were looking at the actual bottle.

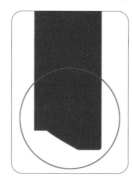

Finally, if you select the wine bottle and examine the Transparency palette (*Shift+F10*), you'll notice the opacity level is set to 85%. Wine bottles are made of

glass, which is semitransparent. This setting will allow you to see through the bottle if you were to place it on top of any other artwork.

3. OK, now that that's out of the way, you're ready to apply the 3D effects. Select the bottle object and choose Effect ➤ 3D ➤ Revolve.

4. In the 3D Revolve Options dialog box, make your settings similar to this reference image. Take particular note of the Lighting Sphere and Surface settings. Be sure to place your light as I have and make sure to change the Highlight settings. Also, note that the Draw Hidden Faces check box is checked. Click OK.

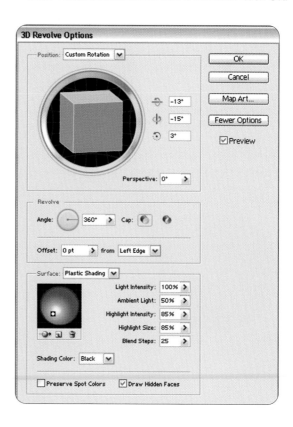

All wine bottles have labels, so your next few steps will entail mapping a label to the wine bottle. I've already created a label for you. All that you need to do is save it to the Symbols palette as you did in the dice exercise.

5. Unhide and unlock the LABEL sublayer and select all of the objects within that sublayer.

6. Choose New Symbol from the Symbols palette (*SHIFT+F11*) flyout menu and enter Label as the symbol name. You should now see your object as a new symbol in the Symbols palette.

7. Select the BOTTLE layer and open the Appearance palette (*SHIFT+F6*). Double-click the 3D Revolve attribute to edit the 3D Revolve settings. Click the Map Art button to view the Map Art dialog box. Be sure the Preview check box is checked.

8. Initially, you'll see a circle map surface. This isn't what you want. Click the Surface Next arrow until the text box reads 6 of 11. Select the Label symbol from the Symbol drop-down list. Position the symbol as I have in the reference image. You may need to resize the image using its bounding box to get it to match the reference image. Also, be sure to check the Shade Artwork check box.

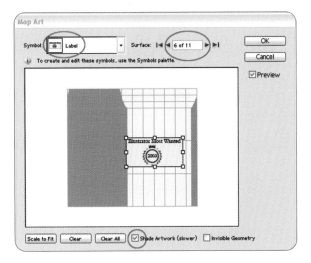

When mapping artwork to 3D objects remember that the white surface map area with the gray grid lines represents the front portion of the artwork you're mapping to. The gray area, in essence, represents the portion of the object that you cannot see.

9. You should add a smaller version of the symbol to surface number 7 as well. When finished, click OK.

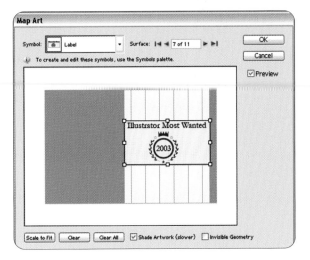

10. Next, you'll work on the cork for the wine bottle.

11. Unhide and unlock the CORK sublayer. Select the object on this sublayer and choose Effect ➤ 3D ➤ Revolve. Make your settings similar to this reference image. Click OK.

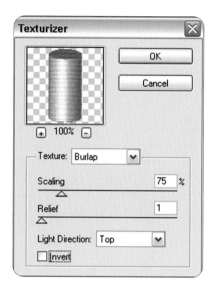

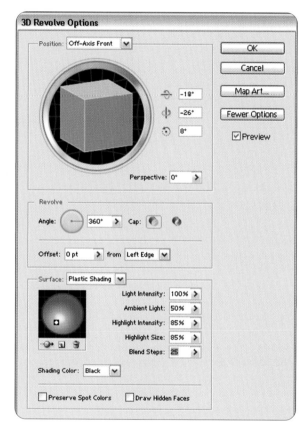

12. With the cork still selected, choose Effect ➤ Texture ➤ Texturizer. Select Burlap for the Texture setting. Set Scaling to 75% and Relief to 1. Click OK.

13. Position the CORK sublayer in place. However, notice how the top of the bottle is visible through the cork. This isn't realistic, as the cork should hide this area.

14. To fix this, select the Knife tool and zoom in on the top of the bottle. Lock all layers except for the CORK layer.

15. Slice through the cork with the Knife tool as displayed in this reference image.

16. This will produce two CORK sublayers—one for the bottom of the cork and one for the top. Name them accordingly (CORK BOTTOM, CORK TOP).

17. Drag the CORK TOP sublayer above the BOTTLE sublayer.

18. Here is the final image. Notice how you can see the cork through the wine bottle. This is because you set the opacity of the wine bottle to 85% and check the Draw Hidden Faces check box in step 4. It really completes the effect.

Summary

You should be well on your way to 3D mastery within Illustrator. The quality of this feature and the effects that it can produce are almost solely worth the upgrade to Illustrator CS. As you've seen in these exercises, the timesaving features and new avenues for creativity provided by the 3D effects will surely give you the ability to produce faster and more innovative artwork. This is new and much anticipated territory for Illustrator. I hope I left you with some key concepts for using 3D effects and inspired you to begin using this tool with your own illustrations.

Chapter 6

ADDING DEPTH AND DIMENSION

Depth effects

One of the greatest features in Illustrator is its flexibility. There is no "Add Depth" tool but there are many tools that can simulate depth and dimension for you. You just need to know where to find them. In this chapter, you'll learn that many of these tools are right at your fingertips and you may, in fact, be using them every day. I'll demonstrate that it's merely a shift in your thought process as to how you view these tools. Gradients, meshes, shadow effects, glow effects, and distort tools all allow you to simulate depth and dimension in Illustrator. Follow along with the exercises in this chapter and you'll learn techniques that can quickly turn your effects into professional-quality illustrations with depth and dimension.

Creating a leaf with the Mesh tool

In this exercise, you're going to create the leaf that you saw back in Chapter 3 during the water droplets exercise. I must first warn you that this exercise isn't for the faint of heart. The Mesh tool is one of Illustrator's most powerful tools—along with that power comes complexity. However, I'll break each step down for you to make it as easy to follow along as possible. Good luck!

1. Open `Chapter_06_MeshLeafStart.ai`. This file contains the outline of the leaf that you saw in Chapter 3.

The first step in this illustration is to decide if your shape will be a good candidate for using the Mesh tool. Unfortunately, this task is very subjective and will depend on the object that you wish to apply a mesh to. For this exercise, I've decided that the stem of the leaf needed to be separate from the actual leaf area. In the following reference image, I've created a mesh using the Mesh tool to help illustrate why.

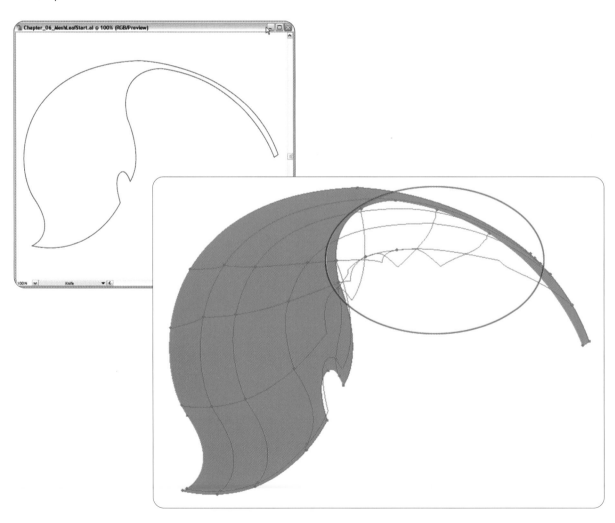

Notice all of the mesh points and lines that exist in the circled area. If you were to leave these points as is, it would wreak havoc on your ability to create a realistic-looking gradient mesh—color transitions would be too sharp and appear distorted. You can't delete them, as you would further deteriorate the mesh. The solution is to break the object apart into a stem and a leaf. Follow along to see how.

2. Duplicate the LEAF layer and name this copy OUTLINE. Drag this new layer below the LEAF layer. Also, lock and hide it for now. The next step will modify the overall shape of the leaf, but you'll want to keep a copy of the outline for later use.

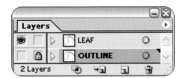

3. Select the Knife tool and slice through the area that you want to separate; the cut doesn't have to be precise.

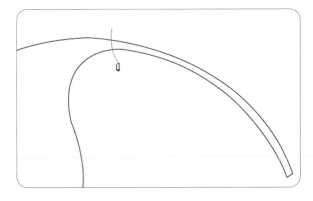

4. Name the sublayer that contains the stem path STEM. Name the other sublayer LEAF MESH.

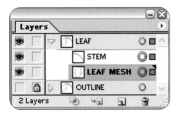

5. Next, select or target the LEAF MESH and STEM sublayers. Fill the shapes with R:72 G:185 B:51 and set the stroke to None.

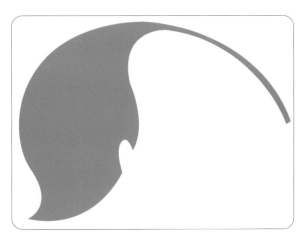

The previous step will aid you in creating the mesh for the leaf. Now you have a base color and you just need to modify the highlights and shadows instead of adding color to the entire leaf.

6. Select the Mesh tool (*U*). Using the following images as a reference, click each of the circled areas once. Precise mesh-point positioning isn't required here, but try to follow along as closely as possible. After each click, your mesh should begin to match the corresponding reference image.

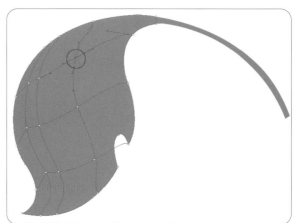

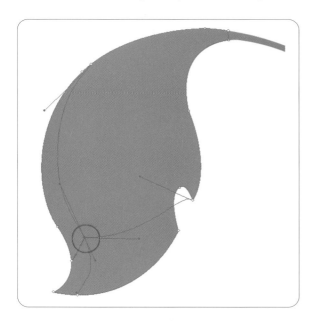

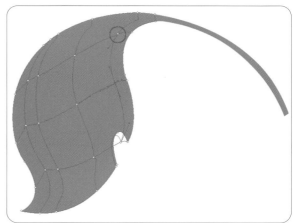

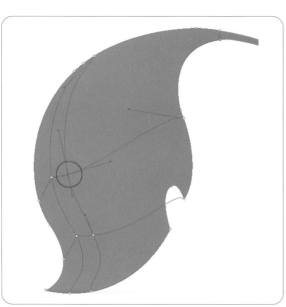

A mesh basically creates, over your object, a distorted grid that follows the contours of its shape. Each time you click with the Mesh tool, you create an additional row or column for that grid. However, if you click along the same path horizontally, you'll only add an additional column to the grid, and the number of rows will remain the same. Alternatively, if you add points vertically along the same path, you'll create additional rows but not columns. Finally, if you add mesh points that aren't on any of the existing vertical or horizontal mesh lines, then you'll create an additional row and column. This is similar to the first three images in the previous step.

Next, you're going to select mesh points within the leaf object and change the colors. This will produce a gradual color shift similar to a gradient. Before you move on to this step, I'd like to first point out a key concept. The wonderful thing about the Mesh tool is that the mesh points it produces are similar to anchor points and paths. You select and manipulate mesh points in the same way that you would a path. See the following reference image for an example.

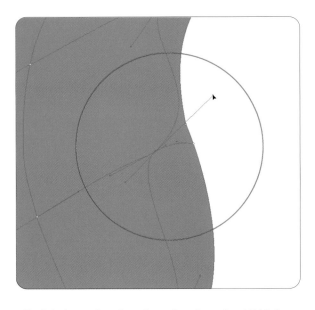

7. If it isn't already selected, select the LEAF layer using the Selection tool or by clicking the meatball in the Layers palette.

8. Select the open arrow Direct Selection tool from the toolbox.

There are actually two methods that you can use when selecting points on an existing mesh. You can use the Direct Selection tool, as suggested in step 8, or the Mesh tool itself. I prefer to use the Direct Selection tool since it will only select points on the mesh. If you use the Mesh tool, you run the risk of adding another mesh line if you accidentally click an open area within the mesh instead of the mesh point. Since Illustrator's anchor points are small and can be difficult to select, this is a very real possibility.

9. Click each mesh point that I've circled in this reference image and change the fill color to R: 233 G:255 B:227.

Turning on Smart Guides (CTRL/CMD+U) for the rest of the exercise may aid you in selecting mesh points.

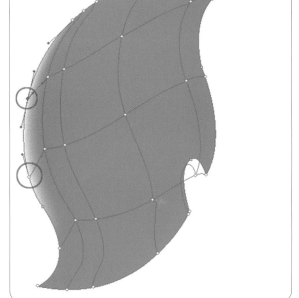

You can change the fill color by using the Color palette, the Swatches palette, or by double-clicking the Fill swatch in the toolbox.

10. Now select the following anchor points.

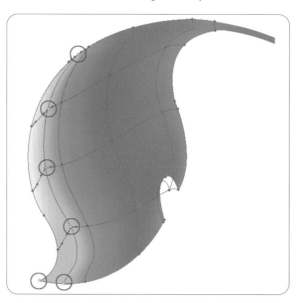

11. Change the fill color of these points to R:192 G:249 B:93.

12. This should produce a nice color shift along the left side of the leaf. It looks pretty good so far, but you have a few more changes to make.

13. Select the points displayed in this reference image.

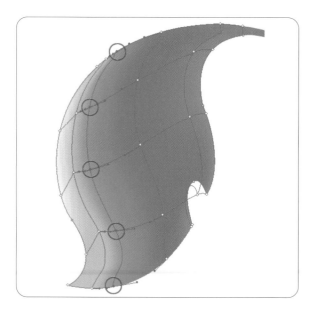

14. Change the fill color to R:98 G:214 B:60.

15. Next, select these points.

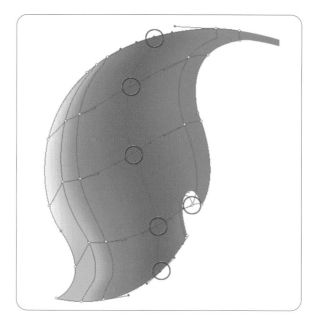

16. Change the fill color to R:51 G:160 B:44.

17. Hopefully, you get the idea. Use this reference image to select the remaining anchor points and change their colors accordingly.

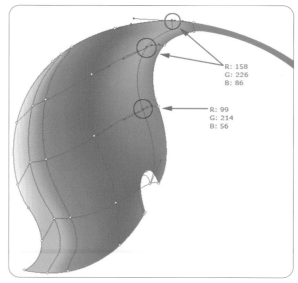

R: 158
G: 226
B: 86

R: 99
G: 214
B: 56

OK, if you've followed along, the hard part is done. All that remains are the veins that run through the leaf. You'll create these using the Pen tool. However, if you have an aversion to (or fear of) this tool, the source file includes a layer named VEINS that you can use without having to actually draw the veins.

18. Create a new layer called VEINS on top of the leaf objects. Select the Pen tool and begin drawing the veins as I have in these reference images. Note that these aren't closed paths. When you wish to end your path, just press the ENTER/RETURN key.

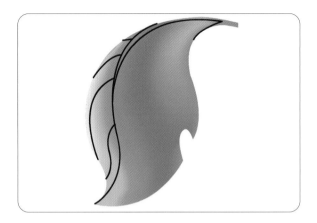

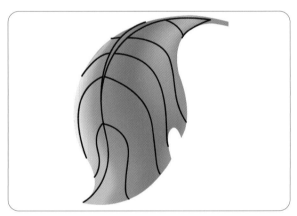

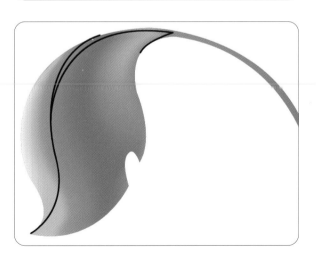

19. Next, select all of the paths on the VEINS layer. Choose Window ➤ Brush Libraries ➤ Artistic_Calligraphic. Select the 3 pt oval brush near the bottom of the palette to apply to your paths.

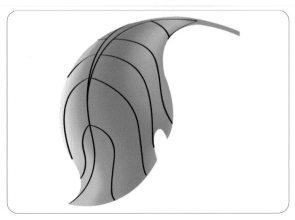

153

20. Finally, unlock and select the OUTLINE layer. Choose the 3 pt oval brush from the same palette to apply to the outline path around the leaf.

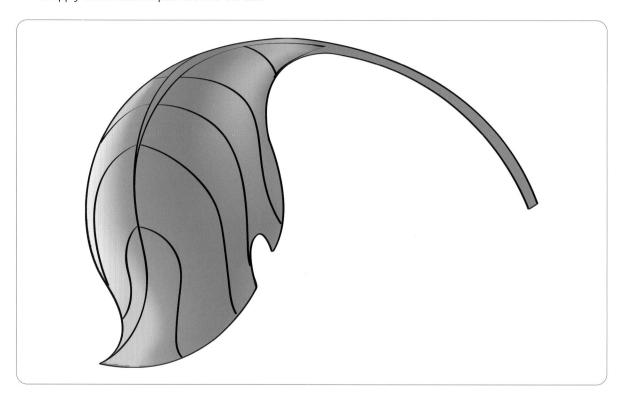

Shadow effects

Often, depth isn't defined only by the highlights and shadows that are produced on an object, but also by the highlights and shadows the object produces on its environment. In this exercise, you'll learn two effects. The first part uses Illustrator's native Drop Shadow effect (Effect ➤ Stylize ➤ Drop Shadow). You've seen this effect used throughout this book in other exercises, and it's very easy to apply. However, the native Drop Shadow effect doesn't always suit your needs. In the second part, you'll actually manipulate and skew a copy of the object itself to cast a shadow on the surrounding area. This is a widely used illustration technique. Although it's more complicated, this method is more versatile and creates more realistic results than the preceding effect.

1. OK, let's dig in. The first effect is simple but you'll look at a couple of variations. Open Chapter_06_ButtonShadowStart.ai. This file contains the aqua gel button that you created in Chapter 4.

2. Examine the Layers palette. Select the bottom layer named BASE. In the Appearance palette, notice the Drop Shadow effect. Double-click this layer. When the dialog box appears, be sure to check the Preview check box.

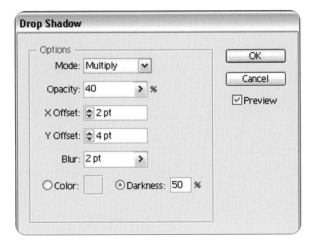

From the settings you chose when you created this button in Chapter 4, you should assume that the light source is shining from the top left. This will cause a shadow off to the bottom right. Examine the Artboard without clicking OK and you'll see what I mean.

3. However, by setting the X Offset value to 0 and the Y Offset value to a positive number, the drop shadow will now be positioned directly below the button. Try this by setting the X Offset value to 0 and the Y Offset value to 15 pt. Also, set the opacity to 30% and the blur to 6 pt.

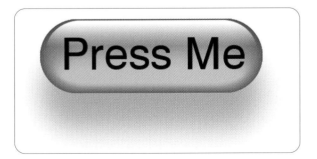

4. You can make the button appear to be raised even higher above the surface by increasing the Y Offset value. In this case, I changed it to 45 pt.

However, keep in mind that as the object gets higher off the surface, the shadow becomes less defined. The intensity of the shadow fades as well. You can simulate this in Illustrator by increasing the Blur setting and decreasing the Opacity setting.

5. While still in the Drop Shadow dialog box, set the Blur setting to 10 pt and the Opacity setting to 20%. Click OK and you're done.

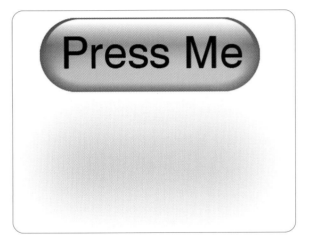

This completes part 1 of this exercise. In part 2, you're going to abandon the native Drop Shadow effect in place of a "manual" process. Don't run away just yet! I know I said manual, but I promise this effect isn't going to be too difficult. In fact, it's a widely used technique, and if you wish to add that extra touch of realism to your illustrations you'll find it very useful.

To begin, I'd like to illustrate why this technique is useful and why it can often be the preferred way to add a drop shadow instead of using Illustrator's Drop Shadow effect. Take a look at this reference image:

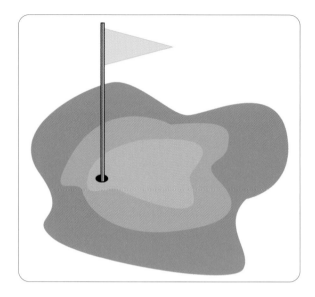

The preceding illustration could benefit greatly from a drop shadow cast by the flag (commonly referred to as a "pin" for all of you non-golf enthusiasts). However, if you add the default drop shadow using Illustrator's Drop Shadow effect, you don't get the effect you're looking for.

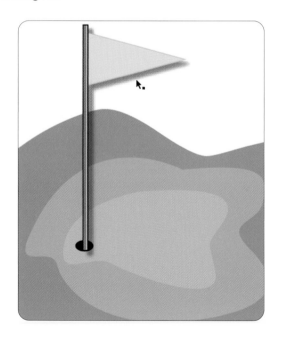

Luckily for you, there is another way. Follow along with the next steps to see how.

6. Open `Chapter_06_GolfFlagStart.ai`. Take note of the layers that exist in this file—GREEN, HOLE, and FLAG, the last two being locked.

7. The first step is to create a copy of the FLAG layer. Duplicate this layer by dragging it to the Create New Layer button at the bottom of the Layers palette. This will produce a layer named FLAG copy. Drag this layer below FLAG and rename it SHADOW.

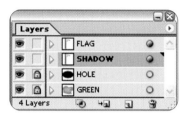

Next, you don't actually need all of the components that make up the flag. You only need the general outline of it.

8. Target the meatball icon for the SHADOW layer to select all of its contents.

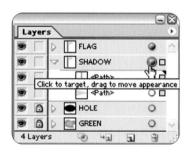

9. Open the Pathfinder palette (*SHIFT+F9*). Hold down the *ALT/OPTION* key and select the Add to Shape Area button to combine all of the shapes. Set the fill color of this path to black and the stroke to None. I've hidden the FLAG layer so you can see the results in this reference image. You'll need to hide it as well to see the effect.

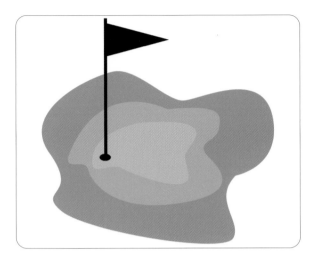

Now that the shape you'll use for the shadow is created, let's position it in place.

10. With the object on the SHADOW layer still selected, choose Object ➤ Transform ➤ Shear. Set the shear angle to 50 degrees and be sure Horizontal is selected. Click OK.

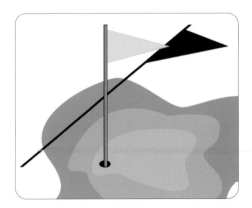

11. Next, choose Object ➤ Transform ➤ Scale. Select Uniform and enter 70 for the Scale setting.

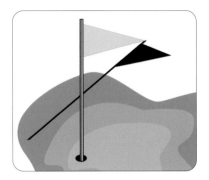

12. Drag the shadow to the right so it appears directly behind the original flagstick as shown in the following figure. Don't deselect the SHADOW layer yet, though.

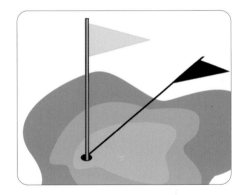

13. Finally, select the Free Transform tool (*E*). Click the top-right corner of the bounding box that surrounds the shadow. Before you move the mouse to transform the flag, hold down the *CTRL/CMD* key. Now drag the corner point downward as I've done here:

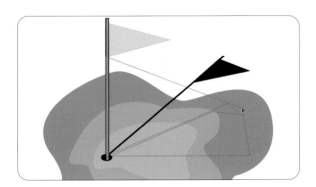

If your transformation doesn't go as planned, you could be holding down the CTRL/CMD key incorrectly. It's very important to click first and then hold down the CTRL/CMD key.

14. You should have something similar to this:

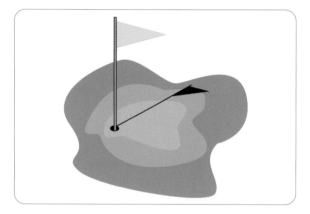

15. Repeat step 13 but drag the bottom-right point of the bounding box this time.

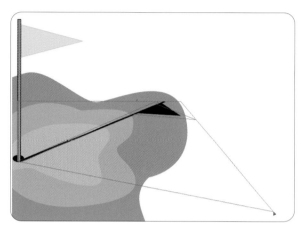

16. Finally, to complete the effect, change the opacity of the SHADOW layer to 50% in the Transparency palette and you're done.

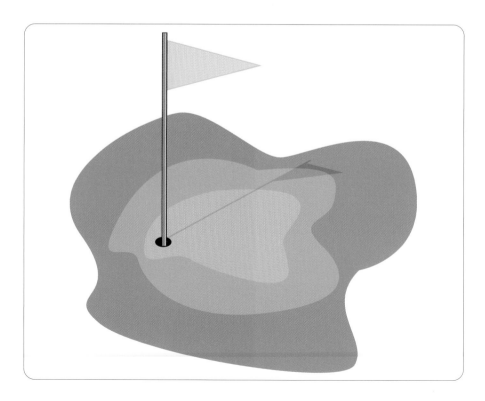

Simulating depth with gradients and glows

The next exercise will walk you through combining one of Illustrator's tools that's commonly used in adding depth and dimension (Gradient) to images and one that isn't (Inner Glow).

1. Open Chapter_06_FishStart.ai. This file contains the outline of a fish shape that I drew for you. As with many of the source files, it's only here to help you jump in and perform the exercises quickly. There are no special tricks to this effect other than taking the time to draw the fish shape.

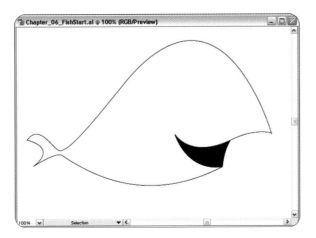

2. The first task is to create a custom gradient. As you may have seen so far, gradients are a great way to add depth to an object. Use this reference image and create a radial gradient to apply to the fish shape.

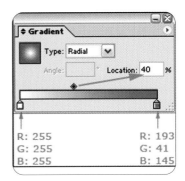

3. Save this gradient for later use by dragging the gradient preview thumbnail (shown in the upper left of the palette) over the Swatches palette and releasing the mouse button.

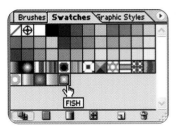

4. Expand the FISH layer to view its sublayers. Select the BODY sublayer. Click the gradient in the Swatches palette to apply it to that shape and set the stroke to None.

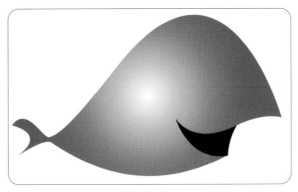

By default, Illustrator aligns the center of a radial gradient with the shape that you applied it to. Since this center point serves as your highlight in this illustration, let's reposition it.

5. With the BODY sublayer selected, select the Gradient tool (G). Position your cursor where you want to define the beginning point of the gradient. Drag across the FISH layer toward the bottom left of the fish shape, as shown in the following image. Release the mouse button where you would like to define the endpoint of the gradient.

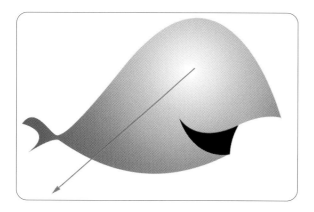

Great! You're now starting to add some dimension to the fish. Next you're going to use an effect in Illustrator that you may not usually associate with depth and dimension—the Inner Glow effect. One main reason why you probably wouldn't associate this effect as being useful in this circumstance is due to the default settings when you choose it. They do very little justice initially, but with some quick modifications you can easily use an Inner Glow effect to add depth to this illustration.

6. Select the BODY sublayer. Choose Effect ➤ Stylize ➤ Inner Glow. Note that the default color setting is a light yellow and the Blending mode is set to Screen.

7. First, be sure the Preview box is checked so you can view your modifications. Change the color to R:124 G:37 B:116 and change the Mode setting to Multiply. Set the Opacity setting to 70% and the Blur setting to 28 pt. Finally, check the Edge radio button.

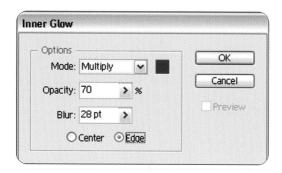

8. Click OK to apply. You should now have something similar to this:

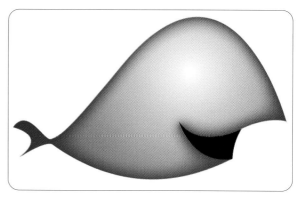

Now, you should really see some depth within the fish object. The final steps are to add a few more depth-related elements such as fins and an eye.

9. Create a new sublayer above FISH and call it FRONT FIN. Draw a simple shape with the Pen tool as I have in this reference image.

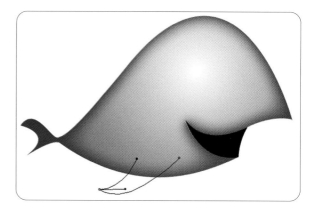

10. Set the fill to the same radial gradient you used for the fish shape in step 4 by clicking the gradient in the Swatches palette.

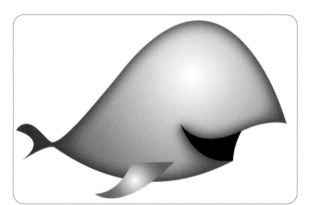

11. Select the Gradient tool and reposition the gradient to your liking, just as you did in step 5.

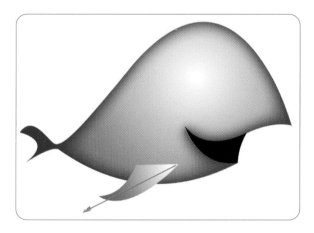

12. Duplicate the FRONTFIN layer and move it below the FISH layer. Name it BACKFIN.

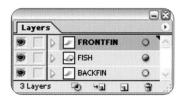

13. Scale the BACKFIN shape down slightly using the Free Transform tool (E). Then drag it over to the right.

14. Finally, select the Knife tool. Slice the fish just to the right of its tail fin.

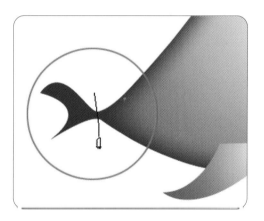

15. The tail fin and the fish shape are actually two separate paths now.

16. Also, note that if you select the tail fin shape, it retains the same effects that were applied to the overall fish shape earlier. This includes the gradient and the Inner Glow effect. You can view this in the Appearance palette (SHIFT+F6).

17. However, the gradient may be difficult to see because the Inner Glow effect is covering it. Back in step 7 you changed the Blur setting to 28 pt. This worked well for the entire fish shape, but the tail fin is much too small for a setting this large.

18. Select the tail fin object. Double-click the Inner Glow effect layer in the Appearance palette to change its settings. Change the Blur setting to 10 pt and click OK.

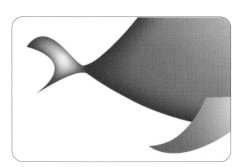

There you have it—a 3D-like illustration using basic gradients and an Inner Glow effect. I've included the eye in the source file for you to complete the fish. It was created in the same way as the fish—radial gradients and an Inner Glow effect. It may also be nice to add some water for the fish to swim in (fish like that, you know).

19. Create a layer below the BACKFIN layer named SEA. Using the Rectangle tool draw a rectangle on the Artboard.

20. Create a radial gradient similar to this reference image and fill the rectangle with it.

21. Finally, reposition the gradient as you've done in other steps so the highlight appears in the top-left corner of the image.

If the fins on the fish look too flat for your taste, you can always apply an Inner Glow effect to them in the same way that you did for the body and tail fin.

Using Liquify tools to simulate dimension

Another popular group of features in Illustrator are the Liquify tools. These tools allow you to step back from the path and anchor-point madness that can sometimes occur so that you can have some plain old fun. Along the way, though, you can produce some astonishing effects with these tools that would have taken a great deal of time with only the Pen tool. In this exercise, you're going to create a simple pattern and modify it with one of the Liquify tools called the Bloat tool. You'll then map this pattern to the fish object you created in the previous exercise to further enhance the illusion of depth and dimension.

1. Open `Chapter_06_FishLiquifyStart.ai`. This is the completed version of the file you used in the previous exercise. I've organized the layers by moving the EYE, BACKFIN, and FRONTFIN layers all within the FISH layer.

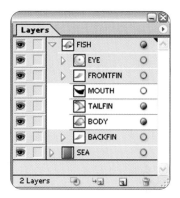

2. Create a new sublayer above BODY called DOTS. Lock all of the other sublayers.

3. Select the Ellipse tool. Draw a circle over the fish body similar to this reference image. Set the fill color to R:158 G:73 B:161 and the stroke to None.

4. Continue drawing circles as I have in this reference image, or duplicate the existing circle and reposition the circles as necessary. This will be the pattern for your fish.

5. Target the DOTS layer by clicking its corresponding meatball icon. Turn the dots into a compound path (*Ctrl/Cmd+8*).

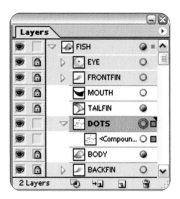

I realize that many of you may not be familiar with polka-dotted fish. However, they're very popular in the waters off the Gulf Coast of Florida where I reside. OK, perhaps that isn't entirely truthful. I have to admit that I've never seen a purple polka-dotted fish before. But I do feel that this pattern portrays this effect very well, so please bear with my genetically altered fish for the remainder of this exercise.

6. Select the Bloat tool. It's located in the Warp tool flyout menu. Alas, there isn't a keyboard shortcut for this one.

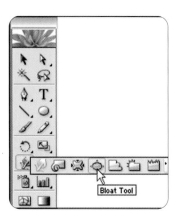

7. Double-click the Bloat tool button in the toolbox to display the Bloat Tool Options dialog box. The Liquify tools are basically brushes with warp effects. They have similar diameter properties, as

well as Angle and Intensity settings. As such, you can modify these settings just as you can a regular brush.

8. Set the Width and Height settings to an amount large enough to cover the dots you just created. If you've been following along, 500 pt should work fine. Also, set the Intensity setting to 25%. Click OK.

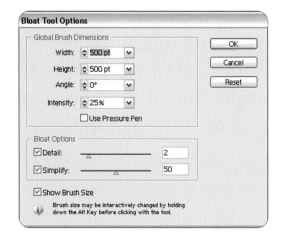

9. Next, quickly click two times over the dot pattern. Notice how the dots appear to expand as if they're exploding. Also, note that the longer you click and hold, the more this affects the shapes.

The final step is to remove the area of the DOTS layer that expands beyond the fish's body.

10. Unlock the BODY layer. Duplicate it by dragging it to the Create New Layer button at the bottom of the Layers palette. You should now have two BODY sublayers in the Layers palette.

11. Select the duplicate body layer's meatball and *SHIFT*-select the DOTS layer meatball as well.

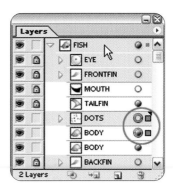

12. Make the Pathfinder palette visible. Hold down the *ALT/OPTION* key and click the Intersect Shape Areas button.

13. This will remove the areas of the DOTS layer that don't intersect with the BODY layer.

14. Your polka-dotted fish should now be complete. One final enhancement would be to change the Blending mode of the DOTS layer to Multiply and the Opacity setting to 50%.

Incorporating depth of field in an illustration

Depth of field refers to the distance between the nearest and farthest points that appear in focus (sharp) in a photograph. Graphic designers attempt to simulate depth of field in their designs in various ways. This usually involves specific paint programs and their corresponding blur effects. Until recently, utilizing this effect in Illustrator was difficult. But with the advent of live effects, you can quickly add this touch of realism to illustrations with little effort. In this exercise, you'll visit the genetically altered purple polka-dotted fish one more time. He was alone in his vast aqua home, so you're going to add some background elements and even a friend to make him feel more at home. Corny, I know, but follow along, as this is an essential technique for adding depth to your illustrations.

1. Open `Chapter_06_FishDepthofFieldStart.ai`. This file contains the same underwater fish scene that you've been working with. Everything has been completed for you up to this point, but feel free to use the same file that you've been working with in previous exercises.

2. Notice the layers within this illustration. The key layer in this illustration is SEA. Lock the other layers and expand the SEA layer to view its sublayers.

3. Create a new sublayer above WATER called BACKHILLS.

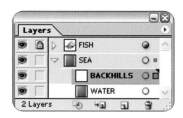

4. Using the Pen tool, draw a jagged, mountainous-type shape similar to this reference image. Notice that this is a closed path, meaning that all the points connect to one another. This allows the shape to accept a fill easily, without allowing any gaps or unintended side effects to occur.

5. Fill this object with the following radial gradient. Use the Gradient tool and mouse to reposition the gradient to your liking. I've included an arrow as a reference for how the gradient was positioned in this example.

6. Next, create another sublayer above BACKHILLS and name it FRONTHILLS. Create a shape similar to the one you created in step 4. Fill this shape with the same radial gradient.

Now it's time to incorporate a Depth of Field effect. To simulate depth of field, you need to decide which object will be in focus. Since the fish has been so dear to your heart in this chapter, let's continue to give him the spotlight. This means that the hills (the BACKHILLS and FRONTHILLS layers) will need to get progressively blurry as the scenery gets farther away.

7. Select the shape on the BACKHILLS layer. Choose Effect ➤ Blur ➤ Gaussian Blur. Enter 10 pixels for the Radius setting.

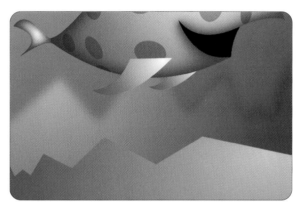

8. Select the shape on the FRONTHILLS layer. Choose Effect ➤ Blur ➤ Gaussian Blur. Enter 3 pixels for the Radius setting.

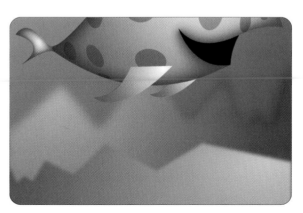

I've purposely varied the settings between the two hill shapes. This is because objects don't instantly become blurred when taking depth of field into account. Everything gets progressively out of focus as you move further away from the focus object. Thus, the hills in front should be slightly more in focus than the hills in back.

Finally, to finish this off, let's add a friend for your fish.

9. Unlock the FISH layer. Duplicate it by dragging the layer over the Create New Layer button at the bottom of the Layers palette. Target the entire contents of the layer by clicking the parent layer's meatball icon.

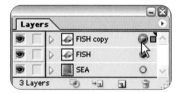

10. Choose Object ➤ Transform ➤ Scale. Enter 35% for the amount and be sure that Uniform is selected. Click OK.

11. Choose Object ➤ Transform ➤ Reflect. Select the Vertical radio button and click OK.

12. Move the new fish off to the left, but don't deselect it yet.

13. Choose Effect ➤ Blur ➤ Gaussian Blur. Set the radius to 5 pixels.

14. This completes the fish illustration. However, I changed the Opacity setting of the FISH copy layer to 75% to make it appear as if the fish was farther in the background, and it began to take on the color properties of the actual ocean surrounding it.

Summary

As you've learned in this chapter, simulating depth and dimension can be accomplished with tools you may use every day. Often, simple changes such as adding a strategically placed gradient or shadow can mean the difference between a mediocre illustration and a professional-looking one. However, if I had to pick one important message from this chapter, it wouldn't be how to use a specific tool or effect. Instead, it would be a concept: highlights and shadows are the key to creating illustrations that appear to have depth and dimension. Our eyes pick up on these elements and translate them into depth, thus the appearance of a 3D object. Study the world around you. Examine how light interacts (or doesn't interact) with objects in your environment. It's this process that will familiarize you with the various highlights and shadows produced on an object. In turn, you'll begin to take control of Illustrator and learn to make the tools work for you when creating illustrations of your own.

Chapter 7

ILLUSTRATOR ANIMATION TECHNIQUES

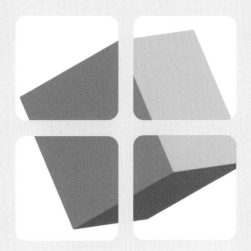

Animation

An often-overlooked feature in Adobe Illustrator is the ability to create animations. Yes, I know—Illustrator isn't actually an animation tool. But the features within Illustrator give you the power to create the image sequences necessary for creating animations. In this chapter, you'll learn various methods that will assist you in creating animation using Illustrator. In some instances, this process can be manual and you must create each individual layer. In others it may be possible to use a custom brush to remove some of the work. But in most cases, you'll use Illustrator's powerful Blend or Transform tools to complete these repetitive steps. You'll then learn to use Illustrator's Release to Layers command to ready the illustration for export. Finally, you'll learn two popular file-saving options when exporting your animation-bound illustrations: SWF and PSD. In the end, you'll have a strong foundation for using Illustrator to help you with animation, and you'll be inspired to use these effects in your own work.

3D rotating box

One of the greatest new tools in Illustrator CS is the 3D effect. Adobe did it right with this new addition. It not only produces stunning 3D images for your static illustrations but it's highly useful in creating animations as well. By using a combination of the Blend tool and 3D effects, you can create animation sequences that previously required many hours of writing code in Macromedia Flash or many dollars spent on a 3D animation tool. In this exercise you'll learn to use the Blend tool with 3D effects. Illustrator doesn't merely create a morph of the two 3D objects being blended, but actually blends them in 3D space. This leaves you with the layers necessary to create simple 3D animations that were previously impossible (or very difficult, to say the least) to create in Illustrator. Finally, you'll export your 3D objects into Flash to create an animation. If you don't have Flash installed on your computer you can download a trial copy at www.macromedia.com/downloads.

1. Create a new RGB Illustrator document. The first half of this exercise is very similar to the beginning steps in the 3D dice exercise in Chapter 5 so I'll move through them quickly.

2. Select the Rectangle tool. Click the Artboard to create a square. Enter 200 pts for the Width and Height settings. Change the fill color of the cube to R:254 G:222 B:88 and set the stroke to None.

3. Name the parent layer 0TO180. Click the arrow on the layer to view the sublayer within. Name this sublayer 180.

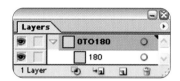

4. Select the 180 sublayer and choose Effect ➤ 3D ➤ Extrude & Bevel. Enter the following settings in the Extrude and Bevel dialog box (shown in the reference image). Take particular note of the Y Axis Rotation value and the Extrude Depth settings. Click OK when you're finished.

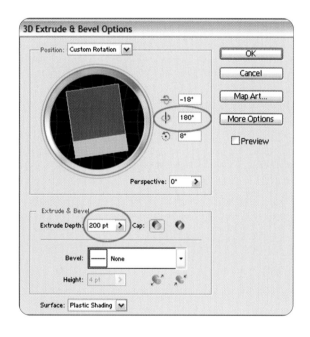

5. Duplicate this sublayer. Name the top sublayer 0 (zero).

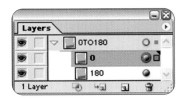

6. Select the 0 layer. Open the Appearance palette (*SHIFT+F6*). Note the 3D Extrude & Bevel layer toward the bottom of the layer stack.

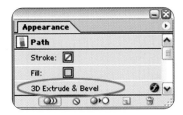

7. Double-click this layer to edit the 3D Extrude & Bevel options. Enter 0 for the Y Axis Rotation setting. Click OK.

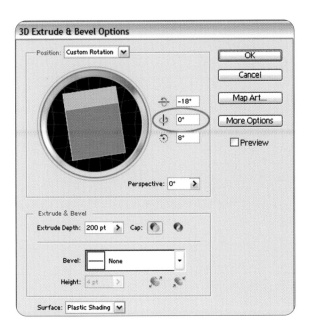

8. Select the two cube layers. Choose Object ➤ Blend ➤ Blend Options. Set the Spacing option to Specified Steps and enter 15 in the text box. Click OK.

9. With the two layers still selected, create a blend between the two (*CTRL/CMD+ALT/OPTION+B*).

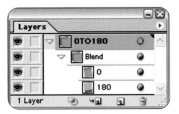

10. Now, duplicate the 0TO180 layer. Name the duplicate 180TO0. Click the expand arrow to view the blend layer and sublayers within. Drag the 0 sublayer below the 180 sublayer. Your expanded Layers palette should now look like this:

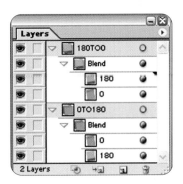

11. Select the 180 sublayer within the 180TO0 layer. Double-click the 3D Extrude & Bevel layer in the Appearance palette to display the 3D settings for this sublayer.

12. Change the Y Axis Rotation setting to −180 and click OK.

Now that the blends are created you need to expand them and make them layers.

13. Select all layers (CTRL/CMD+A).

14. Choose Object ➤ Blend ➤ Expand. This will create two groups instead of blends. Don't deselect the objects yet though.

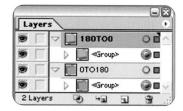

15. Now choose Object ➤ Ungroup (SHIFT+CTRL/ CMD+G). You should now have one sublayer for each step produced by the Blend tool earlier.

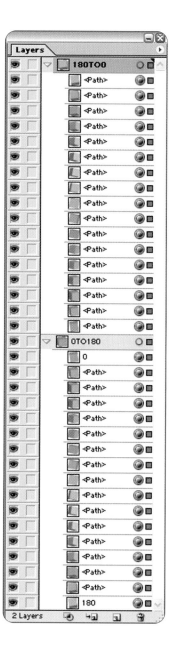

16. Next, deselect all layers (*Shift*+*Ctrl*/*Cmd*+*A*).

17. Click the 180TO0 layer.

> *You aren't selecting anything on this layer. You're just targeting this layer as the active layer but not specifically targeting any objects on it.*

18. Choose Release To Layers (Sequence) from the Layers palette flyout menu.

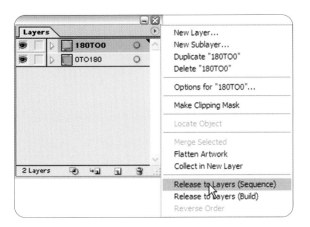

19. Repeat steps 17 and 18 for the 0TO180 layer.

This will complete the process of readying the illustration for export to Flash SWF.

> *If you're wondering why you had to complete step 18, the answer is simple. When Illustrator exports to SWF, it can convert layers to frames. Before step 18, all of the paths were within one layer. The Release to Layers command redistributes them so that they're all actual layers.*

Now you'll begin the process of exporting the layers to an SWF file.

20. Choose File ➤ Export. Pick Macromedia Flash (*.SWF) from the Save as Type drop-down list. Enter 3DrotatingBox.swf as the file name and click Save.

21. Change your settings to appear as the reference image. Take particular note of the Export As setting. Be sure to change this to All Layers to SWF Frames.

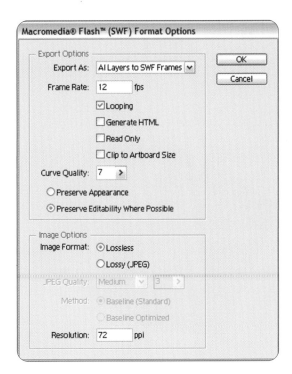

> *The Illustrator help file contains a good description of each setting within the previous dialog box. Within the main index, click M and look for Macromedia Flash File Format.*

22. Next, start up Flash MX. Choose File ➤ New, then choose File ➤ Import. In the Import dialog box navigate to the folder where you stored the exported 3DrotatingBox.swf file. Select the file and click Open.

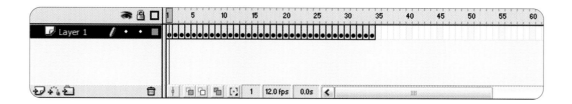

23. Your animation is now in Flash and ready to be tested. Choose Control ➤ Test Movie (*CTRL/CMD+ENTER/RETURN*).

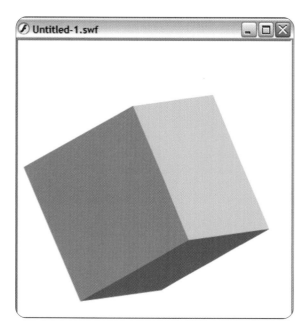

24. Watch in awe as you see what would have taken you a few hundred lines of ActionScript code (or at least a few hundred dollars in purchasing a 3D animation tool) to create.

Text warping

This exercise will walk you through the creation of a simple text animation using Illustrator's text warping effects. While other tools offer text-warping capabilities, it's the Blend tool once again that sets Illustrator apart and makes it a worthwhile contender in creating graphics that are animation bound.

> *Although I love Illustrator, I must give credit where credit is due. If you find yourself performing this type of animation frequently then you should explore the use of Adobe After Effects. It can produce similar effects with greater effectiveness and efficiency than Illustrator. However, if Illustrator is all you have, it's a great alternative.*

1. Create a new RGB Illustrator document. Select the Type tool and set some type using the font of your choice. I've found that thick fonts work best for this exercise but feel free to experiment with other fonts as well. Set this type at a fairly large point size. I used a font called Huggable (download it at www.fontdiner.com) set at 100 pts in this example. I changed the fill color to R:186 G:0 B:255 and set the stroke to None.

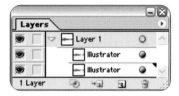

2. Select the text layer and choose Effect ➤ Warp ➤ Fish. Check the Preview check box. Set the Bend setting to 70% and check the Horizontal radio button. Click OK to apply this effect.

3. Duplicate the text by using the Copy (*CTRL/CMD+C*) and Paste In Front (*CTRL/CMD+F*) commands. You should now have two sublayers containing the same text.

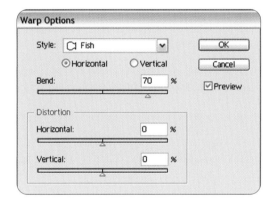

4. Select the bottommost text sublayer. Be sure the Appearance palette (*SHIFT+F6*) is visible and double-click the live Warp effect layer to display the Warp Options dialog box. Change the Bend setting to –70% for this text layer. Click OK. I have hidden the top text layer so you can see the results in this reference image.

5. Select All (*CTRL/CMD+A*). Choose Object ➤ Blend ➤ Blend Options. Set the Spacing option to Specified Steps and enter 20 in the text box beside it.

6. Create a blend between the two text layers (*CTRL/CMD+ALT/OPTION+B*). Don't deselect the text objects yet.

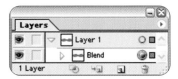

The remaining steps are very similar to the rotating cube exercise. In fact, once you create a blend and decide that you would like to export the blend layers to SWF frames there won't be much deviation from the steps described in these two exercises.

7. Expand the blend by choosing Object ➤ Blend ➤ Expand. This will place all of the blend steps within a group.

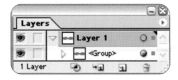

8. Target the group layer and ungroup (*SHIFT+CTRL/ CMD+G*) the objects within. There will now be one grouped sublayer for each blend step produced in step 5. Deselect (*SHIFT+CTRL/CMD+A*) all objects.

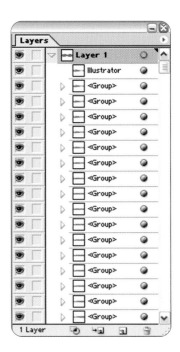

9. Click the parent layer containing the text sublayers produced by the Blend command. Choose Release To Layers (Sequence) from the Layers palette fly-out menu.

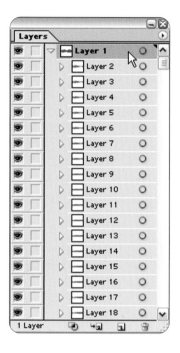

10. To export the layers to Flash SWF complete steps 20–23 from the Rotating Cube exercise. However, in step 21, change the Frame Rate setting in the Export dialog box to 24.

11. Once you've imported your animation into Flash go ahead and test it (CTRL/CMD+ENTER/RETURN).

Looks good, but it's missing something. Since the animation continuously loops, you'll notice that the wave swoops to one side and then jumps back to the beginning. Not very smooth, is it? In the Rotating Cube exercise you took care of this inside Illustrator by creating two blends and changing the order of the layers within the blend. You then exported twice as many layers to Flash but the animation was complete and required no tweaking within Flash. This was required because the cube was in 3D space and needed to be rotated around 360 degrees. However, in this case you aren't dealing with 3D so all that you need to do is duplicate the layers and reverse them to see a complete animation. I chose not to do that in Illustrator in this case to show you how easy it can be to do the same within Flash.

12. Select all of the frames on the Timeline in Flash. Choose Edit ➤ Copy Frames (CTRL/CMD+ALT/OPTION+C).

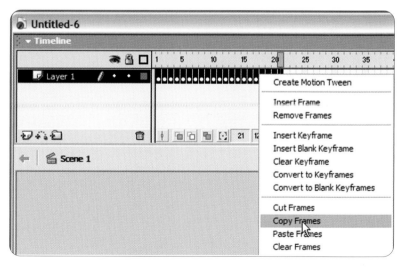

13. Position your cursor on the next empty frame. Choose Edit ➤ Paste Frames (*CTRL/CMD+ALT/OPTION+V*).

14. Select the newly pasted frames.

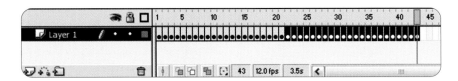

15. Choose Modify ➤ Frames ➤ Reverse.

> *You can also right-click the selected frames and choose* Reverse.

16. This completes the animation. You can now test it and you'll see that the text wave swoops to one side and then back again before repeating itself.

Rotating text around a circle

Up to this point, the exercises in this chapter have utilized the Blend tool to create the graphics needed for animation-bound artwork. This exercise will demonstrate the use of Illustrator's Transform tools and commands in the animation process. Although limited in their options, the various Transform tools are a powerful alternative and sometimes easier to use than the Blend tool.

1. Create a new RGB Illustrator document. Select the Ellipse tool. Click the Artboard and create a circle that is 300 pt by 300 pt in size. The fill and stroke color don't matter for this technique since you're going to be applying text to this circular path. Nevertheless, I set the fill to None and stroke to black for this reference image.

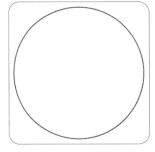

2. Select the Type on a Path tool. Click the circle path and enter the type that you would like to use for this effect. As always, I'm partial to the three words used in the following reference image. The type settings aren't as important for this effect. This type is set at 24 pt Adobe Caslon Pro, a font which ships with Illustrator CS.

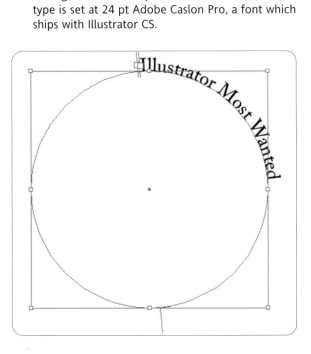

3. Select the type on the path. Choose Object ➤ Transform ➤ Rotate. Enter –30 in the Angle text box and click Copy instead of OK.

4. Press *CTRL/CMD+D* ten times to repeat the Rotate command. This rotates the text 360 degrees around the circle and creates a copy each time. At this point the text should be illegible but that's OK.

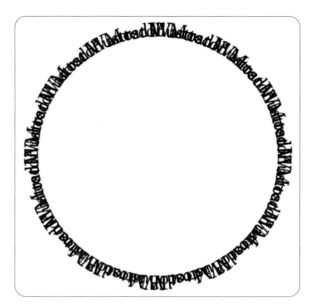

This time you don't need to use the Release to Layers command. You're going to export to a PSD file (Photoshop native file). Illustrator will preserve the text objects as layers in the PSD file, which will work fine for your animation purposes. However, if you wanted to export this as a SWF file you would need to use the release function as you did in previous exercises.

5. Choose File ➤ Export. Choose Photoshop PSD from the Save As Type drop-down menu. Name your file accordingly and click Save.

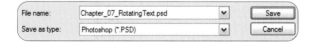

6. When the Photoshop Export Options dialog box appears be sure the color model is set to RGB. Set the Resolution setting to Screen (72 ppi) and be sure that Write Layers, Maximum Editability, and Anti-alias are selected. Click OK when finished.

All that is left is to open Adobe ImageReady and distribute the layers as frames in an animation.

7. Open ImageReady (*CTRL/CMD+O*). Navigate to the folder where you stored the exported PSD file and choose that file to open.

8. Choose Window ➤ Animation to display the Animation palette.

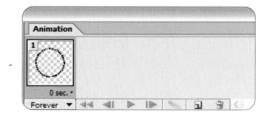

181

9. Click the small arrow at the top right of the Animation palette to view the flyout menu. Choose Make Frames From Layers. This will create a new animation frame from each layer in the Layers palette.

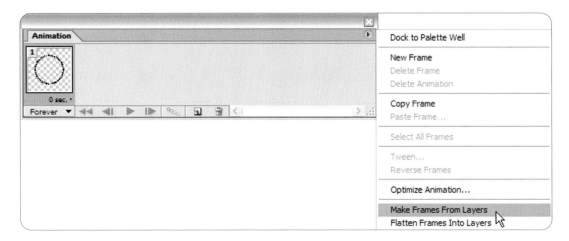

10. All that remains is to test the animation. Do this by choosing File ➤ Preview In ➤ (Your Browser).

11. At this point, you can save this animation as a .GIF file for viewing on the Web. Choose File ➤ Save Optimized to produce a GIF file to insert this into your web pages.

Exploding dots

I love this effect, mainly because the possibilities it opens up are limitless. By using the Liquify tools in Illustrator to produce animations, you can fool people into thinking that you spent hours drawing in Illustrator or writing code in Flash. However, it isn't for the impatient. This exercise is slightly repetitive but the results make it worthwhile; it's difficult to accomplish it in any other way.

1. Create a new RGB Illustrator document. Select the Ellipse tool and set the fill color to R:255 G:153 B:0. Create 8–10 circles of varied size in a small grouped area.

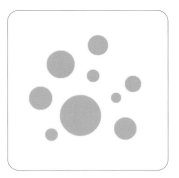

2. Select all circles (*CTRL*/*CMD*+*A*) and group them together (*CTRL*/*CMD*+*G*). Name this layer ORIGINAL.

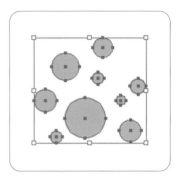

3. Create a duplicate of the ORIGINAL layer. You should now have two groups. Change the name of the topmost layer to PUCKER.

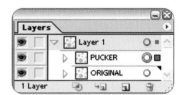

4. Select the Pucker tool. It's located in the Liquify tool's flyout menu.

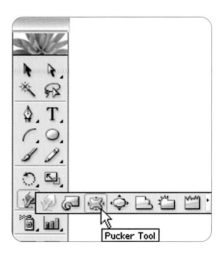

5. Double-click the Pucker tool icon. Change the Width and Height settings to a size large enough to cover the circles that you've created. Change the Intensity setting to 10%.

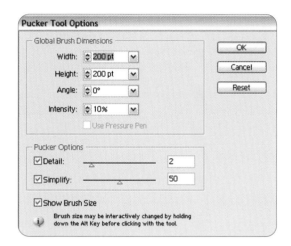

6. Target the PUCKER group layer by clicking its meatball. With the Pucker tool selected, position the brush over the dots and click once. You should have something similar to this (note that I've hidden the ORIGINAL layer so that you could see the result).

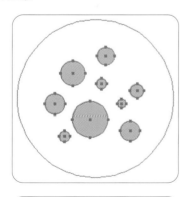

183

This is a time-sensitive tool, meaning that the longer you hold the mouse button down the more of the effect you'll apply to the selected objects. I clicked quickly for the steps in this exercise.

7. Duplicate the new PUCKER group layer and target it so that you can apply the Pucker tool once again.

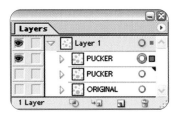

8. Click once over the dots with the Pucker tool. This should make them squeeze together slightly more than previously. Again, I've hidden the previous layers so you can see the effect.

9. Repeat steps 4–7 eight to ten more times or until the dots are nearly invisible. Each time, be sure to duplicate the group you just applied the Pucker tool to so that the dots will get smaller and smaller. From top to bottom your layers should look similar to these reference images.

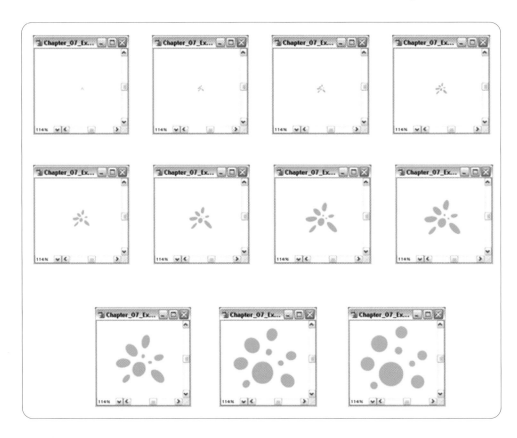

If you were to release the groups to layers at this point and animate them it would look as if the dots were exploding—growing from a tiny group to the fully expanded group. Alone this would be a nice effect, but you can take it a step further. As the dots reach the fully expanded state (the ORIGINAL layer) you can enhance the effect by bouncing the dots into shape at the end.

You can achieve this effect by adding several layers after the final expanded image (ORIGINAL layer) and use the Bloat tool to make them appear as if they expanded even further than the ORIGINAL layer shapes and then bounced back. See the following reference image for a visual.

10. Duplicate the ORIGINAL group sublayer. Select the bottom version of this layer and name it BLOAT1. Select the Bloat tool (next to the Pucker tool in the flyout menu). Double-click the Bloat tool icon and set the Width, Height, and Intensity settings to the same levels that you used in step 5.

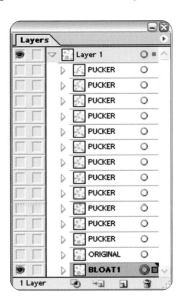

11. With the BLOAT1 group selected, click once with the Bloat tool. The dots should now begin to expand.

12. Duplicate this layer. Select the bottommost copy and name it BLOAT2. Click once with the Bloat tool again.

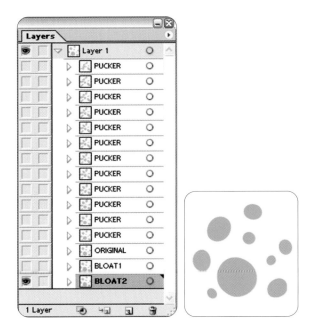

13. Repeat this process one more time so you have a total of three groups that expand beyond the original flat layer. Remember to name the new layer BLOAT3.

14. Create a duplicate of the BLOAT2 group and move it below BLOAT3.

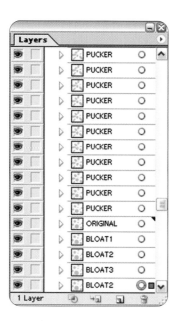

15. Create a duplicate of the BLOAT1 group and move that below the BLOAT2 duplicate group that you just created.

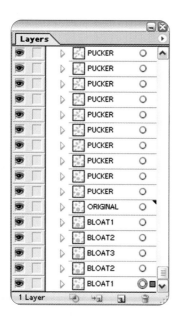

16. Finally, create a copy of the ORIGINAL group and position this at the very bottom of the Layers palette.

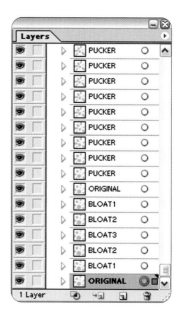

17. Deselect all layers (*SHIFT+CTRL/CMD+A*). Click the parent layer containing all of the sublayers that you applied the Pucker and Bloat tools to. Choose Release To Layers (Sequence) from the Layers palette flyout menu.

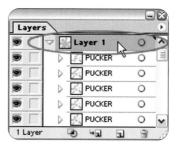

Next you can export the layers to SWF or PSD depending on which type of animation you would like to create. The process is the same as it was in the previous exercises.

Animation with brushes

This exercise will walk you through creating an animation using a custom brush in Illustrator. While somewhat more limited than previous exercises, this exercise has an effect that can quickly produce the graphics necessary for a simple animation. This technique is best applied when trying to animate an object along a particular path. It's true that other animation-specific tools can accomplish this task as well. However, Illustrator's robust brush settings and advanced drawing tools make it a worthwhile, and sometimes more useful, alternative.

1. Create a new RGB Illustrator document. Draw a rectangle encompassing a good portion of the Artboard. Name this layer BACKGROUND. Set the fill color to black and the stroke to None.

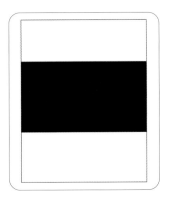

2. Create a new layer above background named ANIMATION. Using the Pen tool, draw a simple curved path. Note that this path isn't closed. When you're done drawing, press *ENTER/RETURN* to end the path.

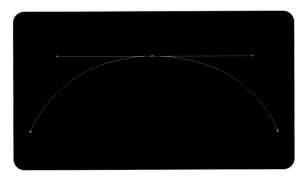

3. Open the Sports_Neon Sports brush palette by choosing Window ➤ Brush Libraries ➤ Sports_Neon Sports.

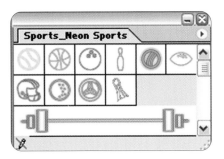

4. Select the path you drew in step 2 and click the football brush to apply it to the path. Note that when you apply this brush to the path, you'll see the football brush appear in your main Brush palette.

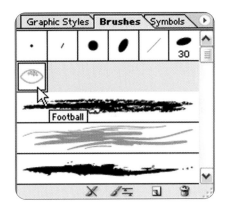

5. Notice how the footballs are scattered along the path.

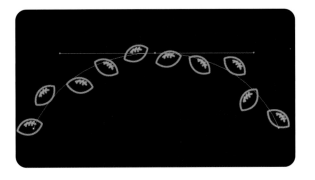

6. This isn't quite the effect you should be looking for. To remedy this, double-click the football brush in the regular Brushes palette, not in the Sports_Neon Sports palette (Window ➤ Brushes or *F5*). This will display the Scatter Brush Options dialog box.

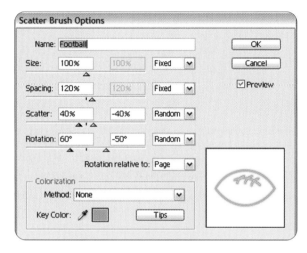

7. To remove the scatter properties of this brush so that it aligns with the path enter 0 in both Scatter text boxes as well as in both Rotation text boxes. Finally, change the Rotation Relative To setting to Path. Click OK when you're done.

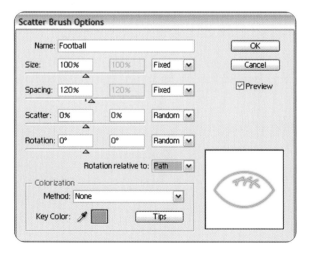

8. When the Brush Change Alert dialog box appears, click Apply to Strokes.

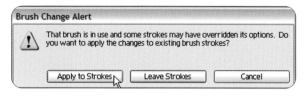

9. Before deselecting, choose Object ➤ Expand Appearance. This will create a group containing the football shapes.

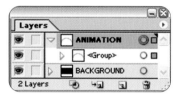

10. Next, ungroup (*SHIFT+CTRL/CMD+G*) the group containing the footballs in the ANIMATION layer.

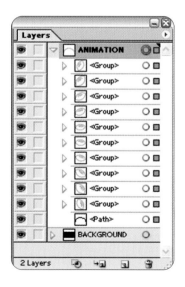

11. Click the ANIMATION layer. Choose Release To Layers (Sequence) from the Layers palette flyout menu.

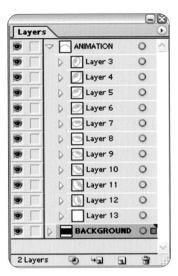

12. Delete the bottom sublayer in the ANIMATION layer. This contains the original path from step 2. Since you expanded the appearance in step 8, you no longer need this layer.

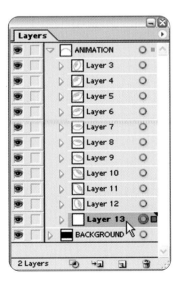

13. The brush animation is now ready for export. You perform this in a way similar to the other exercises. At this point, you could export this animation as an SWF or a PSD file. Either way will work.

> *When exporting this animation, you'll see that it differs from the other in one key aspect. This animation contains a background layer that's separate from the other layers that make up the animation. When Illustrator exports this file it will see the BACKGROUND layer as separate, thus leaving each football layer without a background. To remedy this while in Flash, simply create another layer below the imported SWF file and fill this layer with black. Should you choose to export this to ImageReady, first select the* Make Frames From Layers *command. Select all animation frames in the Animation palette, then click the eye icon next to the BACKGROUND layer to turn it on for all frames.*

Summary

As you can see from the exercises in this chapter, Illustrator CS can be a powerful asset for creating animations for the Web. It not only offers power and flexibility when it comes to actually creating animations, but integrates well with other industry-standard web-animation tools. It's worthwhile to investigate Illustrator CS further for enhancing, streamlining, and inspiring your web-animation tasks.

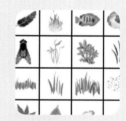

Chapter 8
THE GREAT OUTDOORS

Nature

Nature and outdoor scenery has long been the focus of many illustrators' artwork. This chapter will show you many of the tricks the experts use to illustrate outdoor scenes. Throughout the following exercises, you'll learn techniques to create things such as oceans, skies, clouds, and mountains. As you'll see, many of these scenes are centered on creating gradients to produce the illusion of depth and dimension. This is especially true for outdoor scenery because of the strong light source known as the sun. Thus, it's important to have your gradient skills honed when tackling the following exercises. Finally, this chapter will make extensive use of Illustrator's predefined artwork templates, sample files, and presets.

Until recently, Illustrator had been lacking a variety of predefined artwork samples and templates. This has changed with the CS release. Adobe has gone to great lengths to provide you with a starting point in nearly every area of illustration. Within the Illustrator CS installation folder you'll find a fairly large PDF file. This file is large for a reason: It contains a detailed description of the sample files and presets that ship with Illustrator CS, and there are many. In addition, it contains thumbnails so you can quickly decide which item you want to use. This file is located at the root of the Illustrator CS installation folder and is named Additional Content.pdf. The exercises in this chapter will familiarize you with some of this content. However, I urge you to look at this file to see the abundant material already included with Illustrator CS. It will provide you with a good starting point and a great source of inspiration.

Ocean scenery—water and sky

As the first exercise in this chapter, the following steps will introduce you to the basics for creating outdoor scenery. You'll learn how to use the presets that ship with Illustrator CS and see how a gradient and custom brush can create an entire outdoor scene.

1. Create a new RGB Illustrator document. Using the Rectangle tool (*M*), create a rectangle that spans the dimensions of the Artboard. Name this layer BACKGROUND.

As I mentioned in the opening paragraph of this exercise, many of the effects you'll be creating in this chapter will use some form of a gradient. You could create a gradient from scratch but Illustrator CS offers you many predefined choices, so why not take advantage of them?

2. Choose Window ➤ Swatch Libraries ➤ Other Library. Navigate to your Adobe Illustrator CS install folder. This folder should contain a subfolder named Presets. Within Presets, open the Gradients folder. Select Water.ai and click Open.

> If you can't find any of the presets mentioned throughout this book you may have done a custom install when installing Illustrator CS. If this is the case you may need to do some reinstalling in order to use the Presets folder contents.

3. You should now see the palette that contains 15 different water gradients.

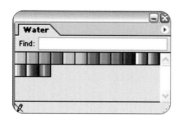

4. With your BACKGROUND layer selected, click the gradient named Water With Horizon 1. Find the name of a swatch by moving your mouse pointer over it. As you do this, a tip box appears with the name.

5. By default, Illustrator will apply a linear gradient with a 0% angle setting to the selection. Therefore you should see something similar to this reference image. To remedy this, simply select the Gradient tool and drag from top to bottom to reposition the gradient. Alternatively, you can enter 270 for the Angle setting in the Gradient palette.

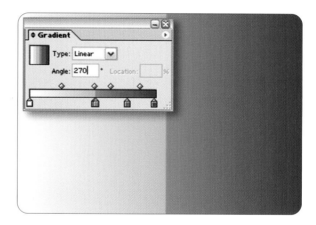

6. You should see an ocean scene appear.

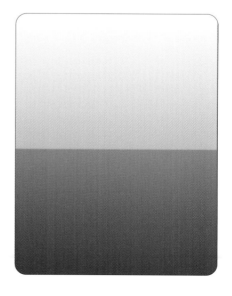

You don't have to use Illustrator's preset gradients for this effect. Feel free to create your own. If you're looking for a source of inspiration, a photo is always a good reference. Scan it in and pick up the colors through the scenery for use in your illustration. In addition, I cannot stress the importance of using Google's Image Search feature. This is an invaluable resource for inspiration and should be used whenever you're in need of ideas.

Now it's time to add some clouds. Fortunately, Illustrator CS also ships with artwork to help you out here as well.

7. Choose Window ➤ Brush Libraries ➤ Water. This opens a palette containing various water-related brushes.

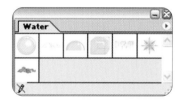

8. Create a new layer above BACKGROUND, and call it CLOUDS.

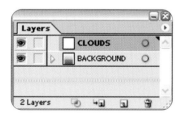

9. Create two wavy, open-ended paths similar to this reference image.

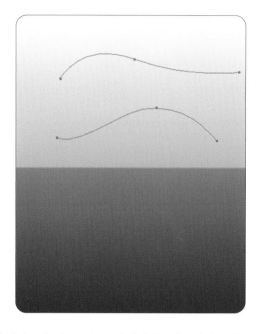

10. Select both paths and click the Clouds brush.

> *You may need to reposition the cloud paths so that they don't overlap the water.*

11. For a slightly stormy weather effect, duplicate the CLOUDS layer. This should produce a layer on top named CLOUDS Copy. Drag this layer below CLOUDS and name it DARK CLOUDS.

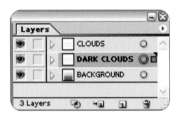

12. Select both paths within the DARK CLOUDS layer. You may need to lock the CLOUDS layer to make your selections. Click the Storm Clouds brush in the Water brush palette. Don't deselect the paths yet.

13. Open the Transparency palette (*SHIFT+F10*). Set the Opacity setting to 30% so that the scene doesn't look too gloomy.

Finally, you're going to add some water ripples.

14. First, create a new layer above BACKGROUND named RIPPLES. Lock the other layers.

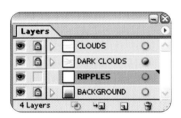

15. Choose Window ➤ Symbols ➤ Libraries ➤ Artistic Textures. Select the Ripples symbol.

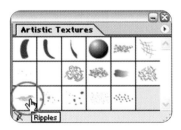

16. Next, select the Symbol Sprayer tool and spray the water ripples over the ocean part of the gradient. If this is new to you, you can click to apply symbols in a concentrated area, or you can click and drag to spread them out, as shown in the figure on the right.

17. By default, the ripples will be somewhat dark. Fix this by selecting the Symbol Stainer tool.

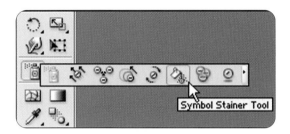

18. Double-click the tool to display the Symbolism Tools Options dialog box. Change the brush diameter to 50 pt. Click OK.

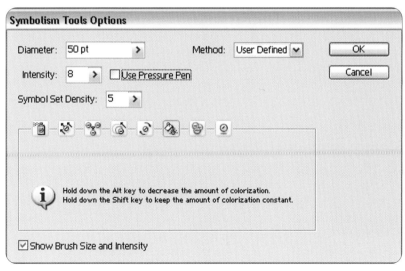

19. Press *D* to set the default colors for fill and stroke in the toolbox (white and black respectively). Click or drag with the Symbol Stainer tool over the ripples to progressively color some of them white for highlights. However, don't color all of them. You'll want to retain some dark ripples as shadows.

> *The longer you hold down the mouse button the whiter the ripples will become.*

20. Finally, select the RIPPLES layer and change the Blending mode to Overlay. Also, change the Opacity setting to 55%.

Desert scenery

The following exercise builds upon the techniques learned in the previous Ocean Scenery exercise. However, you'll begin to use more custom-created elements and rely heavily on the Symbol tools to quickly build a detailed desert scene.

The sky

1. Create a new RGB Illustrator document. Using the Rectangle tool, create a rectangle in the center of the Artboard that will contain the sky. Don't worry about the Fill and Stroke settings at this point. Name the layer that contains this rectangle SKY.

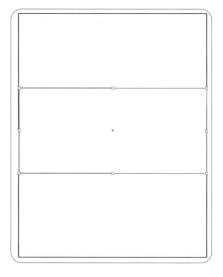

2. Load the Sky gradients by choosing Window ➤ Swatch Libraries ➤ Other Library. Navigate to your Adobe Illustrator CS install folder. This folder should contain a subfolder named Presets. Within Presets, open the Gradients folder. Select Sky.ai and click Open.

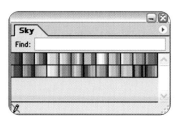

3. With the SKY layer selected, click the Sky 4 gradient to apply it. Also be sure that the stroke is set to None for this shape.

4. If you need to reposition this gradient to appear like the reference image, select the Gradient tool and drag from bottom to top or enter 90 degrees for the Angle setting in the Gradient palette.

The ground

5. Create a new layer above SKY called GROUND. Using the Rectangle tool, create a new rectangle for the ground.

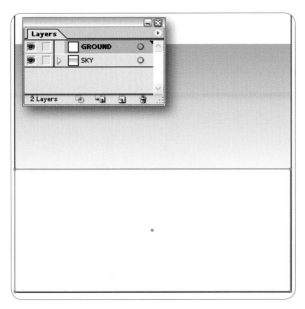

6. Choose Window ➤ Swatch Libraries ➤ Other. Once again, navigate to the Gradients folder and select Earthtones.ai. Click Open.

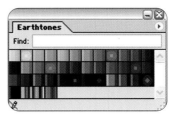

7. Fill the rectangle within the GROUND layer with the Earthtone 2 gradient (third swatch in the palette). Position this gradient as I have in the reference image by selecting the Gradient tool and dragging from the top left to the bottom right.

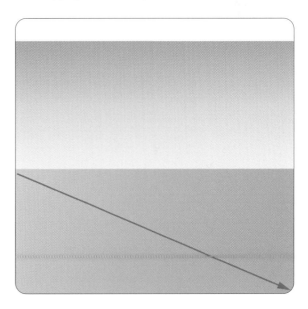

The mountains

8. Create a new layer above SKY but below GROUND. Name this layer MOUNTAIN.

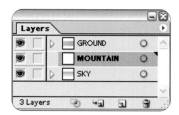

9. Select the Pen tool. Draw a jagged mountainous shape similar to the reference image. Be sure it's a closed path so that there are no fill problems popping up. Enter R:169 G:119 B:93 for the fill settings. There's no need to spend a great deal of time on this shape. I clicked very quickly with the Pen tool to create straight path segments. Occasionally, I spent extra time in certain areas to add more detail to the path.

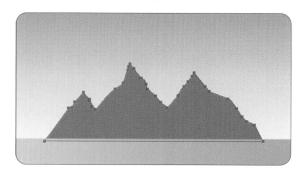

10. Select or target the mountain shape. Choose Object ➤ Path ➤ Offset Path. Enter 4 pt for the offset value. Set the Joins drop-down list to Miter and the Miter Limit text box to 4. Click OK.

11. This will create a new sublayer below the original mountain shape. Set the fill as follows: R:231 G:185 B:138.

12. Name the new sublayer HIGHLIGHT. Also, name the darker mountain shape above this sublayer MIDTONE. Lock the MOUNTAIN layer at this time.

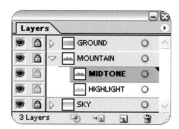

13. Create a new layer above MOUNTAIN named CUTOUT. Using the Pen tool, draw small, closed-path cutout shapes. These shapes will eventually be subtracted from the MIDTONE sublayer shape to allow the areas from the HIGHLIGHT layer to show through. Keep this in mind as you create and place these shapes. Note that I've filled them with white to make them easier to see. However, the fill color doesn't matter in this step.

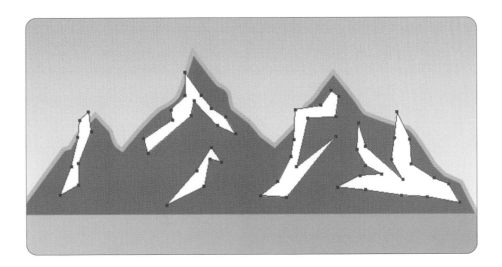

14. Unlock the MOUNTAIN layer. Using the Layers palette, target the new layer so all of the small cutout shapes within are selected. Then *Shift-click* the MIDTONE sublayer's meatball.

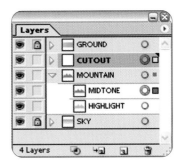

15. Open the Pathfinder palette (*Shift+F9*). Hold down the *Alt/Option* key and choose Subtract From Shape Area. You should now be able to see the HIGHLIGHT mountain shape in place of the small cutout shapes you created.

16. The previous step will have merged all sublayers within the CUTOUT layer into one compound path sublayer. To keep things orderly in the Layers palette, drag this layer within the MOUNTAIN layer but above the HIGHLIGHT sublayer and rename it MIDTONE.

17. Create a new sublayer above MIDTONE and name it SHADOW.

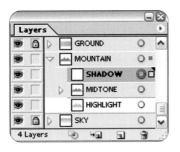

199

18. Using the Pen tool, create small, jagged, closed paths. Set the fill to R:138 G:100 B:74. These shapes will serve as shadows within the mountain.

19. Next, you need to add the drop shadow that the mountains will cast on the desert. Create a new layer above GROUND named DROP SHADOW. Make a copy of the HIGHLIGHT sublayer (*CTRL/CMD+C*) from within the MOUNTAIN layer. Lock all layers except for DROP SHADOW. Use the Paste In Front command (*CTRL/CMD+F*) to paste the copy on the DROP SHADOW layer.

20. Select the shadow shape. Fill it with black and set the stroke to None. Then choose Object ➤ Transform ➤ Reflect. Select the Horizontal radio button and click OK.

21. Select the shadow shape. Choose Object ➤ Transform ➤ Scale. Under the Non-Uniform options group, enter a value of 80% in the Vertical text box and click OK.

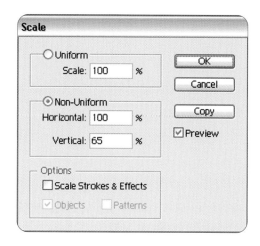

22. Choose Object ➤ Transform ➤ Shear. Set the shear angle to –60 degrees. Be sure Horizontal is selected and click OK. Finally, drag the shadow shape over and down so it lines up with the base of the other mountain shape.

23. With the SHADOW sublayer still selected, use the Transparency palette (*SHIFT+F10*) to change the Blending mode to Overlay and the Opacity setting to 50%.

24. The mountains are now complete.

Clouds

25. You'll use a slightly different method to add clouds to this illustration from what you used in the Ocean scene.

26. First, create a new layer above SKY but below MOUNTAIN named CLOUDS.

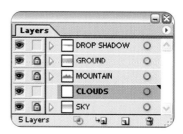

27. Choose Window ➤ Symbol Libraries ➤ Nature to open the various nature symbols that ship with Illustrator CS.

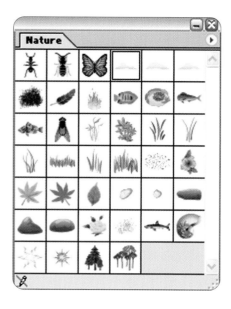

28. Click the Cloud 1 symbol from the palette. Select the Symbol Sprayer tool and drag across the sky area to add a few clouds.

29. For an added effect, you can select the remaining two cloud symbols (Cloud 2 and Cloud 3 respectively) and add a few more clouds. They are just smaller versions of the Cloud 1 symbol.

Foliage

The remaining steps will focus on adding some detail on the ground.

30. Create a new layer above GROUND called FOLIAGE. Open the same Nature symbols palette that was used for the clouds previously in this exercise.

31. Select the Grass 2 symbol. Using the Symbol Sprayer tool, add some grass throughout the illustration on the ground.

32. Select the Symbol Sizer tool.

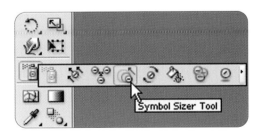

33. Click grass symbols in the foreground to enlarge them slightly, then hold down the ALT/OPTION key and click the symbols toward the background to reduce their size. Repeat this process of enlarging and reducing size until you achieve the desired result.

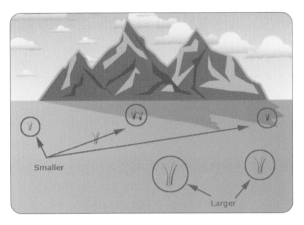

34. Next, to add some variety, select the Grass 4 symbol and apply it to the illustration as well.

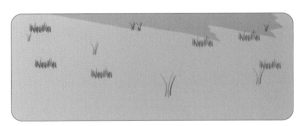

35. Use the Symbol Sizer tool and size these symbols similar to the way you did in step 10.

36. Repeat this process by selecting the Foliage 2 symbol and applying it toward the front.

Be sure to arrange the sublayers containing your symbols in the appropriate order. For example, the rocks should be behind the foreground foliage symbols but in front of the small grass symbols in the background. Similarly, the Dirt symbols should be below all symbols.

37. The remaining steps are the same. I've applied the Dirt symbol and the Rock 3 & 5 symbols in a similar way.

Underwater scene

1. Create a new RGB Illustrator document. Using the Rectangle tool, create a rectangle around the top half of the Artboard to serve as the surface of the water. Name this layer SURFACE.

2. Fill this rectangle with a linear gradient that uses the following settings:

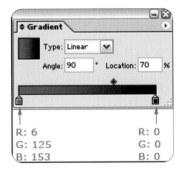

3. Select the SURFACE layer and choose Effect ➤ Distort ➤ Glass. Enter the following settings. Don't deselect yet.

4. Next, with the rectangle still selected choose Object ➤ Expand Appearance.

> The previous step served an important purpose. If you were to continue without expanding the SURFACE layer, then whenever you made changes to the rectangle, the Glass effect would redraw itself to the new shape. Part of this effect involves resizing this shape significantly to produce the desired effect. By expanding the appearance first, you can manipulate and distort the Glass effect without it redrawing itself to conform to the new shape.

5. Select the Free Transform tool (*E*). Position your cursor over the bottom-center handle of the bounding box that appears and drag upward, thereby reducing the size to nearly 25% of what it was previously.

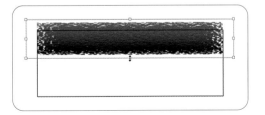

6. Continue using the Free Transform tool to size the shape so that none of the white artifacts that appear as a result of the Glass filter appear within the Artboard. You only want to see the ones on the bottom; these will be hidden in the next step.

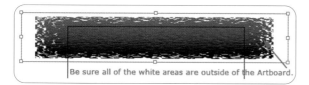

Be sure all of the white areas are outside of the Artboard.

7. Create a new layer above SURFACE called WATER. Create a rectangle that encompasses the remainder of the Artboard and extends slightly outside of it on all sides. Fill it with the same gradient used in step 2 but reverse the gradient direction this time so the black area of the gradient is on top.

Note how the top of the rectangle extends over the SURFACE layer.

8. Select the new rectangle on the WATER layer and choose Effect ➤ Blur ➤ Gaussian Blur. Enter 10 for the Radius setting. This softens the transition between the WATER and OCEAN layers so that they blend together nicely.

Next, you'll create the ocean floor with a similar technique.

9. Create a new layer above WATER named BOTTOM. Create a rectangle on this layer toward the bottom of the Artboard and fill it with a new gradient.

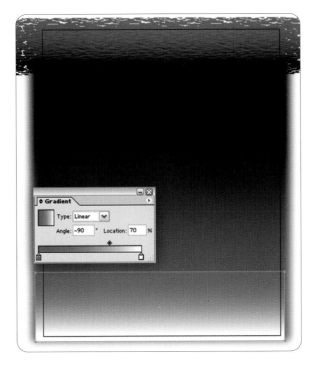

> *This is the same gradient except the right color stop is white instead of black.*

10. Choose Effect ➤ Blur ➤ Gaussian Blur. Enter 10 for the radius. Again, this step softens the edges of BOTTOM layer so it matches seamlessly with the OCEAN layer.

11. Choose Effect ➤ Texture ➤ Texturizer. Set the scaling to 70% and the relief to 2. Leave the Light Direction setting at Top and be sure the Invert check box isn't checked.

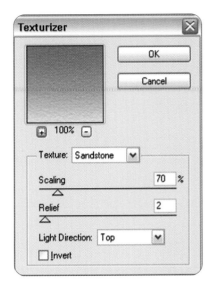

207

Next, you'll add some rays of sunlight that fade as they get closer to the bottom. This effect is similar to the spotlight effect used in Chapter 3 so I'll discuss it quickly.

12. Create a new layer above BOTTOM and name it SUNLIGHT. Using the Ellipse tool, create a small circle positioned above the top of the illustration outside of the Artboard boundaries. Fill this circle with white and set the stroke to None.

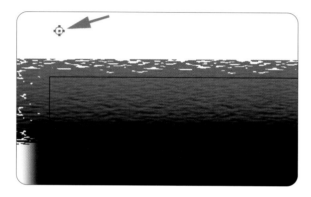

13. Create another larger oval shape positioned below the bottom of the illustration also outside of the Artboard boundaries.

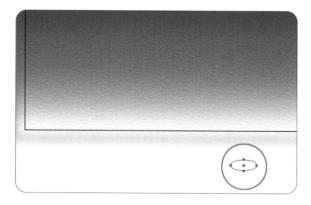

14. Choose Object ➤ Blend ➤ Blend Options. Choose Specified Steps and enter 200 in the text box.

15. Select both circles and create a blend between them (*CTRL/CMD+ALT/OPTION+B*). Don't deselect yet.

16. Choose Effect ➤ Blur ➤ Gaussian Blur. Enter 20 for the Radius setting.

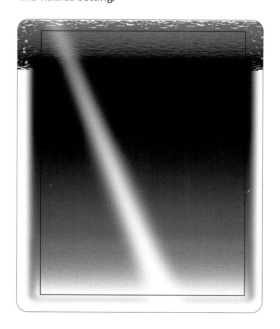

17. Click the small arrow on the left side of the Blend layer to view its contents. Target the circle at the bottom of the Artboard in the blend group and change its Opacity setting to 0%.

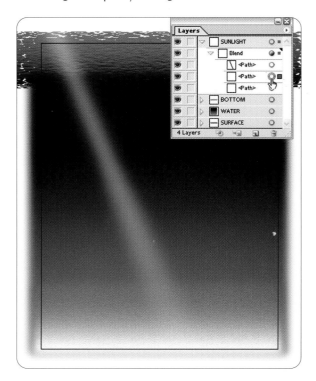

18. Duplicate the SUNLIGHT layer several times. Use the Free Transform tool (*E*) to rotate and reposition each ray of light as I have in this reference image.

19. Finally, to finish the effect off, add some fish to enjoy the new ocean home. In this example, I chose Window ➤ Symbol Libraries ➤ Nature. This library contains a few fish that will work great for this illustration.

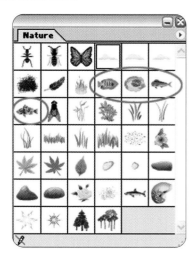

20. I created a new layer below SUNLIGHT but above BOTTOM called FISH.

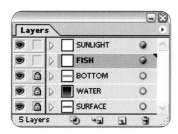

21. Using the Symbol Sprayer tool, I added various fish to this layer, each on its own separate sublayer.

22. Next, reduce the opacity of the entire FISH layer to 50%. Then selectively run the Gaussian Blur effect on each set of fish. Set the radius from 3–4 for the fish that you would like to appear in the distant background (the orange fish). Set the radius from 1–2 for any fish that you would like to appear slightly closer (the round blue and yellow fish) and leave the remaining fish alone.

Summary

As this chapter comes to a close, I hope that I've left you with a strong foundation for how to create outdoor scenery effects in Illustrator. If you choose to continue with this type of illustration, you should already have a good starting point after you've completed the preceding exercises. By using the presets that Illustrator CS ships with, you can create some astonishing effects right out of the box. In addition you can draw from these presets for inspiration when you create your own library of effects. However, whether you decide to use the artwork included with Illustrator CS or create your own, I urge you to explore the content that Adobe has provided you. It can offer many timesaving effects and serve as a learning tool as well as a source of inspiration.

Chapter 9

CARTOON AND GAME EFFECTS

With Macromedia Flash games and cartoons becoming so popular, the need for scalable vector graphics has increased. This, coupled with Illustrator CS's Flash-exporting capabilities, make it an ideal place to create graphics for your Flash games and cartoons. While animation tools such as Flash do offer drawing capabilities, you'll find that none offer the power, control, and flexibility you get from Illustrator. And with the latest versions of Illustrator, you can export your art-work to Flash in a snap. This chapter will show you techniques on how to quickly and professionally draw, color, and manipu-late your work in Illustrator. You'll learn techniques that demonstrate Illustrator's prowess in path manipulation tools, stroke options, layer maintenance, and live effects. Finally, you'll see how Illustrator's guides and 3D effects can help your game and cartoon illustrations achieve perspective that was previously difficult to create.

Cartoon faces: Eyes, nose, and mouth

Online Flash cartoons have become extremely popular over the years. They allow designers to animate a variety of objects, scene elements, and characters. This exercise will teach you a few different methods for creating various expressions on your cartoon faces. Pay close attention to the techniques that use the Pathfinder palette, as the palette isn't available in many animation tools. Also note the various brush and stroke options used throughout this exercise. Programs such as Flash do offer stroke options but none of them compare to the variety and flexibility you get by using Illustrator.

Flat eyes

1. Open Chapter_09_CartoonFaceStart.ai. This file contains a cartoon head that has already been drawn for you. I've included this to give you a jump start on the exercises, but feel free to draw your own if you wish.

2. Create a new layer above HEAD called EYES. Select the Ellipse tool.

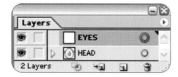

3. Draw an oval to create the basic outline for an eye. Fill the shape with white and set the stroke color to

black. Also, be sure the Weight setting in the Stroke palette is set to 1 pt.

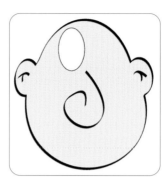

4. Open the Brushes palette (*F5*). With the oval shape selected, click the 6 pt Flat brush.

5. Next, draw a smaller oval. Fill this shape with black and set the stroke to None. Notice that I've positioned this oval slightly toward the inside of the eye. You'll make your cartoon character slightly cross-eyed. Feel free to experiment with your own placement.

6. Target the entire EYES layer by clicking its meatball icon.

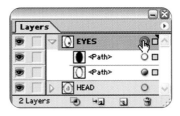

7. Choose Object ➤ Transform ➤ Reflect. Check the Vertical Axis option and click COPY. This will create a copy of the eye and flip it so it matches correctly on the other side of the face. It will also leave it selected, which works out well for the next step.

8. Drag the selected eye to the other side of the face and position it in place.

Another variation on this is to create both eyes at the same time and merge them so that they appear as one shape.

9. Using the Ellipse tool, create two ovals that overlap each other.

10. Select the two oval shapes. Hold down the *ALT/OPTION* key and click the Add to Shape Area button in the Pathfinder palette.

11. Then add the small black ovals in the center of the eyes.

Eyelids

12. Complete the first part of the previous exercise by creating two eyes.

13. Next, create a duplicate of one of the large white eye shapes by dragging the sublayer over the Create New Layer button at the bottom of the Layers palette.

14. Create a new sublayer above the duplicate you just created. With the Pen tool, draw a shape to simulate the eyelid closing over the eye. The only area you need to concern yourself with is the actual shape of the bottom of the eyelid. Be sure it has a nice downward curve to it. The portions of this shape that extend outside of the actual eye will be removed, so don't worry if you go over the outline of the basic eye shape. Fill this shape by entering the following: R:249 G:237 B:199.

15. Select or target the eyelid shape and the duplicate eye shape.

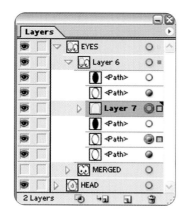

16. Hold down the *ALT/OPTION* key and click the Intersect Shape Areas button in the Pathfinder palette.

17. Repeat this process for the other eye.

18. You may need to move the small black ovals so that they can be seen underneath the eyelid. Looks sleepy, doesn't he?

3D eyes

3D eyes are just a variation on the same techniques you've been using for the other eye effects.

19. First, be sure to complete the first exercise by creating two eyes. However, don't stroke the white oval shapes with any color at this time.

20. Select the white oval shape on the right side of the face. Choose Effect ➤ Stylize ➤ Inner Glow. You want to simulate shadows and depth so change the Mode color to black. Set the Mode setting to Normal, the Opacity setting to 40%, and the Blur setting to 12 pt. Finally, be sure the Edge radio button is selected and click OK.

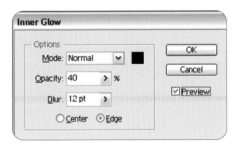

21. Instant 3D eye!

22. Next, add a drop shadow behind the eye by choosing Object ➤ Stylize ➤ Drop Shadow. Enter the following settings and click OK.

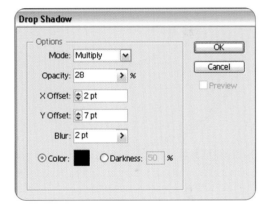

23. Finally, add a small highlight over the black part of the eye by creating another small oval and filling it with white. Be sure to set the stroke to None as well.

24. Duplicate these steps for the other eye, or better yet, delete the other eye and just duplicate the completed 3D eye. Don't forget to use the Reflect transformation to maintain symmetry.

Noses

Noses are actually pretty easy. You have a lot of flexibility when creating cartoon noses because they are just that—cartoons.

As you can see, I've created one nose for you on the HEAD layer. I drew this with the Pen tool, set the fill color to None, and set the stroke with the 6 pt. Oval brush located in the Brushes palette.

Front view nose

While the other nose was viewed from the front, it wasn't symmetrical. It almost implied a side or three-quarter view. Here is another alternative.

25. Hide the NOSE1 sublayer within the HEAD layer. Create a new layer above HEAD named NOSE2.

26. To create a symmetrical front view nose select the Ellipse tool and draw an oval the size of the nose you would like to create.

27. Draw another oval at the top (as shown). This will serve as the shape used to cut out of the other oval.

28. Select both oval shapes and click the Subtract From Shape Area button in the Pathfinder palette.

29. Using the open arrow Direct Selection tool, click the center anchor point located in the top portion of the nose path.

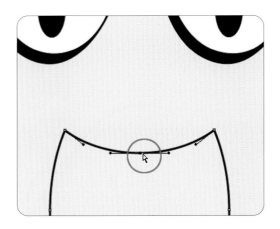

30. Press the *DELETE* key to remove that anchor point and leave an open-ended path.

31. Since the nose will be the same color as the face, you don't have to set a fill color. However, set the stroke to the same 6 pt. Oval brush that you used previously.

Free-formed nose

Finally, you can create a slightly quirky free-formed nose.

32. Hide the previously created NOSE2 layer and create a new blank layer named NOSE3. Using the Pen tool, create a shape similar to this reference image.

219

33. Once again, set the stroke to the 6 pt. Oval brush located in the Brushes palette.

34. Finally, duplicate the sublayer containing the nose and place the copy directly above the original. Select the bottom copy of the nose and nudge it down and to the left several times with the arrow key.

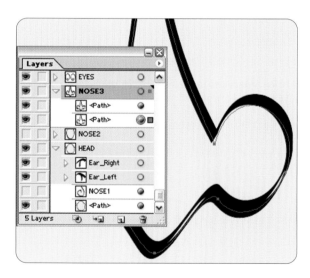

35. Set the Opacity setting of the duplicate to 40% in the Transparency palette.

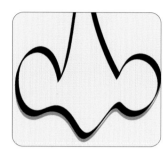

Mouth

Mouths are just as simple. Follow along and you'll see three quick ways to create mouths.

36. You can create a mouth by just creating a wavy line with the Pen tool. Set the fill to None and the stroke to black. Also, set the stroke's Weight setting to 2 pt.

37. To vary this technique, set the stroke to one of the calligraphic brushes located by choosing Window ➤ Brush Libraries ➤ Artistic_Calligraphic. A 5–7 pt. Flat or Oval brush work well in this case.

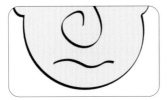

The next technique simulates an open mouth.

38. Create a circle or oval shape using the Ellipse tool and fill it with black. Set the stroke to the 6 pt. oval brush used in previous examples.

39. To add to this effect, use a radial gradient for the fill instead of only black. This example uses a red to black radial gradient to simulate the color of the inside of a mouth.

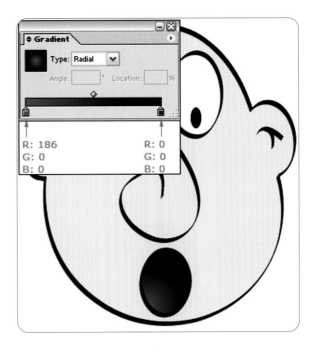

Finally, you can add a mouth with teeth. This technique is very similar to the way the eyelids were created earlier.

40. Create the base shape for the mouth. Set the fill color of the shape to black and the stroke to black as well.

41. On a sublayer above the mouth shape, use the Pen tool to draw a shape for the teeth. Much like the eyelid, the only part that matters for this shape is the area that intersects with the mouth. The rest will be removed. Fill this shape with white and set the stroke to None.

42. Duplicate the original mouth shape and paste the copy in front of the original. Select the duplicate and the teeth shape just created. Hold down the ALT/OPTION key and choose the Intersect with Shape Area button from the Pathfinder palette.

Using a perspective grid

Creating cartoons and games with complex background scenery can often become difficult when maintaining perspective is involved. Illustrator allows you to create custom guides and use the Snap and Smart Guides features to align your artwork with those guides. This helps tremendously when you create complex perspective illusions in your illustrations. This exercise will demonstrate how to create a vanishing point with guides in Illustrator. You'll learn how to actually create your own guides out of any path and how to align your artwork to them to take away the guesswork involved in being precise.

1. Create a new RGB Illustrator document.

2. Select the Rectangle tool. Click the Artboard once and enter 610 pt for the width and 250 pt for the height. Name this layer SKY.

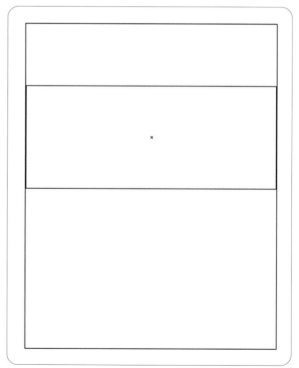

3. Next, fill the SKY layer with the following linear gradient and set the stroke to None.

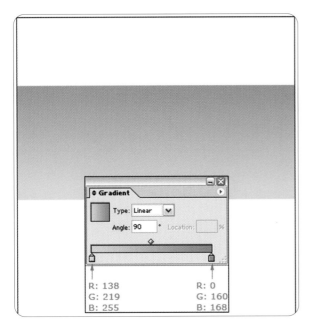

Next, you're going to create some guides to help you align your objects in the correct perspective. Guides are lines that appear to float over the entire image but will not print or be visible over the final image output. In Illustrator there are two ways to create guides. First is the method in which you drag guides vertically or horizontally from the ruler (CTRL/CMD+R). This will only allow for gridlike guides to be created. The second method entails drawing paths and converting them to guides. In this method you can draw a path with any of the path tools and convert it to a guide.

4. Choose View ➤ Show Rulers (CTRL/CMD+R).

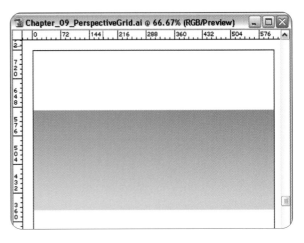

5. Position your mouse over the horizontal ruler at the top. Click and drag downward and you'll see a guide appear. Position this guide approximately at the bottom of the SKY rectangle. This will serve as your horizon line.

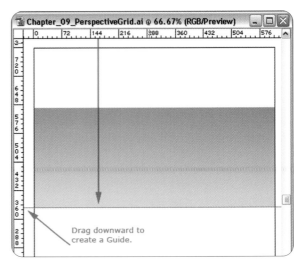

Drag downward to create a Guide.

223

6. Create a new layer above SKY. Name it GRASS.

7. Create a new rectangle by clicking and dragging on the Artboard. Position the rectangle so the bottom is even with the outlines of the Artboard and the top is even with the guide. Fill the GRASS layer rectangle with the following gradient and set the stroke to None.

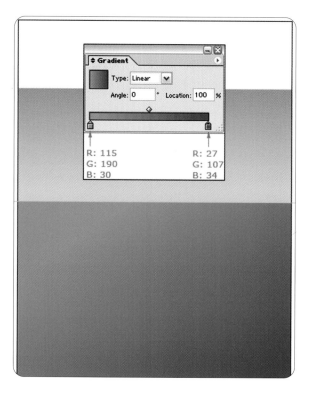

8. Next, you need to create some more guides. Create a new layer at the bottom of the Layers palette named VANISHING POINT. Lock the SKY and GRASS layers.

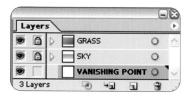

9. Select the Pen tool and draw two diagonal lines from the outside left area of the Artboard to the point where the horizon line and rectangle intersect. These guides will serve as the road. Note that I've hidden the GRASS layer so that you can see the lines in the reference image.

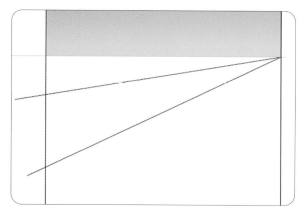

10. Then draw two more lines that are positioned as closely to the center of these two lines as possible. These will be used for the center white line in the road.

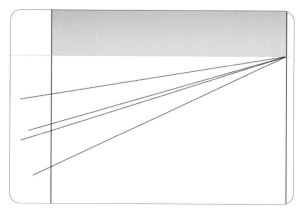

11. Since everything besides the VANISHING POINT layer should be locked, go ahead and Select all the layers (*CTRL/CMD+A*). Choose View ➤ Guides ➤ Make Guides. This will turn your paths into guides.

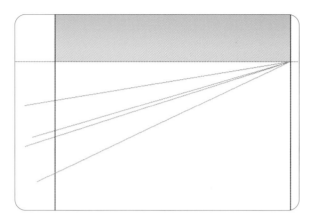

By default, guides are cyan in color. This makes them somewhat difficult to see at times and even more difficult to display in reference images for a book. Because of this, I've changed the guide color to red by choosing Edit ➤ Preferences ➤ Guides & Grid. The resulting dialog box contains a Color setting allowing you to change the color of the guides.

12. Create a new layer above GRASS named ROAD.

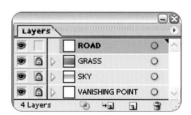

13. Turn on Smart Guides (*CTRL/CMD+U*) and select the Pen tool. Draw a three-sided shape that follows the two outside diagonal lines. Fill this shape with R:165 G:165 B:165 and set the stroke to None.

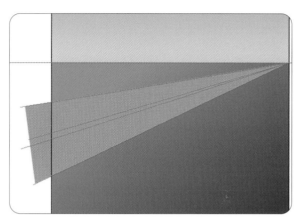

14. Next, do the same for the two inner guides and fill this shape with white. This will be the center line of the road.

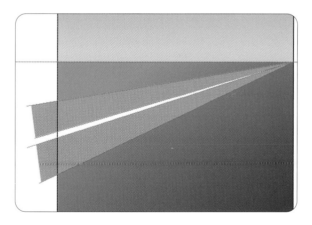

Next, you need to create the wooden posts that will be positioned along the side of the road. All you need to do is create one and use the Transform effect to create the rest.

15. Create a new layer above ROAD named POSTS. Create a wooden post shape similar to mine. I used the Rectangle and Ellipse tools to create this shape and merged them with the Add to Shape option in the Pathfinder palette.

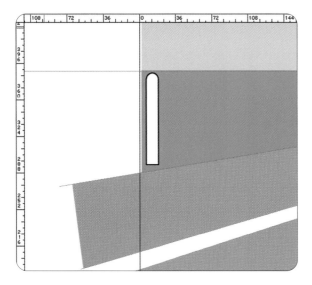

16. Choose Window ➤ Swatch Libraries ➤ Other Library. Navigate to the Gradients folder within the Presets folder and choose Wood.ai. Apply the Poplar gradient to this post and set the stroke to None.

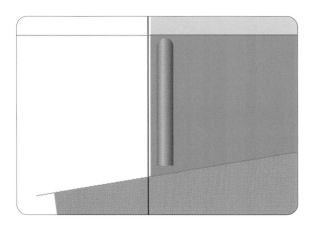

17. Select the post shape and choose Effect ➤ Distort & Transform ➤ Transform. Enter settings similar to this reference image and click OK. Note that your settings may differ slightly depending on the proportions and size of other elements in your illustration.

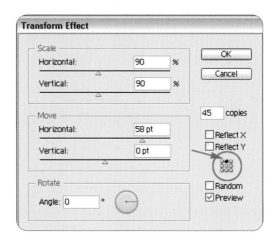

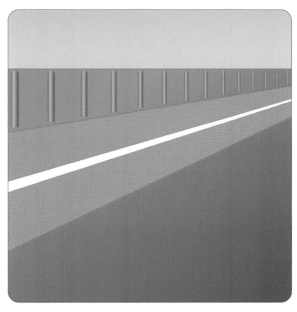

18. Your illustration is now ready for animation. Choose View ➤ Guides ➤ Hide Guides to hide the guides. This would be a great technique for an animation of a car driving down the road. You could create the car in Illustrator, export it to Flash, and create a tween of the car that gets smaller as it drives into the distance.

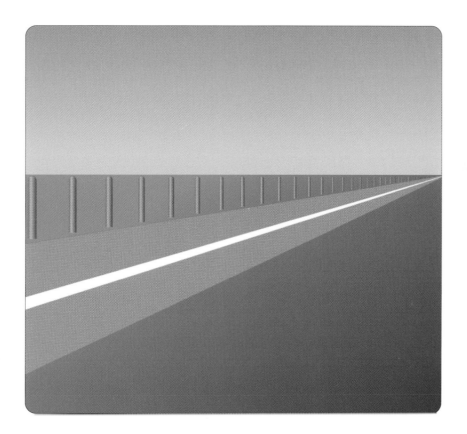

Background scenery for games

Many games incorporate the old Donkey Kong–style theme. This is characterized by a static background image, with a variety of moving or still platforms and game elements for the character to interact with (often referred to as a "sprite" in game development). This exercise will teach you some great techniques for creating these types of games.

Once again, you'll use timesaving tools within Illustrator that simply aren't available in Flash. In the end, you'll have quickly produced an environment suitable for export to Flash for further game development.

1. Create a new RGB Illustrator document.

First, you'll create the background elements.

2. Using the Rectangle tool, draw a rectangle for the sky. Fill it with the following gradient. Name this layer SKY.

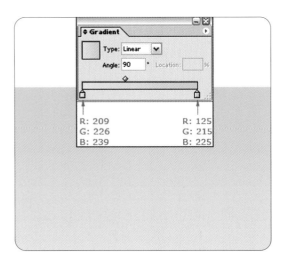

3. Create a new layer above SKY named WATER. Create a rectangle once again and fill it with this gradient. Note that the SKY and WATER rectangle shapes don't need to match up perfectly in this illustration. You'll be putting mountains in front of them.

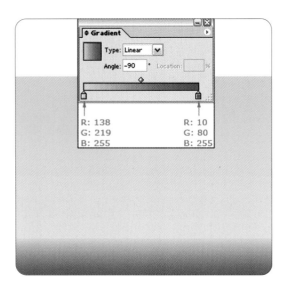

4. Create a new layer below WATER but above SKY and name it MOUNTAIN. Draw a mountain with the Pen tool similar to the way that you did in Chapter 8 for the desert scenery effect. Fill this shape with the following settings: R:127 G:127 B:127. Name the sublayer BASE.

5. Create a new sublayer above BASE called SHADOWS. Select the Pencil tool and draw a jagged shape that creeps up the mountain from the bottom. Set the fill color of this shape to R:102 G:102 B:102 and set the stroke to None.

6. Select the SHADOWS layer and choose Effect ➤ Stylize ➤ Drop Shadow. Enter the following settings. Click OK.

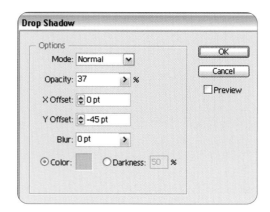

7. Take note of the new layer that is added to the Appearance palette.

8. Duplicate this layer in the Appearance palette by dragging it over the Duplicate Selected Item button at the bottom of the palette.

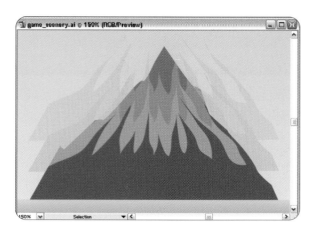

9. Move back to the Layers palette. Duplicate the BASE sublayer. Drag the duplicate above the SHADOWS layer.

10. Select or target the topmost duplicate BASE sublayer and the SHADOWS sublayer below it. Choose Make Opacity Mask from the Transparency palette's (SHIFT+F10) flyout menu. This will restrict the SHADOWS sublayer to the shape of the BASE sublayer.

Next, you'll complete the mountain by create a snowy peak.

11. Create a new sublayer above SHADOWS named PEAK. Draw a jagged snowcap shape and fill it with white. Don't worry if you extend beyond the mountain shape.

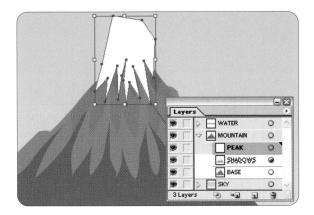

12. Duplicate the BASE sublayer. Select the duplicate and the PEAK sublayers by targeting one meatball in the Layers palette and *SHIFT*-clicking the other to target it as well.

13. Hold down the *ALT/OPTION* key and click the Intersect Shape Areas button in the Pathfinder palette. This will conform the PEAK sublayer shape to the BASE sublayer shape.

14. Create two duplicates of the MOUNTAIN layer and scale them down using the Free Transform tool (*E*). Position the large mountain layer in the center and on top of the other two. Position the remaining two layers to the left and right, respectively.

15. Next, target the two smaller MOUNTAIN layers by clicking the parent layer's meatball icon and *SHIFT*-clicking the other.

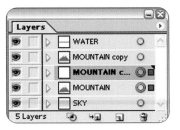

16. Using the Transparency palette, set the opacity of the two layers to 70%. This adds some atmospheric volume to the illustration.

> *Atmospheric volume is the phenomenon that causes objects to blend with the environment as their distance increases. Mountain ranges are a perfect example of this. The mountains up close are usually brighter and more colorful. But the mountains in the distance usually become less saturated with color and may appear lighter.*

17. Create a new layer above SKY named SUN.

18. Within the SUN layer create a circle using the Ellipse tool. Fill this circle with a yellow to orange gradient.

19. Create a new sublayer within the SUN layer but underneath the circle created in the previous step. Name it RAYS OF LIGHT.

20. Add some rays of light behind the sun using the technique in the Ray of Light exercise in Chapter 3.

This takes care of the scenery for the background of the game. Next, you'll create some game elements for the sprite to interact with.

21. Create a new layer above WATER named PLATFORMS.

22. Create a long thin rectangle and fill it with the following settings: R:237 G:146 B:36. Set the stroke to None.

23. Select the rectangle and choose Effect ➤ 3D ➤ Extrude & Bevel. Enter the following settings. Click OK but don't deselect yet.

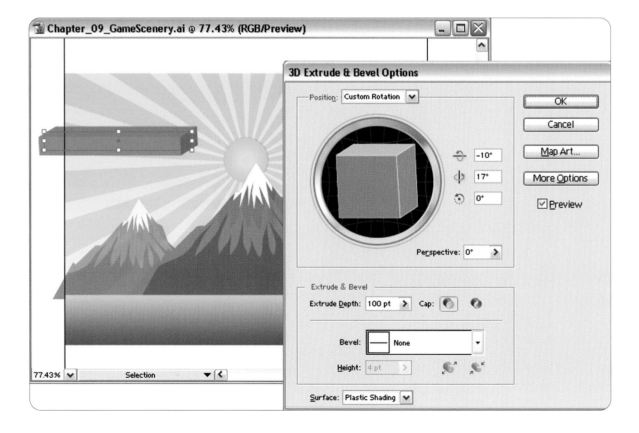

24. Choose Effect ➤ Distort & Transform ➤ Roughen. Enter these settings and click OK.

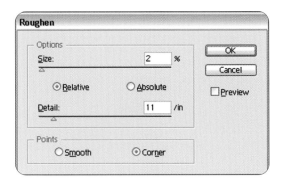

25. Take note of the Appearance palette. You should see something similar to this reference image. If not, you may not have selected the rectangle.

26. Duplicate the sublayer containing the rectangle shape in the PLATFORMS layer. Position several duplicates throughout the Illustration and resize them using the Free Transform (*E*) tool. Make some longer or shorter.

27. To finish off the game settings, you should add some symbols from the Nature Symbols palette (Window ➤ Symbol Libraries ➤ Nature) that your sprite will interact with.

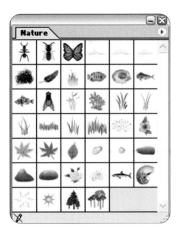

28. There you have it. Your game is ready. Just add a game character and export your elements into Flash or whatever tool you choose.

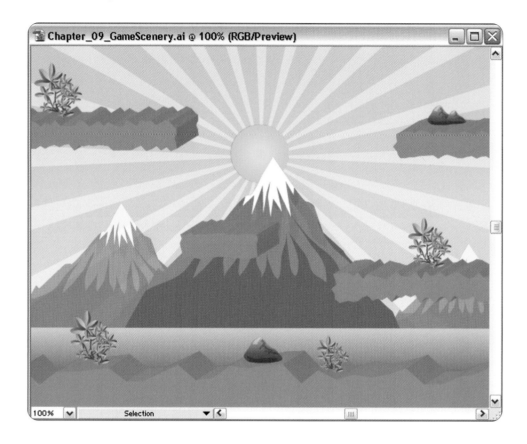

Isometric scenes

Isometric scenes are quite popular within the gaming world. Without bogging you down with too much technical jargon, you should know that an isometric scene basically means that there's no vanishing point. These scenes are very popular with games because they allow the player a top-down view of the entire environment but still maintain an angle at which to see game details (since looking at the top of your game character's head doesn't sound like much fun).

How does this translate to Illustrator? Well, creating this type of artwork once entailed editing Illustrator's Smart Guides preferences and restricting your paths to specific angles. However, with the release of Illustrator CS, all of this can be done with 3D effects. This exercise will walk you through the creation of a simple isometric world. Along the way, you'll learn to harness Illustrator's Extrude and Bevel effects, and learn a few simple modifications to quickly build the environment.

1. Create a new RGB Illustrator document.

2. Name the existing layer FLOOR. Select the Rectangle tool and click the Artboard. Enter 350 pt for the Width setting and 600 pt for the Height setting. Click OK and fill this rectangle with the following settings: R:255 G:250 B:182. Set the stroke to None.

3. Select the rectangle and choose Effect ➤ 3D ➤ Extrude & Bevel. The only two modifications you need to make to this dialog box are to the Position drop-down list at the top and the Extrude Depth drop-down list at the bottom. Change the Position setting to Isometric Top and set the Extrude Depth setting to 25. Click OK.

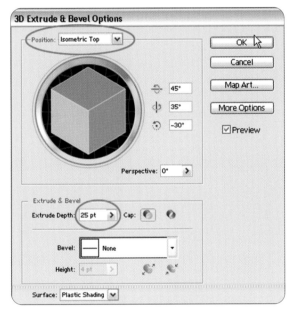

4. Create a new layer above FLOOR named RIGHT WALL. Select the Rectangle tool again. Click the Artboard and enter 300 pt for the width and 300 pt for the height. Click OK. Set the fill color of this shape to R:0 G:164 B:255 and the stroke to None.

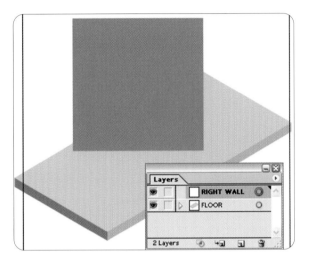

5. Select the new rectangle and choose Effect ➤ 3D ➤ Extrude & Bevel. The only two modifications you need to make to this dialog box are to the Position drop-down list at the top and the Extrude Depth drop-down list at the bottom. Change the Position drop-down list to Isometric Left and set the Extrude Depth setting to 25. Click OK.

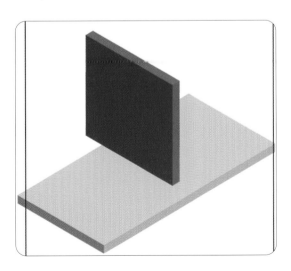

6. Position the RIGHT WALL layer so that it fits evenly with the top-right side of the FLOOR layer.

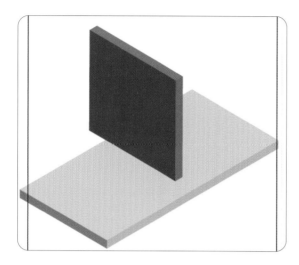

7. Create a new layer above RIGHT WALL named LEFT WALL. Once again, select the Rectangle tool. Click the Artboard and enter 575 pt (600 pt less the 25 pt extrude depth taken up by the RIGHT WALL layer) for the width and 300 pt for the height. Click OK. Set the fill color of this shape to R:0 G:164 B:255 and the stroke to None.

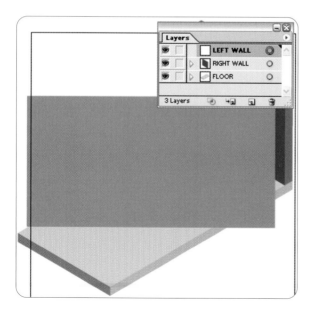

8. This time, create four smaller rectangles (actually, create one and duplicate it three times) in sublayers on the top of the left wall shape. Space them evenly so they appear similar to this reference image. These shapes will enable you to create a window on this wall.

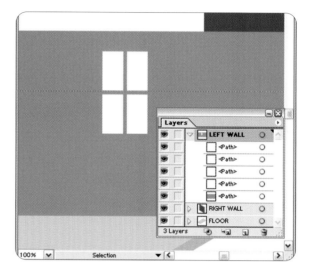

I've filled the small rectangles with white. However, the fill color doesn't matter at this time since you'll be deleting this area from the original shape.

9. Select the entire LEFT WALL layer. Choose the Subtract from Shape Area button in the Pathfinder palette (*SHIFT+F9*).

10. Select the left wall and choose Effect ➤ 3D ➤ Extrude & Bevel. In the Position drop-down list, select Isometric Right and set the Extrude Depth drop-down list to 25 pt. Click OK.

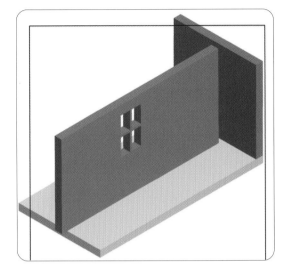

11. Position the LEFT WALL layer so that it fits evenly with the top-left side of the FLOOR layer as well as the top-right side of the RIGHT WALL layer.

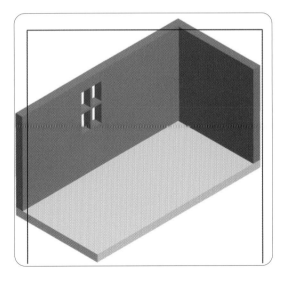

A bookcase on the wall can be created in the same way the left wall was created.

12. First, you create a rectangle shape on a new layer and set the fill to the following settings: R:239 G:219 B:34. Then, you add six smaller rectangle shapes in the same way that you did in step 9 for the window. These shapes will become shelves.

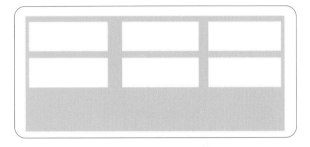

13. Repeat the same process that you followed in step 9 to subtract the small rectangle shapes from the larger shape.

14. Finally, add three rectangles at the bottom to serve as drawers (R:191 G:172 B:38). Then use the Rounded Rectangle tool to create drawer handles over each drawer shape.

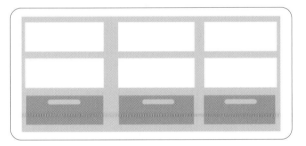

15. Select all of the bookcase objects and group them together (*Ctrl*/*Cmd*+*G*). Don't deselect them yet.

16. Choose Effect ➤ 3D ➤ Bevel & Emboss. Enter Isometric Right in the Position drop-down list and 50 pt in the Extrude Depth drop-down list. Click OK.

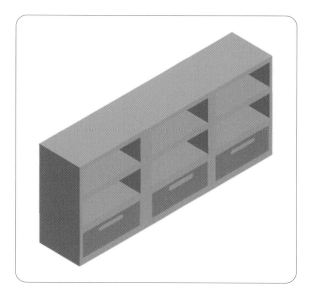

17. For an added effect you can add a stroke to the bookcase shape. Do this by duplicating the 3D BOOKCASE layer. Delete the drawer shapes so only the bookcase shape remains in the group.

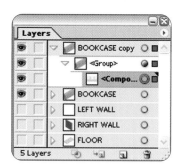

18. Set the fill to None and the stroke color to R:124 G:113 B:50. In the Appearance palette, double-click the 3D Bevel & Emboss layer for this shape to display the dialog box. Change the Extrude Depth setting to 0 pt and click OK. Finally, reposition the new shape using the Selection tool or the arrow keys until it matches the bookcase.

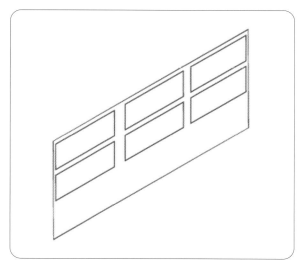

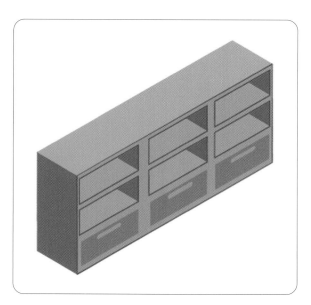

To finish the exercise off, let's add a few people. As you can imagine the process is very similar.

19. Choose Window ➤ Symbol Libraries ➤ People to open the People Symbols palette.

20. Drag the Hands on Hips symbol from the Symbols palette to the Artboard. Resize the symbol accordingly, but don't deselect it yet.

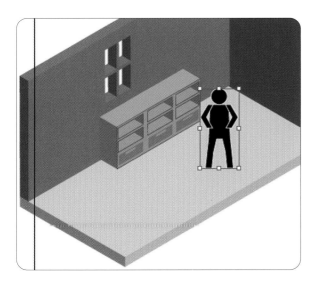

21. Open the Symbols palette (*SHIFT+F11*) and click the Break Link to Symbol button at the bottom of the palette.

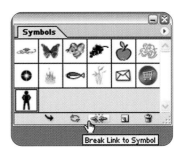

22. Change the fill color to R:234 G:155 B:15 and set the stroke to None.

23. Apply the Extrude & Bevel 3D effect to this symbol. Set the Position drop-down list to Isometric Right and the Extrude Depth setting to 10 pt.

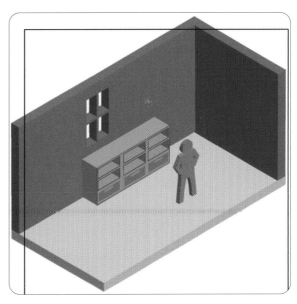

24. Repeat the previous four steps for another person shape from the People Symbols palette. However, change the Position drop-down list to Isometric Left for this shape.

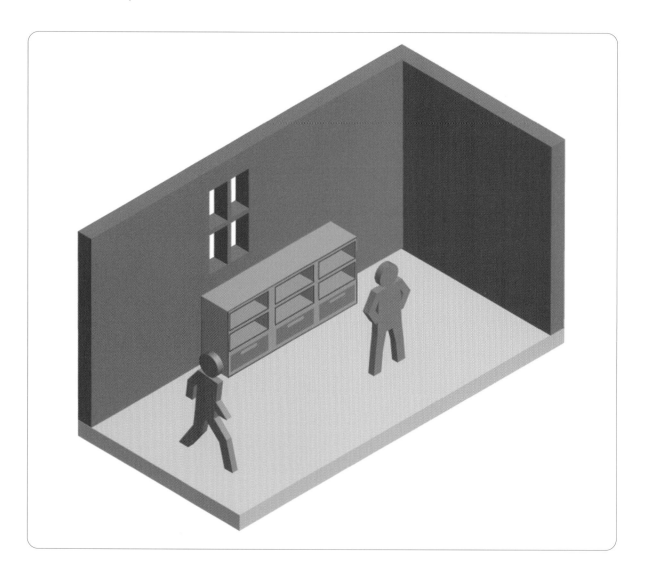

Summary

Online cartoons and games are indeed revolutions that will be with us for some time to come. If you're new to this topic, I hope that I've given you some basic concepts and inspiration to help you move forward with cartoon or game design. If you're experienced, I hope that I've left you with a new perspective on how to use other tools in combination with Flash. Regardless of your proficiency, it's difficult to overlook Illustrator as a formidable tool for the creation of graphics and illustrations for cartoons and games. This isn't to say that Flash is any less of a tool. Many illustrators feel very comfortable with (and are very good at) creating cartoon and game artwork in Flash. I've seen some astonishing work that was created using only Flash's drawing tools (Visit Adam Phillips' website at www.biteycastle.net for some incredible examples). However, the main goal of this chapter was to present you with another strong alternative—one that not only saves you valuable time, but presents you with more options and flexibility for creating your online illustrations.

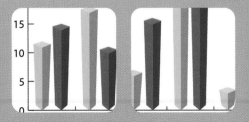

Chapter 10

THE BUSINESS SIDE OF ILLUSTRATOR

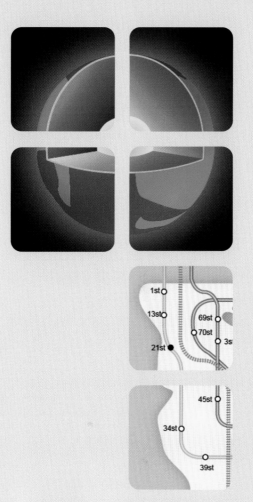

You can arguably consider all of the techniques within this book to be business related. This largely depends on the type of work you do and the nature of your clients. However, the topics within this chapter tend to be more "businesslike," whereas the others seem to fall into a more artistic category. Make no mistake though; creating graphs, maps, and technical illustrations can take just as much skill as any of the other effects portrayed throughout this book. As you complete the following exercises, you may begin to view Illustrator in a different way. However, whether you're creating a retro-style background pattern for your personal website or a technical illustration for a client, you'll see that the techniques used are all similar. Everything builds upon the basic foundation of drawing and manipulating paths and working with color. The final output may change but the way you get there doesn't.

Custom designs for bar graphs

In this exercise, you'll delve into the Graph tools within Illustrator—specifically, the Column Graph tool. By realizing the capabilities that exist for customization and creativity when using this tool, you'll be presented with an entirely new world.

1. Create a new RGB Illustrator document. Select the Column Graph tool.

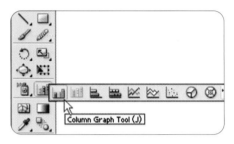

2. Click the Artboard. In the Graph dialog box, enter 410 pt for the Width setting and 250 pt for the Height setting. Click OK.

> Alternatively, you can create a graph by selecting the appropriate Graph type and dragging on the Artboard in the same way that you would create a rectangle with the Shape tool.

3. The resulting window is called the Graph Data window. You can manually enter data to populate the graph or import data from an external source such as a tab-delimited text file or spreadsheet file (Microsoft Excel, Lotus 1 2 3, and so on).

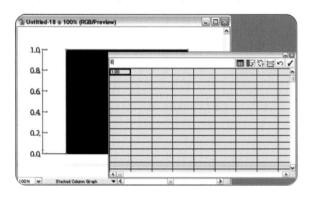

4. For this exercise, you're going to enter the data manually. Using the screen reference, enter the appropriate data for this graph. Also note that by entering two columns of data, a side-by-side double-column graph will be created.

12				
12.00	15.00			
18.00	11.00			
7.00	16.00			
25.00	20.00			
4.00	8.00			

5. When you're done, click the small check box button at the top right of the Graph Data window. This will update the graph with your data. Finally, close the window.

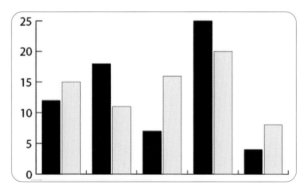

OK, now that you have your graph, you have to admit that it looks very plain and boring. It certainly isn't going to be wowing any clients in a sales presentation. However, Illustrator offers you the flexibility to change many attributes for this graph. First, you'll see how to change the colors of the columns and then you'll add your own custom column to really make this graph stand out.

6. To change the colors of individual columns, select the open arrow Direct Selection tool.

7. Click the inside of one of the columns in the graph. You have now selected only that column and any changes you make will only be reflected for that specific selection.

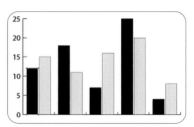

If you attempt to use the regular Selection tool to select columns you'll notice the entire graph is selected. If you wished to make a global change to the entire graph this would be the process. However, in this instance, you must use the Direct Selection tool to select single columns. Also, be sure to only click the inside of the column. If you click the edges or strokes of the column you'll only select that path segment and not the whole column.

8. Hold down the *SHIFT* key and *SHIFT*-click with the Direct Selection tool on the remaining left-side columns in the graph.

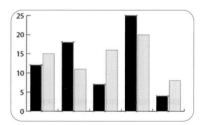

9. Next, apply a global change to them by clicking a blue swatch in the Swatches palette. Set the stroke to black.

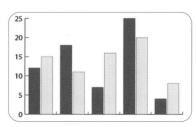

10. Repeat this process for the right columns. However, choose a red swatch for the color.

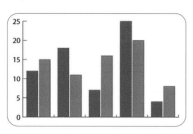

Great. You've modified the graph to make it somewhat more appealing. Remember, you have several options when performing these steps. Feel free to substitute the solid fill color with a gradient or even a pattern (yes, I know the jaguar pattern used in the following reference image doesn't make for the best-looking graph, but hopefully you get the point).

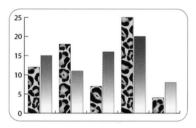

Next, you're going to create a custom column to be used in the column graph.

11. Save this file as `Chapter_10_ColumGraph.ai`. There's no need to close it at this point. It's just a good habit to save often. Also, this will allow you to know exactly what document to return to after you complete the remaining steps.

12. Create a new RGB Illustrator document.

13. Select the Rectangle tool and click the Artboard. Enter 78 pt for the width and 78 pt for the height. Set the fill color to R:225 G:225 B:62 and the stroke to None.

14. Select this shape and choose Effect ➤ 3D ➤ Extrude & Bevel. There are quite a few changes for this one so pay close attention. Take particular note of the Surface options area. Notice that I've added two additional lights and positioned them in different places on the Lighting Sphere. Click OK when you're ready.

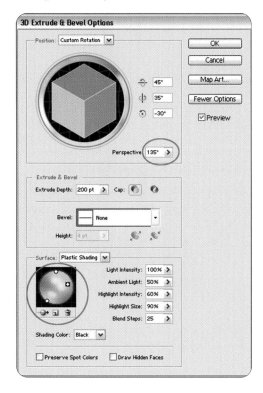

15. With the extruded bar still selected, choose Object ➤ Graph ➤ Design. This will display the Graph Design dialog box. Click the New Design button to confirm your selection as a design. You should see your bar appear in the Preview box at this time.

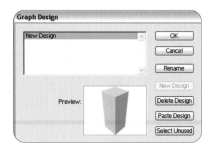

16. Click the Rename button and enter Left Column in the text box. Click OK to confirm the name change. Then click OK once more to exit the dialog box and accept your changes.

> *For more information on creating custom column designs see Illustrator's help file. Search for "Creating Graphs" and you'll find a great deal of information relating to the creation and customization of graphs.*

17. You have now created a custom column that can be used in your column graphs. Repeat steps 13–16 to add another column. However, in step 13, set the fill color to R:255 G:0 B:0 this time. Also, set the name to Right Column when you reach step 16.

18. Switch back to the Chapter_10_ColumnGraph.ai file but keep this file open.

> *The file containing your custom column must remain open for Illustrator to recognize your custom column design, and Illustrator allows the design to be available when creating graphs in other files. If you close this file, you will no longer see either design in the dialog box when you try to complete the following steps.*

19. Using the Direct Selection tool, select the leftmost column in each grouping, similar to the way you did in step 8.

20. Choose Object ➤ Graph ➤ Column. The resulting Graph Column dialog box will display all column types available to you.

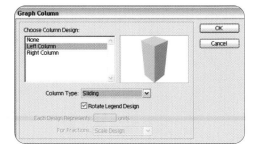

21. Select Left Column from the Choose Column Design list. Set the Column Type to Sliding and click OK.

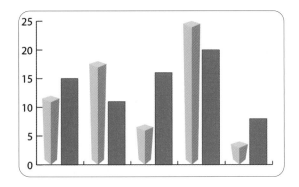

22. Next, repeat this process for the rightmost columns in each grouping within the graph. However, when viewing the Graph Column dialog box, select Right Column from the list box before clicking OK.

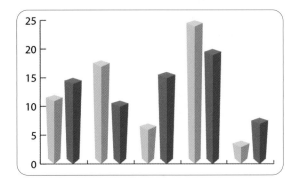

23. Finally, on a new layer, create miniature versions of your columns at the bottom of the graph to serve as a legend. Enter the appropriate text and you (or your client) are ready to win that big sales presentation. Who can resist 3D extruded column charts?

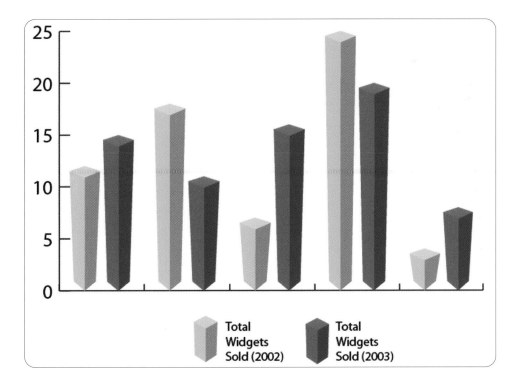

Creating maps

Illustrator's advanced drawing and brush capabilities make it a great tool for mapmaking. In the following exercises, you'll learn to harness Illustrator's power by creating several maps. Using basic layer techniques along with custom brushes and strokes, you'll create some city maps. Once again, you'll notice the final output may be quite different than what you're used to seeing in this book, but the techniques used to achieve these results are all very similar to ones that you've used previously.

Creating the map

1. Create a new RGB Illustrator document. I've included a source file (`Chapter_10_TampaBayMapStart.ai`) for you to start with if you choose. It includes the water and basic county shapes you'll create in the next few steps. If you use this file, you can skip to step 4.

2. Using the Rectangle tool, draw a square in the center of the Artboard that is 500 pt in width and 300 pt in height. Fill this shape with R:185 G:229 B:251 and set the stroke to None. Name this layer WATER.

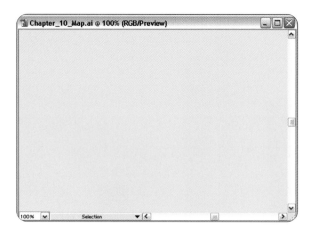

3. Create a new layer named COUNTY. Draw the shapes that will make up the areas in which you would like to map. For this example, I've chosen the Tampa Bay area and drew two counties on two different sublayers. I filled one county with a pastel yellow (R:255 G:244 B:210) and another with a pastel orange (R:255 G:224 B:191).

Maps that are similar in nature tend to use pastel colors. If you find yourself working with maps often, Illustrator offers Swatch palettes that contain only pastel colors, which may speed up the process.

4. Set the stroke color of both shapes to R:21 G:172 B:232. Note how this stroke separates the area between the two counties where they connect.

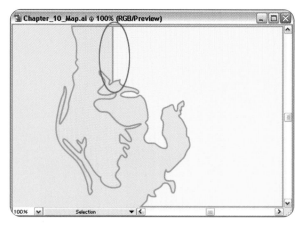

5. This isn't the ideal way to display this connection between the two counties. You want the blue stroke to outline the entire map area, not individual counties. To fix this, simply select the Add Anchor Point tool within the Pen tool flyout menu. Add an anchor point in between the top and bottom points along the lines where the counties meet, as shown in the reference image overleaf.

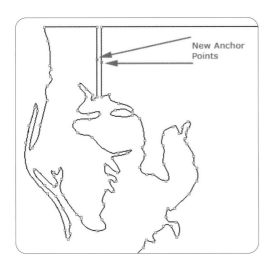

New Anchor
Points

7. Next, using the Pen tool or Line Segment tool, draw a straight line between the two counties. Set the fill color to None and the stroke to R:170 G:170 B:170. In the Stroke palette, set the stroke weight to 2 pt and select the Dashed Line check box. Enter 12 pt in the first text box under Dashed Line.

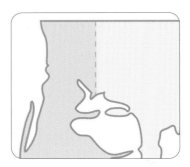

6. Select the anchor point (using the Direct Selection tool) along each side of the counties in question and delete them by hitting the *DELETE* key. I've provided several screen references to portray this as well as a picture of the map in outline view so you can better visualize the results.

8. Finally, create a new layer named INFO. Within this layer, create text sublayers that contain any city, county, or geographical information needed for the map. Here are the settings I used for each category:

- County—Myriad—Bold—35 pt—R:165 G:165 B:165
- City Names—Arial—47 pt—Black
- Water Names—Times New Roman—Italic—47 pt—R:39 G:147 B:201

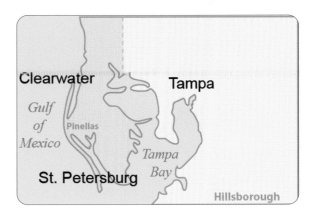

Creating roads

1. The next part of this illustration will deal with creating roads. Start out by creating a new layer, under INFO, named INTERSTATES.

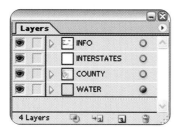

2. Using the Pen tool, draw any Interstate roads that may exist within your map area. Set the fill color of the paths to None and the stroke color to R:255 G:0 B:0. Set the Stroke Width setting in the Stroke palette to 8 pt.

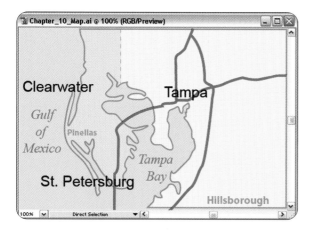

3. Next, create a new layer below INTERSTATE, named HIGHWAY.

4. Add highways in the same way as interstates. However, set the Stroke Width setting to 4 pt instead of 8.

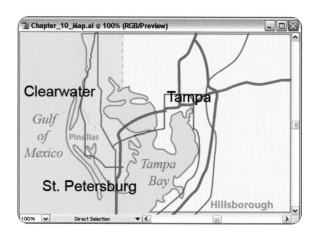

5. Finally, create a new layer below HIGHWAY, named STREET. Using the Pen tool, create any main streets throughout the map area. Set the fill color to None and set the stroke color to R:150 G:150 B:150 or any shade of gray that integrates well with your map.

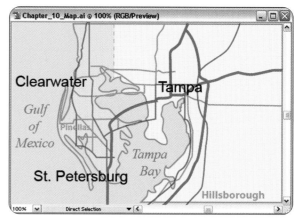

Generally, maps display major highways and interstates in red and minor roads in shades of gray.

Adding icons for places of interest

1. Choose Window ➤ Symbol Libraries ➤ Maps to open the Maps symbols palette.

2. Create a new layer under INFO named ICONS.

3. Using various symbols within this palette, add icons for places of interest throughout the map. When adding interstate icons, be sure to create a text layer above them for the interstate number. In this example I used a bold, sans-serif font set at 12 pt.

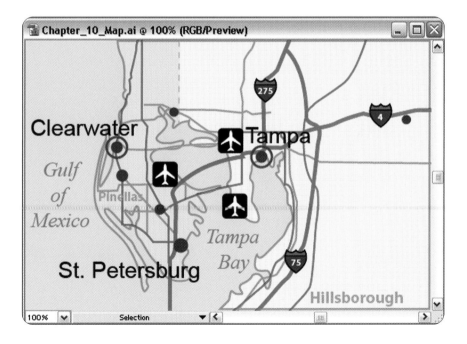

Creating Railways

1. Open the source file for Chapter 10 named `Chapter_10_RailwaySystemStart.ai`. This file contains the outline of a city that you'll use for a railway system.

2. Be sure the CITY layer is locked and create a new layer on top of it. There is no need to name this layer specifically, as it will only contain a custom brush that you'll create.

3. On the new layer, select the Rectangle tool and create a rectangle 11 pts in width and 2 pts in height. Create this shape off to the side of the Artboard, as you don't want this included with your illustration. Set the fill color to R:175 G:175 B:175 and the stroke to None.

You may need to zoom in to see this object well. The reference images for this exercise are taken at a 600% zoom level.

4. Duplicate this shape and use your arrow keys or Selection tool to move it down slightly.

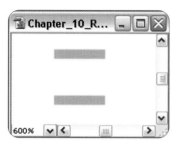

5. Next, create another rectangle shape over the two gray shapes. Make this shape 5 pts in width and 18 pts in height. Set the fill color to R:169 G:119 B:93 and the stroke to None.

6. Select all the layers (CTRL/CMD+A). This should only select the three shapes just created since the CITY layer is locked.

7. Make sure your Brushes palette is visible (F5) and drag the three shapes over this palette. Alternatively, you can click the small arrow at the top right of the Brushes palette to display the fly-out menu and select New Brush. Either way, the following dialog box will appear.

New Brush

Select a brush type:

- New Calligraphic Brush
- New Scatter Brush
- New Art Brush
- New Pattern Brush

OK
Cancel

8. Select New Pattern Brush and click OK. The next dialog box will display the Pattern Brush options. Enter Railroad in the Name text box and leave the remaining settings at their defaults. Click OK.

Now that you have your brush created, you can begin to add railroads to the map.

9. Hide or delete the layer that was just used to create the railroad brush. Create a new layer on top of the CITY layer named RAILROAD.

10. Using the Pen tool, create a path similar to this reference image. Be sure the fill color for this path is set to None. Don't deselect the path yet, though.

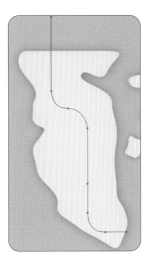

11. With the path still selected, click the new Railroad brush to apply it to the path.

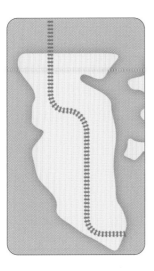

12. You can also adjust your stroke Weight settings for this path to vary the size of the railroad. I set the Weight setting to .5 in this example.

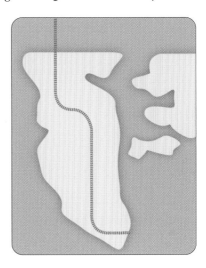

Next, you'll create some subway lines. Fortunately, they are even easier to make.

13. Lock the RAILROAD layer. Create a new layer under RAILROAD named SUBWAY.

14. Using the Pen tool, create a rounded path that spans throughout the city. Set the fill to None and the stroke color to R:0 G:122 B:255. Also, set the stroke Weight settings for this path to 9 pt.

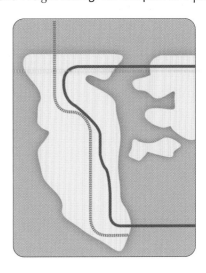

15. If the path is no longer selected, select the path with the Selection tool or target its sublayer within the Layers palette.

16. Open the Appearance palette. You should see something similar to this reference image.

17. Click the small arrow at the top right of the palette to display the flyout menu. Select Add New Stroke. Click the stroke on the top layer in the Appearance palette and set the stroke color to R:138 G:219 B:255 and the stroke Weight to 3 pt.

18. Repeat this process throughout the map with various colors.

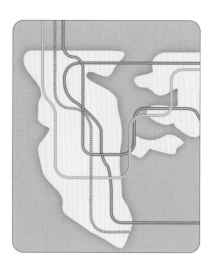

19. All that remains is to create the subway station symbols and their corresponding labels on new layers. You could create your own symbols, but the Town symbol within the Maps symbols palette that was used previously works fine.

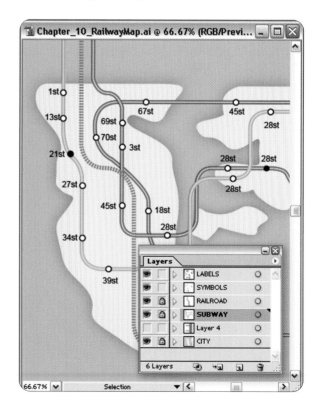

Technical illustration

1. Create a new RGB Illustrator document.

2. Using the Pen tool, draw a flat shape that roughly illustrates the continents of the earth. There's no need to be detailed, as most of this shape will be hidden later in the exercise. Fill this shape with R:13 G:223 B:0 and set the stroke to None.

3. Select all of the elements. Drag them to the Symbols palette. Later in the exercise, you'll map this symbol to your illustration of the earth. You can delete the green shapes at this time as well.

4. Using the Ellipse tool, create a circle 285 pts in width and height. Fill this circle with R:10 G:80 B:255 and set the stroke to None. Name this layer EARTH.

5. Create a duplicate sublayer of this circle and hide it. You'll use this later as well.

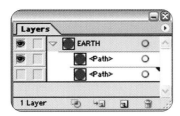

6. Using the Direct Selection tool, select the leftmost anchor point of this circle and press the *Delete* key. As you do this, the full circle becomes half.

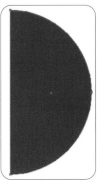
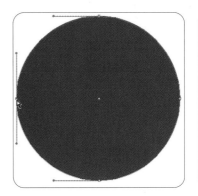

7. Select the circle and choose Effect ➤ 3D ➤ Revolve. Set your settings similar to the reference image. Be sure to add another light source as I have. Don't click OK yet.

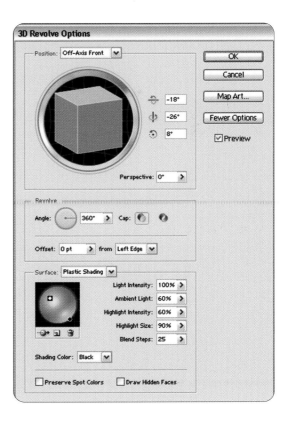

8. Click the Map Art button. Select the green land symbol that you defined as a symbol in step 3. Click the Scale To Fit button and make sure that the Shade Artwork button is checked. Click OK to close the Map Art dialog box and then click OK again to accept the overall Revolve settings.

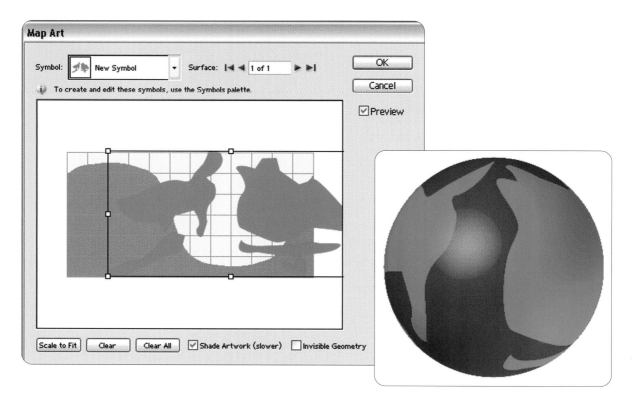

9. Create a new layer named INNER EARTH above the EARTH layer.

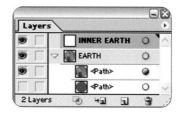

10. Create another circle 285 pts in width and height. Name this sublayer CRUST. Fill this shape with white and set the stroke to None. Position this circle directly above the earth shape but nudge it down slightly so that you can see a small area of the earth showing behind it.

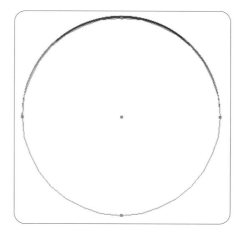

11. Select the CRUST sublayer. Choose Object ➤ Transform ➤ Scale. Select Non-Uniform and enter 87% in the Horizontal text box and 100% in the Vertical text box. Click OK.

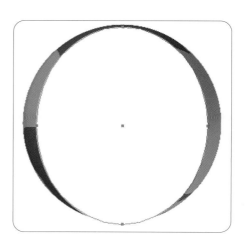

12. Create a large oval shape above the CRUST sublayer that's 525 pts in width and 360 pts in height. Fill it with any red color (the red will help you distinguish this circle; it won't be used for this illustration). Position the bottom point of the oval just below the center point of the CRUST sublayer. This oval will serve as a cutout shape for the following Pathfinder operation.

Feel free to use Smart Guides to help you align this shape.

13. Select both sublayers within the INNER EARTH layer. Hold down the *ALT/OPTION* key and click the Intersect Shape Areas button in the Pathfinder palette. Leave red as the fill color of this shape and set the stroke color to R:255 G:169 B:110.

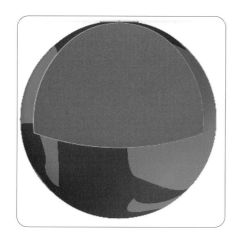

14. Note that the resulting sublayer has been named <Path>. Rename this sublayer CRUST.

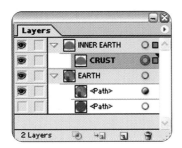

Next, you're going to break the CRUST shape up into three parts.

15. Turn on Smart Guides (*CTRL/CMD+U*) and select the Line Segment tool. Using the Smart Guides, position the crosshairs over the center point of the earth. The guides should look this reference image when you have the correct point.

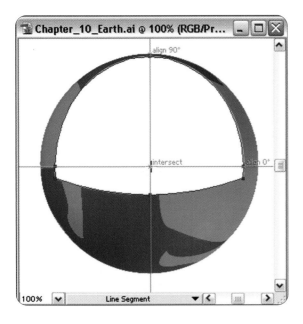

I've changed the fill color of the CRUST shape to white in the following reference images. This allows you to better see the guides for illustrative purposes.

16. Click and drag a line toward the bottom right point of the CRUST sublayer. Again, use the Smart Guides as a reference to know when you're over the correct point. The color of this line doesn't matter at this point.

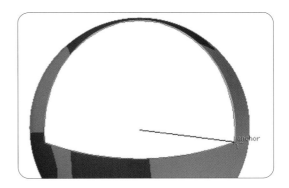

17. Repeat the process but create a line from the center to the bottom left point of the CRUST sublayer this time.

18. Finally, create a line from the center to the top point of the CRUST sublayer shape.

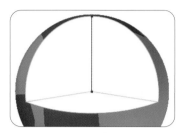

19. Create a duplicate of the CRUST sublayer and select the top version of this shape. *Shift*-click the meatball icons of the three line shapes to select them as well.

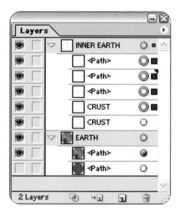

20. Hold down the *Alt/Option* key and click the Divide button in the Pathfinder palette. This will create three distinct shapes. You can view this by expanding the group in the INNER EARTH layer.

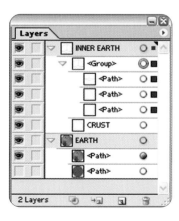

21. Fill each shape with the Sensual Red linear gradient located in the Swatches palette. Also, set each shape's stroke to None. You'll need to reposition the gradient for each shape to give the appearance of perspective To aid you with this task, I've provided several reference images with red arrows to show you which direction the gradient was dragged for each shape.

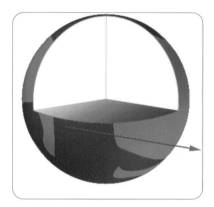

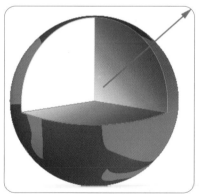

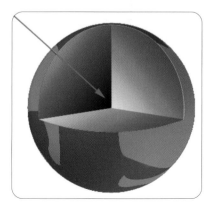

22. Select the CRUST sublayer. The stroke color should already be set to R:255 G:169 B:110. However, set the stroke weight to 6 pt at this time.

Next, you'll create the Earth's core.

23. Create a new sublayer at the top of the INNER EARTH layer. Name this sublayer CORE. Create a circle that is 85 pts in width and height and position it in the center of the earth. The fill and stroke colors don't matter at the moment.

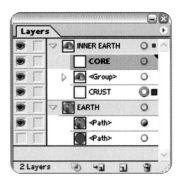

24. Use the same technique as in step 13 to cut out the bottom portion of the circle. When performing this step, try to make the point at which a corner is formed on the CORE shape intersect with the lines that separate the CRUST of the earth. See the accompanying reference images to help with this.

25. Fill the new core shape with a yellow-to-orange radial gradient. If all went well you should now have something similar to this.

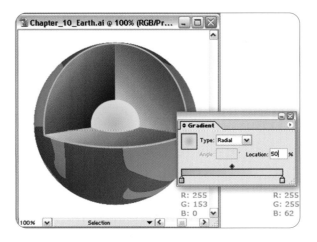

26. Finally, create a new layer below EARTH and name it ATMOSPHERE. Create a sublayer containing a black rectangle to simulate the darkness of space.

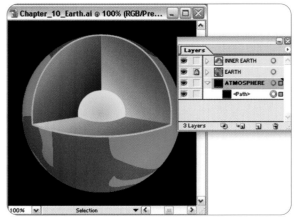

27. On top of the black rectangle, create a new circle the same size as the earth. This fill color doesn't matter because this shape is hidden. Set the stroke to None.

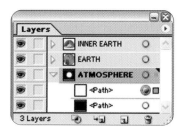

28. Select this circle and choose Effect ➤ Stylize ➤ Outer Glow. Change the color to R:250 G:252 B:190, set the mode to Normal, the opacity to 100% and the blur to 50 pt. Click OK.

All that remains is to add the technical text elements to your illustration. A common (and nice) touch is to create a zoomed-in cutout of a specific area of the illustration. This allows for greater detail to be observed in key areas of the illustration. Here's how.

29. Duplicate the INNER EARTH layer and place the copy on top of the original.

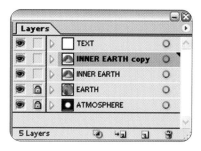

30. Create a new layer above the duplicate INNER EARTH layer named ZOOM. Then use the Rectangle tool to create a square in the new layer.

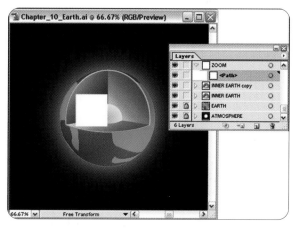

31. Target both the ZOOM layer and INNER EARTH copy layers by clicking their meatball icons.

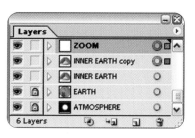

32. Hold down the *ALT/OPTION* key and click the Crop button in the Pathfinder palette. This will leave you with a group sublayer containing the inner earth area that was under the square. To keep things tidy, delete the INNER EARTH copy layer as well.

33. Duplicate the <Group> sublayer within the ZOOM layer and target the bottom copy of the group. Hold down the *ALT/OPTION* key and click the Add to Shape Area button in the Pathfinder palette. Without deselecting the resulting path, set the fill to None and the stroke color to white. Also, set the stroke weight to 4 pt.

34. Finally, select the ZOOM layer and use the bounding box or Free Transform tool (*E*) to increase the size of the square. Also, move it to the bottom left of the illustration.

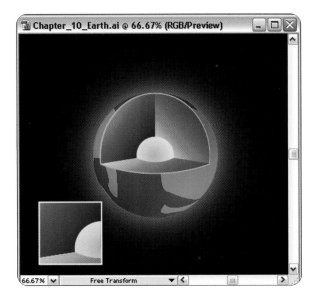

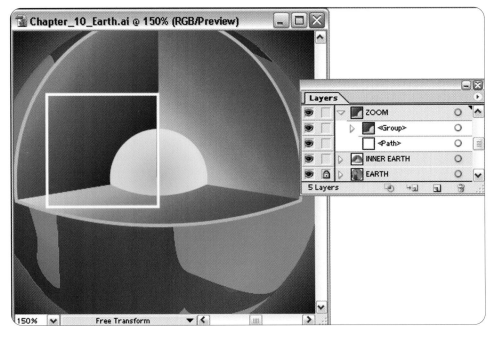

35. Add some extra text and you're finished.

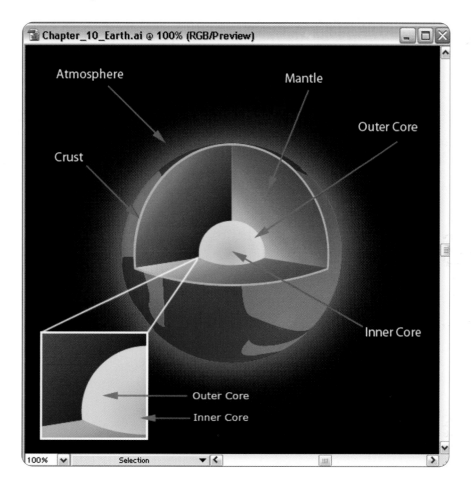

Summary

This chapter has taught you that Illustrator CS can indeed be an excellent tool for creating business-related and technical illustrations. As you've seen, the same basic tools are used to create this type of illustration—they're just applied in a different way. Although some may not view this to be the most glamorous task for an illustrator, this type of illustration can take just as much skill to create as any artistic illustration. If done correctly, illustrations that are businesslike or corporate in nature can result in some of the most stunning artwork, both visually and technically.

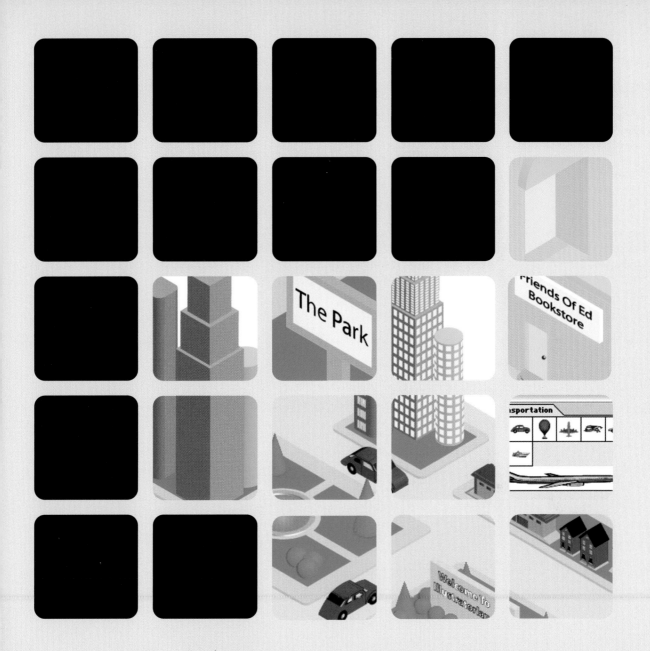

Project 1

ISOMETRIC CITY

Sim City illustration style

When I first began writing the outline for this book (before I got my hands on the beta version of Illustrator CS), I wanted to include the following content as an exercise because I felt that it warranted the "Most Wanted" title. However, I was a bit nervous since setting up isometric Sim City–like drawings in Illustrator can be tedious and time-consuming. But alas for you, the reader, I was prepared to do it (melodramatic tone intended). To my delight, Illustrator CS's 3D tools include settings that automatically position your objects at isometric angles with only the click of a button. As a result, this exercise went from showing you the basics of creating an isometric city to the full-blown project that it is today. So follow along as I play God and create a flourishing city.

1. Create a new RGB Illustrator document. Using the Rounded Rectangle tool, create a new rectangle 410 pt width and 350 pt height. I set the corner radius to 17 pt for this example. Set the fill color to R:229 G:226 B:198 and the stroke to None. Name this layer CITY BLOCK and name the sublayer within it SIDEWALK.

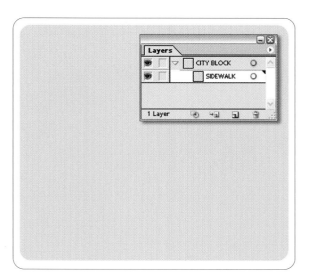

2. Create a new sublayer within the CITY BLOCK layer but on top of the SIDEWALK sublayer. Name this sublayer GRASS.

3. Create a rectangle (not rounded) with the Rectangle tool that is 365 pt by 310 pt in size and position this shape in the center of the SIDEWALK shape. Set the fill color to R:50 G:224 B:14 and the stroke to None.

4. Select the SIDEWALK sublayer and choose Effect ➤ 3D ➤ Extrude & Bevel. Set the Position setting to Isometric Top, the Extrude Depth setting to 8 pt, and the Ambient Light setting to 85%. Leave all other settings at their defaults and click OK.

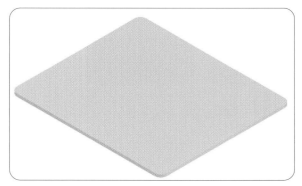

5. You're going to use this effect several times throughout this project so go ahead and create a graphic style so you can apply the settings in just one click. Select the SIDEWALK sublayer and click the New Graphic Style button at the bottom of the Graphic Styles palette or drag the thumbnail from the Appearance palette to the Graphic Styles palette. Name this style SIDEWALK.

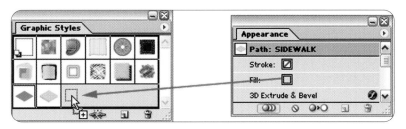

6. Select the GRASS sublayer and choose Effect ➤ 3D ➤ Extrude & Bevel. Set the Position setting to Isometric Top and the Extrude Depth setting to 0 pt. Leave the remaining settings at their defaults and click OK.

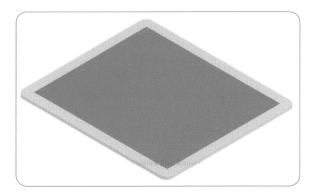

7. Repeat step 5 and create a graphic style from this sublayer's settings.

Next, you need a sign welcoming people to your city.

8. Lock the CITY BLOCK layer and create a new layer on top of it named SIGN. Using the Rectangle tool, draw a rectangle 250 pt by 145 pt in size. Set the fill color to R:242 G:238 B:187 and the stroke to None.

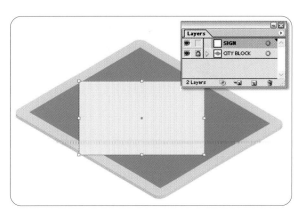

9. Apply a 3D Extrude & Bevel effect to this shape. Set the Position settings to Isometric Left, the Extrude Depth setting to 20 pt, and the Ambient Light setting to 85%. Position this shape in the center of the city block shape.

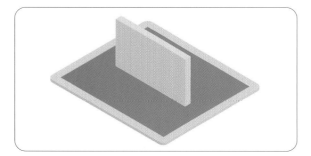

10. Create a new sublayer within the SIGN layer and add some text as a welcome message. A bold sans-serif font set at 36 pt works well (Myriad was used here). Press the *D* key to set the text color and stroke to their defaults.

11. Apply the 3D Extrude & Bevel effect to the text. Set the Position setting to Isometric Left, the Extrude Depth setting to 0, and the Ambient Light setting to 100%. Position the text accordingly on your sign.

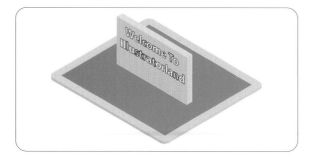

Next, you'll add some trees and bushes.

12. Create a new layer named FOLIAGE. Using the Ellipse tool, draw a circle approximately 40 pt in width and height. Fill this circle with a green radial gradient as shown in this reference image. Name this sublayer BUSH.

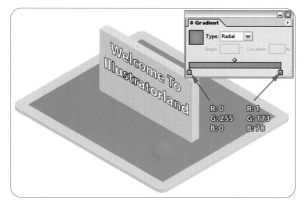

13. If you're happy with the flat appearance of this bush then skip this step. However, you may wish to add some texture to the bush to give it some depth. To do this, select the BUSH sublayer and choose Effect ➤ Texture ➤ Texturizer. Enter the following settings and click OK.

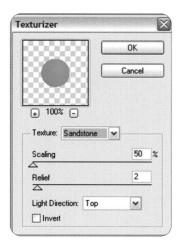

14. Next, choose Effect ➤ Stylize ➤ Drop Shadow. Enter the following settings and click OK.

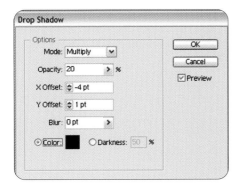

15. You should now have something similar to this reference image.

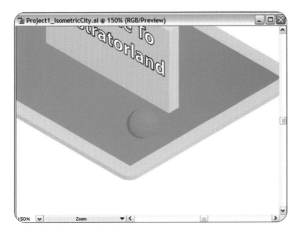

16. Duplicate the bush shape and place bushes of various sizes throughout the illustration.

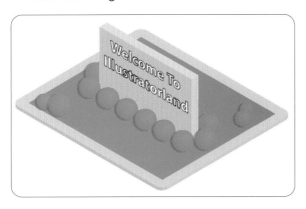

Use the Blend tool to save you time if you wish to place them along a specific path. Also note that you may need to position bushes within other layers in order to make them appear behind the sign.

17. To add some taller trees, create a new sublayer within FOLIAGE named TREE.

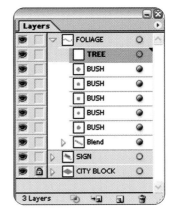

18. Using the Pen tool, create a shape similar to this reference image and fill it with R:32 G:255 B:0. Set the stroke to None.

19. Choose Effect ➤ 3D ➤ Revolve. Set the Position setting to Isometric Right and the Ambient Light setting to 70%. Click OK.

269

20. Add texture to the tree by using the Texturizer effect once again with these settings.

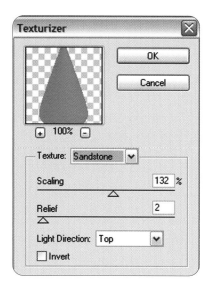

21. Make duplicates of the TREE sublayer and position them around just as you did the bushes. Remember, you may need to adjust the layer order of certain layers to create the proper perspective.

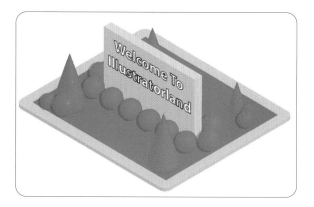

22. Finally, I created a parent layer named WELCOME and put the FOLIAGE, SIGN, and CITY BLOCK layers inside of it. This gives you an organized way to build your city within one file and yet maintain the flexibility needed to move an entire city block around later if needed.

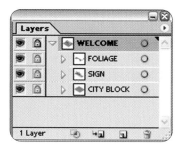

Next, you're going to create another city block. This time, you're going to take advantage of some of the presets that Illustrator ships with.

23. Lock and hide the WELCOME layer. Create a new CITY BLOCK layer.

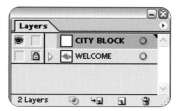

24. Create another rounded rectangle to serve as the sidewalk shape just as you did in step 3. This shape should be approximately 560 pt in width and 225 pt in height. There is no need to set the fill color at this time.

25. Select the shape and click the Sidewalk graphic style to apply it.

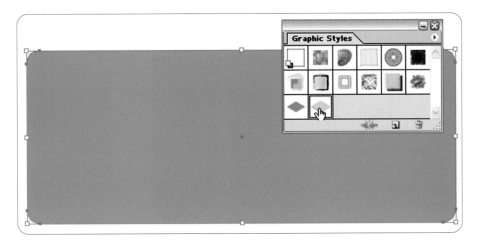

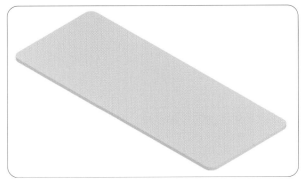

26. Create another grass sublayer positioned on top of it. Click the Grass graphic style to apply it. Hopefully you can see the benefits of graphic styles at this point and how they have saved you the time of reapplying the same settings as before.

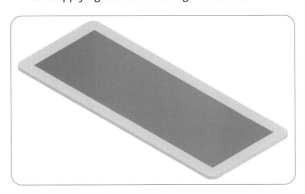

27. Next, open the preset building shapes that Illustrator CS ships with by choosing Window ➤ Symbol Libraries ➤ Buildings.

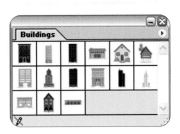

28. Create a new layer named BUILDINGS. Drag the Factory symbol from the palette on to the Artboard. Open the Symbols palette (*SHIFT+F11*) and click the Break Link to Symbol button at the bottom of the palette.

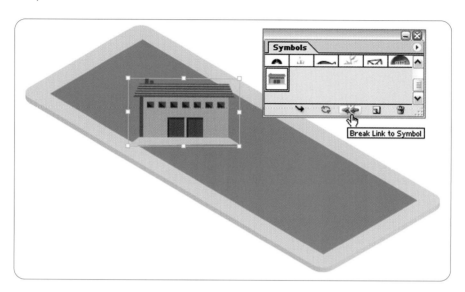

29. Select the Factory shape and choose the Free Transform tool (*E*). Make the Factory shape slightly wider by dragging the side handle to the right.

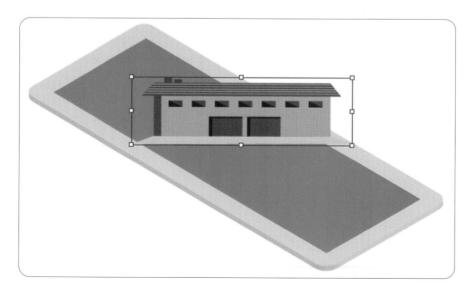

30. Select the Factory shape and apply a 3D Extrude & Bevel effect to it. Set the Position setting to Isometric Left and the Ambient Light setting to 90%. Click OK and position the building to the far left of the city block.

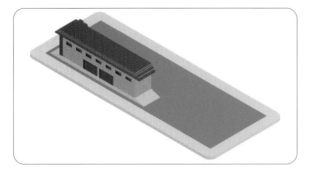

31. Repeat this process with the Townhouse, Store, and Office Building 4 symbols. Position them through the city block as displayed in this reference image.

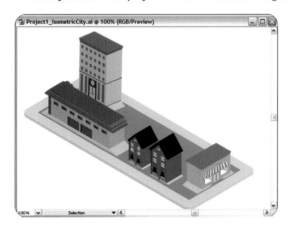

32. Create a new parent layer named FACTORIES and drag the BUILDINGS and CITY BLOCK layers into it so that you can maintain the layer organization mentioned earlier.

Next, you're going to create a city block that contains some larger skyscrapers.

33. Create a new city block in a way that's similar to what you did in the first two parts of this project. The size of the sidewalk shape should be 315 pt in width and 260 pt in height. Don't forget to use the preset graphic styles for the sidewalk and grass.

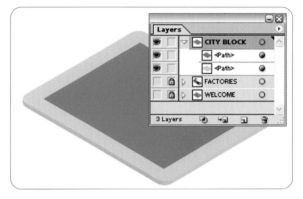

34. Create a new layer named SKYSCRAPERS. Start out simple by creating a 75 pt circle with the Ellipse tool. Fill this circle with the following settings: R:255 G:255 B:62.

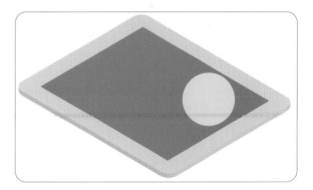

273

35. Select the circle shape and apply a 3D Extrude & Bevel effect to it. Set the Position setting to Isometric Top, the Extrude Depth setting to 300 pt, and the Ambient Light setting to 70%. Click OK and position the round building accordingly.

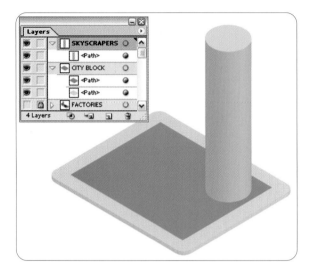

36. Next, select the Rounded Rectangle tool. Click the Artboard to create the rectangle. Enter 80 pt for the Width setting and 65 pt for the Height setting. Set the Corner Radius setting to 17 pt and the fill color to R:138 G:219 B:255.

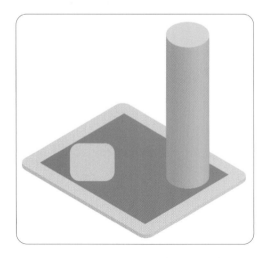

37. Add a 3D Extrude & Bevel effect to this shape as well. Change the Position setting to Isometric Top, the Extrude Depth setting to 450, and click OK.

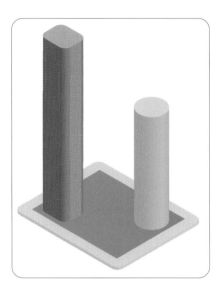

Next, you'll create a giant skyscraper.

38. On a sublayer below the previous two skyscrapers, use the Rectangle tool to create a square 100 pt in width and height. Set the fill color to R:215 G:215 B:215 and the stroke to None.

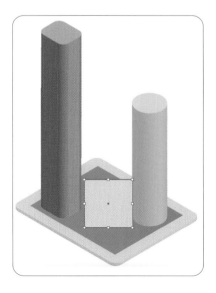

39. Apply a 3D Extrude and Bevel effect to this square with the following settings. Set the Position setting to Isometric Top, the Extrude Depth setting to 365, and then click OK when you're done.

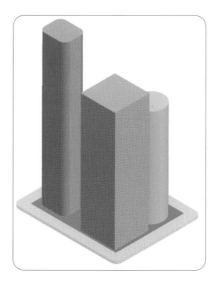

40. Duplicate this shape and use the Free Transform tool. Scale the square down to about 90 pt in width and height. Don't forget to hold down the *SHIFT* key to maintain the proper proportions of the square.

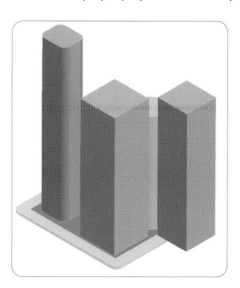

Use the Info palette (F8) to observe the size of the square as you're scaling it.

41. Select the duplicate shape that was just scaled down. Open the Appearance palette and double-click the 3D Extrude & Bevel effect to modify the settings. Change the Extrude Depth setting to 100 pt. Click OK to accept the changes.

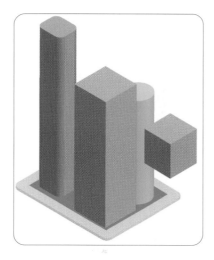

42. Position the smaller shape above the larger one as I have in this reference image.

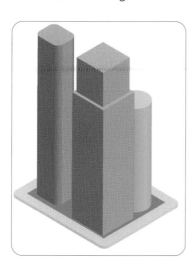

43. Duplicate this shape. Scale the duplicate down to 65 pt in width and height and leave the Extrude Depth settings at 100 pt. Position the duplicate above the other two square shapes as I have in this reference image.

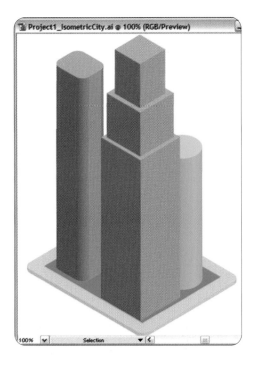

44. Finally, to create the top of the skyscraper, use the Pen tool to create a triangle. Fill this triangle with the same gray used in step 38.

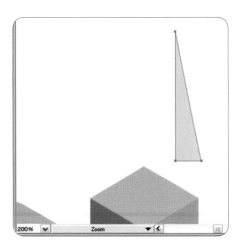

45. Select the triangle and choose Effect ➤ 3D ➤ Revolve. Change the Position setting to Isometric Left and leave all other settings at their defaults. Click OK and position the cone shape at the top of the building.

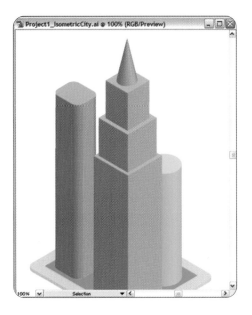

OK, the skyscrapers are looking good but they're missing something: windows. To add them you're going to define a symbol that contains a group of small rectangles. Then you'll edit the Extrude & Bevel settings of each building to map the symbol to them.

46. Create a new layer named WINDOWS. Using the Rectangle tool, create a new rectangle that's 12 pt in width and 19 pt in height. Set the fill color to R:220 G:248 B:255 and the stroke to None.

47. With the small rectangle selected, choose Effect ➤ Distort & Transform ➤ Transform. Make your settings similar to this reference image and click OK. However, don't deselect the window shape yet.

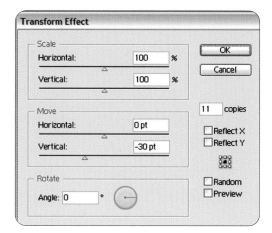

48. With the window still selected, choose Effect ➤ Distort & Transform ➤ Transform once again. A window will pop up and will ask you if you wish to apply another instance of this effect. Click the Apply New Effect button to open the Transform Effect dialog box. This time enter these settings and click OK.

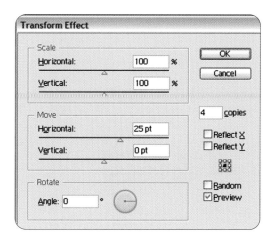

49. You should now have something similar to this reference image. Note that I've changed the fill color to a deeper blue so you can see it better in this book.

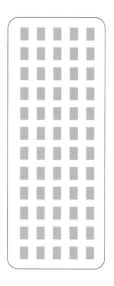

This will be the art that you map to the surface of the buildings. However, if you recall from the dice exercise in Chapter 5, any artwork that you wish to map to a 3D object must first be saved as a symbol.

50. Select the window shape and drag it to the Symbols palette.

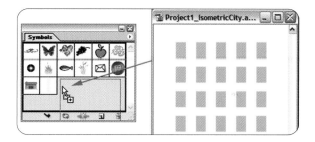

You're now ready to map the windows to the buildings. The rounded rectangle blue building is the most difficult to map to so let's cover that one.

51. Select the rounded blue building. In the Appearance palette, double-click the 3D Extrude & Bevel layer to edit the 3D effects for this object.

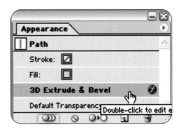

52. Click the Map Art button to open the Map Art dialog box. Before moving on, check the Preview check box so that you can view your changes without exiting the dialog box.

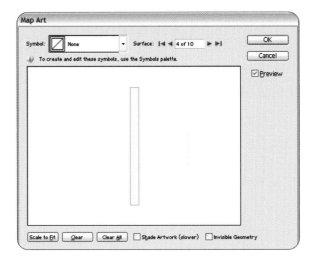

Illustrator breaks this object into ten surfaces instead of six as the typical cube shape. This is because it's treating the rounded corners as a surface.

53. Click the Next Surface (the right arrow) button to cycle through the surfaces until you reach surface 4.

54. Select the window symbol that was added to the Symbols palette in step 50 from the Symbol dropdown list. Use the bounding box around the symbol to scale it into place so it fits within the rectangle.

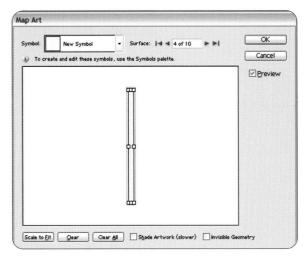

55. Click the Next Surface button until you reach surface 6. Repeat the previous step and map the windows onto this surface as well. When you're finished, click OK to return to the 3D Extrude & Bevel dialog box. Click OK once again to accept the changes.

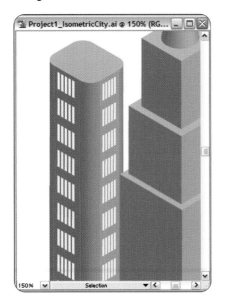

56. Repeat this process for the remaining skyscrapers. The square objects are simple, as they don't have the rounded sides to work with. The circle shape is even easier, as it only has one side to map to.

57. Finally, I selected each shape associated with the large gray skyscraper and grouped them together (*CTRL/CMD+G*). I then moved this skyscraper behind the others so it appears at the back of the illustration.

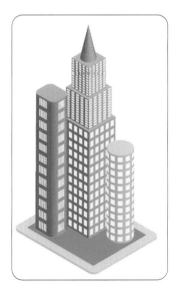

In the following steps of this project you'll construct a park for all of your isometric city people to play in.

58. Create a new layer named PARK. Using the Rounded Rectangle tool, create a new city block in a similar way as the first parts of this project. Make this block 640 pt by 465 pt in width and height with a corner radius of 17 pt. Name this sublayer SIDEWALK.

59. Apply the SIDEWALK graphic style to the SIDEWALK sublayer and lock it.

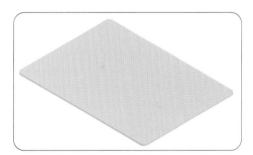

60. Create a new sublayer above SIDEWALK named GRASS. Create a rectangle that's 530 pt wide and 350 pt in height. The fill and stroke settings don't matter at this point.

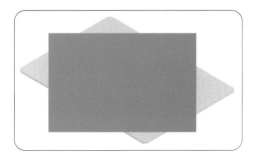

279

Next, you're going to deviate from the normal steps that you've been taking in the past to create the grass on top of the sidewalk. Instead of applying the preset graphic style at this time, you're going to make a few modifications to the grass first.

61. Using the Rectangle tool, create a rectangle that is 30 pt in width and 370 pt in height. Position this rectangle in the center of the GRASS sublayer.

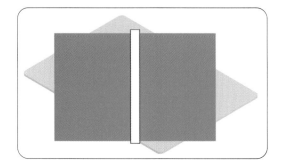

> Use the Align palette to help you position the rectangle in the exact center of the GRASS sublayer.

62. Create a new rectangle that is 550 pt in width and 30 pt in height. Again, position this rectangle in the center of the larger GRASS sublayer.

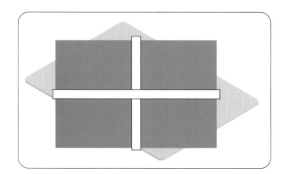

63. Select all layers (CTRL/CMD+A). Since the SIDEWALK sublayer should be locked, this will select the GRASS sublayer as well as the two rectangles you've just created.

64. Hold down the ALT/OPTION key and choose Subtract from Shape Area from the Pathfinder palette. You should now have a shape similar to this reference image.

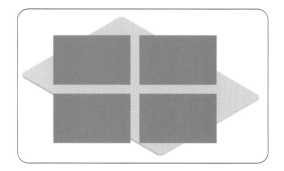

65. This will produce a GROUP sublayer that contains four rectangles. Rename this sublayer GRASS at this time.

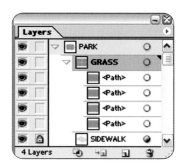

66. Next, on a new sublayer above GRASS, create a circle with the Ellipse tool that is 200 pt in width and height. Position this circle in the center of the GRASS sublayer. Press D to set the fill and stroke settings to their defaults.

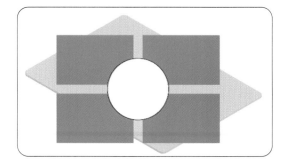

67. Select the circle and choose Object ➤ Transform ➤ Scale. Be sure Uniform is selected and enter 85% for the Scale setting. Click the Copy button.

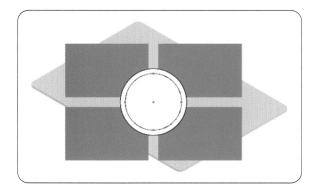

68. This will produce a smaller version of the circle created in step 66. Hide this sublayer at this time.

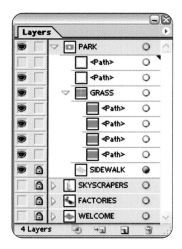

69. Select the GRASS sublayer and the larger circle or press *CTRL/CMD+A* to select all layers, because the other layers are either hidden or locked.

70. Hold down the *ALT/OPTION* key and choose Divide from the Pathfinder palette. This will create yet another GROUP sublayer.

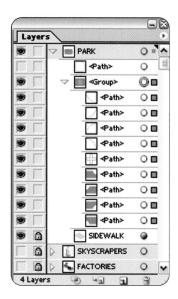

71. Expand the GROUP sublayer at this time. Select all of the small inner wedge shapes from this group and delete them so that you're left with a shape similar to this reference image.

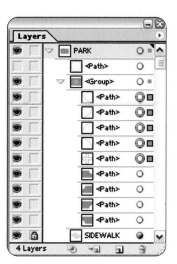

72. Rename this GROUP sublayer to GRASS once again. Your image should now look similar to this reference image.

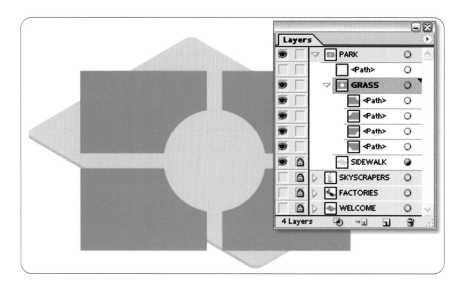

73. Next, unhide and select the circle shape that was hidden in step 68. Choose Object ➤ Transform ➤ Scale. Select the Uniform radio button and enter 85% for the Scale setting. Click Copy.

74. Select both of these circles, hold the *ALT/OPTION* key down, and choose the Subtract from Shape Area button in the Pathfinder palette. This will produce a Compound Path sublayer. Name this path FOUNTAIN at this time.

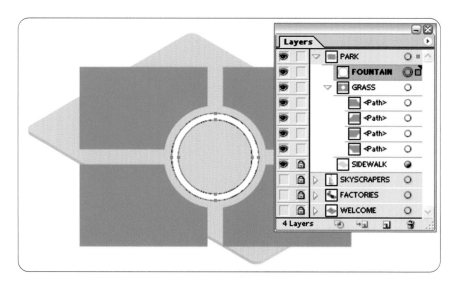

75. Set the fill color of the FOUNTAIN path to R:206 G:206 B:206 and the stroke to None.

76. Select the GRASS sublayer and apply the preset graphic style you've used in the past to create the grass on top of the SIDEWALK layer. Position the grass so that it's in the center of the sidewalk shape.

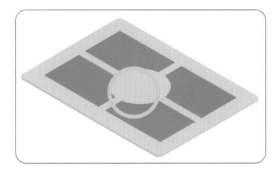

77. Select the FOUNTAIN sublayer. Choose Effect ➤ 3D ➤ Extrude & Bevel. Make your settings similar to this reference image. Don't forget about the extra light source that was added to the Lighting Sphere. Click OK when you're done.

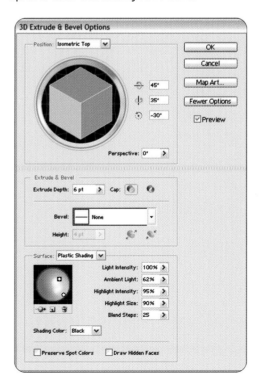

78. Position the fountain in the center of the park.

79. Create a new sublayer below FOUNTAIN named WATER. Using the Ellipse tool, create an ellipse that encompasses the area at the bottom of the fountain. Be careful that this ellipse doesn't extend beyond the fountain shape, though. Set the fill color to R:85 G:170 B:255 and the stroke to None.

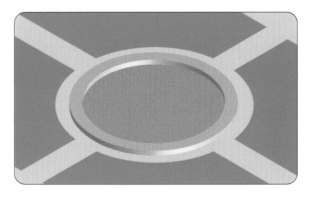

80. Select the WATER sublayer and choose Effect ➤ Artistic ➤ Plastic Wrap. Use the following settings and click OK when you're done. Change the Highlight Strength setting to 6, the Detail setting to 12, and the Smoothness setting to 13.

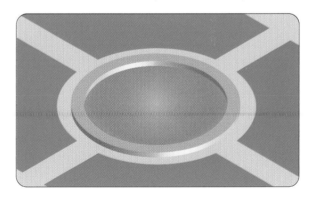

Next, you'll create small sign for the park.

81. Create a new layer named PARK SIGN.

82. Create two rectangles—one for the actual sign and one for the signpost. Use the Add To Shape Area command in the Pathfinder palette to combine these shapes. Fill the new shape with R:231 G:185 B:138 and set the stroke to None. Name this sub-layer SIGN.

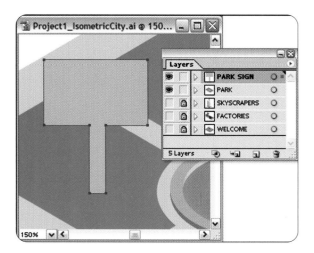

83. Create another rectangle on top of the sign. Fill this shape with white and set the stroke to None as well. Name this sublayer POSTER.

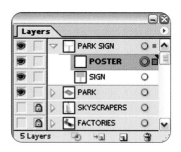

84. Create a text layer above POSTER and type in a name for your park. I used a sans-serif font set at 24 pt.

85. Select both the SIGN and POSTER and text sub-layers. Group them together (*CTRL/CMD+G*).

86. Select the <Group> layer and choose Effect ➤ 3D ➤ Extrude & Bevel. Enter the following settings and click OK:

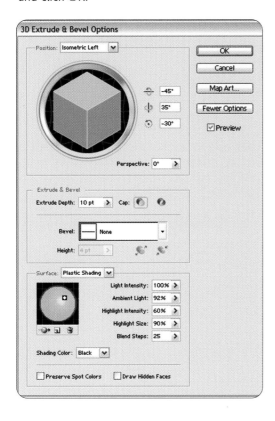

87. You should now have something similar to this reference image.

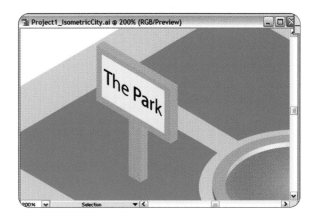

88. To finish up the park, create a new layer named FOLIAGE. Add some of the trees and bushes that you used in the first part of the project.

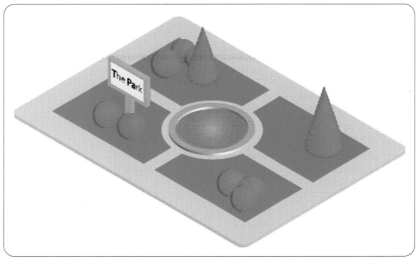

89. Lastly, move all of the park-related layers into one parent layer named PARK.

In the following steps of this project you'll construct another building using the Bevel & Extrude effects. Instead of using Illustrator's preset symbol for this building, you're going to create your own building complete with a walkway, steps, and a sign. This process is very similar to the isometric exercise in Chapter 9. You're going to build walls for your building instead of just using one square shape and extruding it. The reason for this is that if you were to add door and window shapes to the square shape and extrude it, you would end up with something like this:

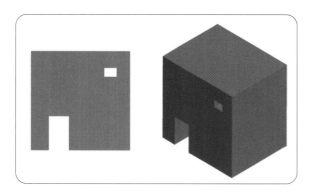

As you can see, this isn't exactly the effect you should be after. This is mainly because you would only be able to add door and window shapes to one side of the object. Another reason is because the door and window shapes on the cube in the above reference image go straight through the object. If you were to rotate this object around in 3D space you would see the same window and door on the opposite side of the building. As a result, you must take the long way.

90. Create a new layer above the others and call it STORE.

91. Using the Rectangle tool, create a square that is 300 pt in width and height. Press *D* to set the fill and stroke colors to their defaults for now. Name this sublayer LEFT WALL.

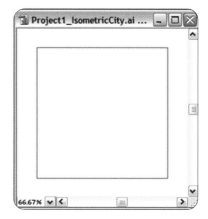

92. Create another rectangle shape for the door. Use the Subtract from Shape Area command in the Pathfinder palette to remove this shape from the LEFT WALL sublayer. This will rename the sublayer to Compound Path. Change the name back to LEFT WALL again.

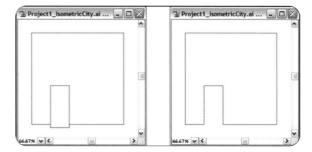

93. Repeat this process and create a RIGHT WALL sublayer. This time use the Rectangle tool to create a window instead of a door.

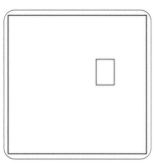

94. Select both the LEFT WALL and RIGHT WALL sublayers. Set their fill colors to R:222 G:255 B:176 and their strokes to None.

95. Select the LEFT WALL sublayer and apply a 3D Extrude & Bevel effect to it. Change the Position setting to Isometric Left, the Extrude Depth setting to 20 pt, and the Ambient Light setting to 85%.

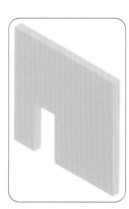

96. Do the same for the RIGHT WALL sublayer by changing the Position setting to Isometric Right, the Extrude Depth setting to 20 pt, and the Ambient Light setting to 85%.

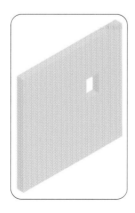

97. Using the Selection tool, drag both walls and match them together so that there's no seam between the two.

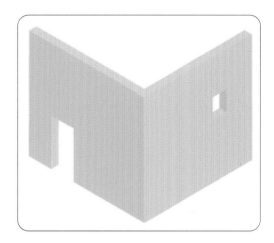

98. Create a new sublayer named ROOF above the LEFT WALL and RIGHT WALL sublayers. Create another rectangle. Set the width to 320 pt and the height to 312 pt. Set the fill color to R:255 G:255 B:62 and the stroke to None.

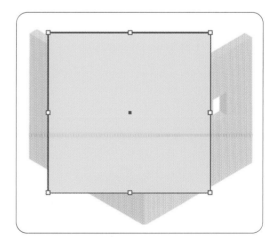

99. Apply a 3D Extrude & Bevel effect to the ROOF sublayer by changing the Position setting to Isometric Top, the Extrude Depth setting to 20 pt, and the Ambient Light setting to 85%.

100. Position this shape above the walls so that it looks similar to this reference image. Note that the overlap is intentional and is meant to enhance the architecture of this building.

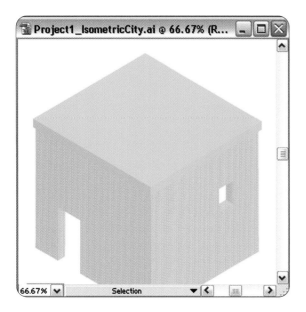

Next, you need to create a window and door. Unfortunately, you cannot use the 3D effects for everything in your isometric town. You must now resort to the Pen tool to customize this building.

101. Create a new sublayer above the RIGHT WALL sublayer and call it WINDOW.

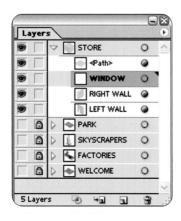

102. Use the Pen tool to draw a shape that's similar to this reference image. The shape should cover the window. Set the fill color to R:138 G:219 B:255 and the stroke to None. Finally, reduce the opacity of this shape to 50%.

103. Repeat this process and create a DOOR sublayer. However, set the fill color of this shape to the same yellow used for the roof and don't reduce the opacity.

104. Create a small circle and fill it with the White, Black Radial gradient located within the Swatches palette.

Finally, you're going to add some steps in front of the door and some shades over the windows.

105. Create a new sublayer called STEPS, and add it above the others located within the parent STORE layer.

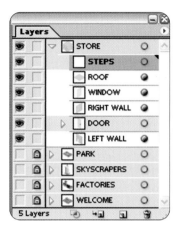

106. Create a circle 80 pt in width and height. Set the fill color to R:224 G:224 B:224 and the stroke to None.

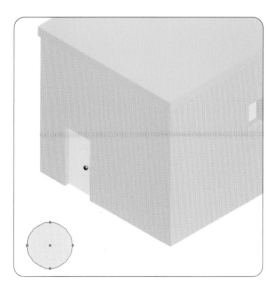

107. Create a rectangle over the top half of the circle and use the Subtract from Shape Area command in the Pathfinder palette to remove half of the circle.

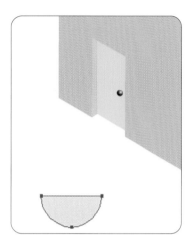

108. Apply a 3D Extrude & Bevel effect to this shape by changing the Position setting to Isometric Top and the Extrude Depth setting to 3. Click OK when you're done.

109. Position the step just at the bottom of the door.

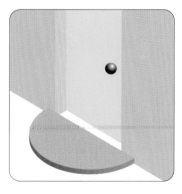

110. Select the half circle shape and choose Object ➤ Path ➤ Offset Path. Enter –3 for the Offset setting. This will produce a smaller half circle shape with no 3D effect applied to it.

111. Apply the same 3D Extrude & Bevel effect as in step 108 and position this shape on top of the larger version as I have in the reference image. You should now be able to see how the steps are being built.

112. Repeat this process one or two more times depending on how high you would like your steps.

Finally, let's create some shades to go over the windows.

113. By using the same process you used in the steps you've just created, you're going to create some awnings to go over the windows. Create a circle 40 pt in width and height. This time, create a rectangle over the bottom half of the circle and use the Subtract from Shape Area command in the Pathfinder palette to remove the bottom half.

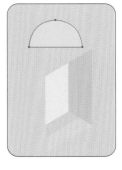

114. Select the half circle shape and apply a 3D Extrude & Bevel effect to it by changing the Position setting to Isometric Right, the Extrude Depth setting to 5 pt, and the Ambient Light setting to 85%. Click OK when you're done.

115. Add a sidewalk layer below the store just as you did with the other city blocks. If you've followed along with the sizes that I've used for the store, then you should make this shape 450 pt in width and height.

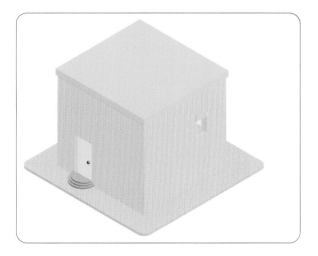

116. A sign above the door always helps, too.

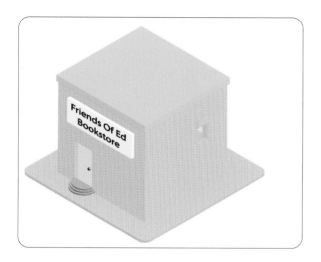

OK, you're pretty much finished with your city. The next step is to combine all of the city blocks into one illustration. If you've been careful about keeping your city blocks within separate layers this should be a simple task of selecting layers and moving them around appropriately. After you've done this, add a layer at the bottom of the entire city and create one last isometric shape filled with white to serve as the road. Once you apply the Extrude & Bevel effect to it, the road will become a darker shade of gray.

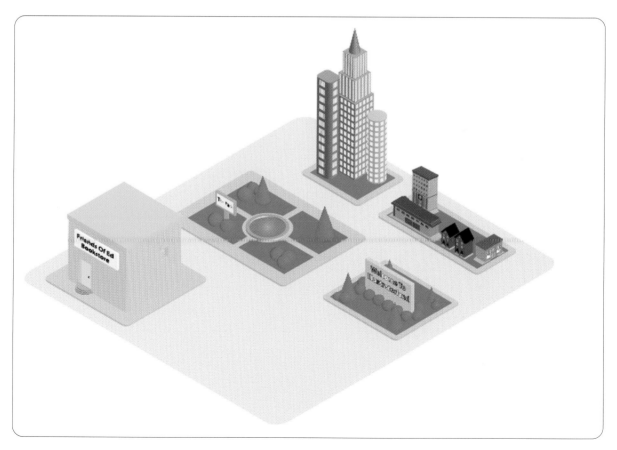

One final effect would be to add artwork to bring the city alive—people, cars, trucks, and so on. This process is very similar to the other effects used in this project. Illustrator CS even ships with a few symbols and shapes that can easily be extruded or you can create your own flat objects to extrude. I'll cover a simple way to add some cars in the following steps.

117. Choose Window ➤ Brush Libraries ➤ Transportation to display the Transportation Brush palette. Note the Car brush.

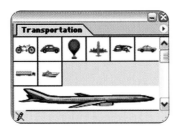

118. Create a new layer above all other layers named AUTOMOBILES. Drag this brush on to the Artboard and size it according to your city streets.

119. Select the car object and choose Effect ➤ 3D ➤ Extrude & Bevel. Enter the followings settings and click OK.

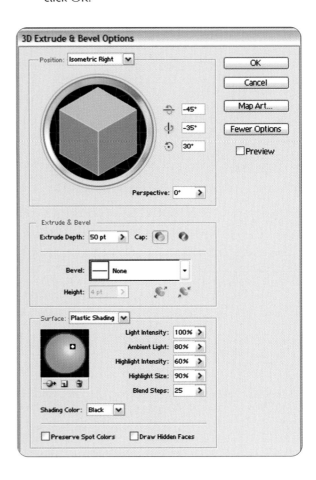

120. Position the car on the city street wherever you feel it fits.

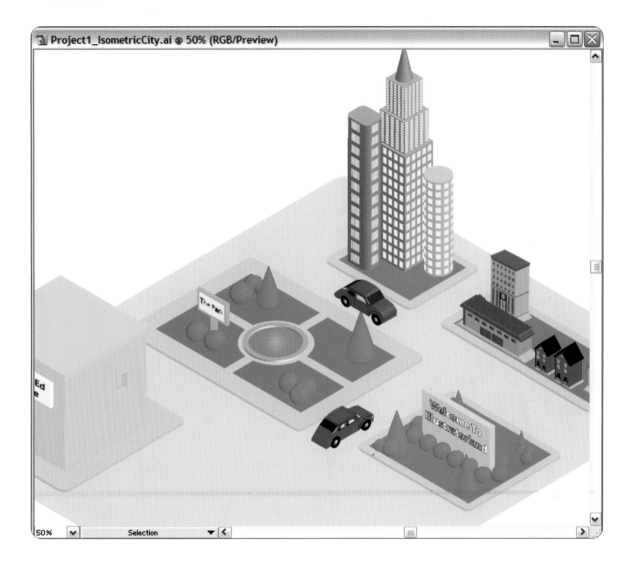

Summary

I hope you've had as much fun as I've had working through this project. This is one of my favorite techniques in illustration and the possibilities for using it are endless. I urge you to stop by the forums at www.friendsofed.com/forums and post your creations. I'd love to see what you come up with.

Project 2

VECTORIZING A PHOTO

From photo to vector

Vectorizing photographs has become an extremely popular technique. In this project you'll learn how to use an ordinary photograph as a reference image and you'll convert it to a stylized vector illustration. The key to this project is to realize it isn't a photorealistic technique—meaning that you aren't trying to perfectly re-create the photograph so that someone cannot see the difference between the illustration and the actual photo. Instead, this process uses only key details from the original photograph and eliminates those details that aren't. These details allow the subject in the photograph to remain distinguishable, but they leave many characteristics to the viewer's imagination. So follow along as I re-create a photograph that was kindly provided by photographic illustrator Kevin Ames. Kevin's work is well known and his gallery is definitely worth viewing (www.AmesPhoto.com).

1. First, find a photograph that's suitable for vectorizing. I've included one with the source files for this chapter. If you decide to pick your own, keep a few things in mind:

   - Your photograph can never be of too high a quality. The higher the resolution, the easier it will be for you to work with.

   - Try to be sure your photograph has a decent amount of detail—mainly in the eye, nose, and lips areas. The more detail you have to work with the better the decisions you can make about what to keep and what to discard.

   - Watch out for hair. If you choose a photograph with hair blowing in the wind, be prepared to spend a lot of time re-creating it.

2. Import the reference photograph into Illustrator as a template by selecting File ➤ Place. (Refer to Chapter 1 for a detailed exercise on how to accomplish this.)

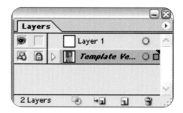

Now that your reference photo is in place, it's time to begin tracing. In the first steps you'll define the major shapes and colors within the illustration. After that, it's much easier to add details. So let's begin with the face, body, hair, and any clothes that the person in the reference photo may be wearing.

3. First, you'll start with any skin that exists in the photo. It's helpful to use multiple paths to complete this process. However, even though the face and the neck may be distinctly different body parts, they are all skin as far as the illustration is concerned and will only have one shape created for them. For instance, when viewing this reference photo I can see that I'll need to create one shape for the right arm, and one for the face and neck.

4. Create a new layer named ARM and trace the outline of the woman's arm with the Pen tool. As you're tracing, you may be tempted to follow the jagged, pixelated outlines of the photo if you're zoomed in. Try to resist this urge and only approximate the outline of the object you're tracing. Also, you may want to set the fill to None and the stroke to black so that you can see the path. When you're finished, fill this shape with the following settings: R:250 G:202 B:159.

Illustrator does offer autotracing tools that may be helpful in some circumstances. However, these tools have a few key drawbacks. First, they tend to create paths with too many anchor points. They also don't leave you with much control when creating paths. In the end, you may spend just as much time adjusting the autotraced path as you would have spent had you used the Pen tool initially.

5. Next, create another layer named HEAD. Repeat the tracing process but be sure to include the neck and upper chest area as well. However, there's no need to worry about the detail around the hair. You're going to create another layer on top of the HEAD layer for the hair. For now, just extend your path far enough into the hairline so you won't have to manipulate it later when you add hair. Fill this shape with R:250 G:202 B:159.

297

6. Create another layer named SHIRT above the others. Use the Pen tool to trace the outline of the shirt. Fill this shape with R:0 G:170 B:255.

> *When creating the* SHIRT *layer, you'll need to be more precise with the lines you draw since the shirt overlaps the skin layers. Keep this in mind as you create this type of illustration. You'll tend to have more flexibility when drawing objects that are underneath other objects. It's the objects that overlap other objects that usually require more detail.*

Next, you need to work on the hair. This part is slightly more difficult than the others. The hair is a very important part of the illustration. If it isn't traced with enough detail, the overall effect of the entire illustration can be diminished. However, this isn't to say you should spend three hours tracing every stray piece of hair. Just try to create the major details.

7. Create a new layer above the others named HAIR.

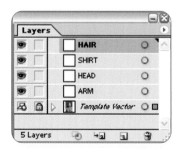

8. Trace the outline of the hair using the Pen tool. Fill this shape with R:18 G:16 B:14 and set the stroke to None.

Now that you have the basic outline of the figure, let's add some of the facial details. The eyes are the most difficult part and I usually like to get them out of the way first, so let's start there.

9. Create a new layer named RIGHT EYE below the SHIRT layer but above the HEAD layer. Zoom in on one of the eyes. Trace the actual shape of the eye. Fill this with black and set the stroke to None. Name the sublayer EYE OUTLINE. Note that you'll need to hide the HEAD layer in order to see the eye.

As always, working in separate layers is very important but it's especially so in this project. Be sure to create new layers for each part of this illustration and be aware of what layer you're working on. This will make life much easier later in the illustration when you may need to go back and fix certain areas or move objects around.

10. Create another shape for the white area of the eye. Don't worry if you go outside of the previous black shape. You'll take care of that with a Pathfinder command. Name this sublayer EYEBALL.

As mentioned in the previous step, the white eyeball shape most likely extends beyond the actual outline of the eye. As you're creating shapes within this illustration, you'll often need to do this. Otherwise, you would spend hours trying to get an overlapping path to match exactly with the one below it. Fortunately, you have the Pathfinder palette and can easily remove the excess area.

11. Create a duplicate of the EYE OUTLINE sublayer. Select the duplicate and the EYEBALL shape. Hold down the *ALT/OPTION* key and click the Intersect Shape Area button in the Pathfinder palette. This will remove the areas of the white eyeball shape that extend beyond the overall black eye shape.

Next you'll create the iris (the colored part of the eye) and the pupil (the black part within the iris).

12. Create a black circle with the Ellipse tool. Again, don't worry if it extends beyond the shape of the eye.

13. Repeat step 6 to remove the area of the circle that extends beyond the white eyeball shape. This time, you'll have to duplicate the eyeball shape, select the duplicate and the black circle, and use the Pathfinder palette's Intersect command to remove the excess area.

14. Create a smaller circle on top of the black one. Name this sublayer IRIS. Fill this shape with the following settings: R:109 G:75 B:44. Repeat the process to remove the area of this shape that extends beyond the eyeball shape.

15. Create a small black circle on top of the iris. Name this sublayer PUPIL. You shouldn't need to perform any Pathfinder commands on this shape.

16. Finally, create a small white circle on top of the pupil. Name this sublayer HIGHLIGHT.

17. Use the Pen tool to create the eyebrow. Fill this shape with black.

18. Next, create a thin black crescent shape just over the eye but below the eyebrow.

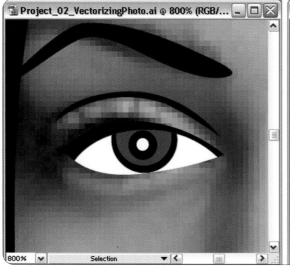

At this point, the eye is looking pretty good. However, there are some shadows around it that you'll need to create in order to make the eyes look more realistic.

19. First, create a new sublayer below EYE OUTLINE and call it EYE SHADOWS.

20. Use the Pen tool to trace the two shadows around the eye. One is an overall shadow around the entire eye and the other is a small shadow just below the eyeball. Fill these shapes with the following settings: R:222 G:171 B:127.

Now for the other eye. If you're lucky, your subject will be looking straight at you and you can just duplicate the eye layer and move it over to the other side of the face.

21. Drag the RIGHT EYE layer over the Create New Layer button at the bottom of the Layers palette to create a duplicate. Name the new layer LEFT EYE.

22. Click the LEFT EYE layer's meatball to select the entire LEFT EYE layer. Select Object ➤ Transform ➤ Reflect. Select the Vertical radio button and click OK. Don't deselect yet.

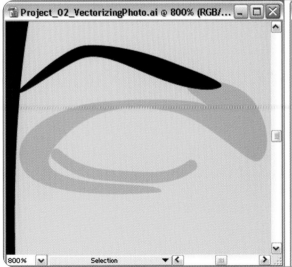

23. Drag the LEFT EYE layer over to the other side of the face.

If you aren't so lucky, you'll have to re-create another eye for the other side of the face. However, the same steps apply. Just be sure to create the eye on a new layer and name your layers accordingly.

Next, let's move on to the lips.

24. Create a new layer named LIPS. This layer can be above or below the eye layers but it must be above the HEAD layer.

25. Using the Pen tool, trace the general outline of the lips.

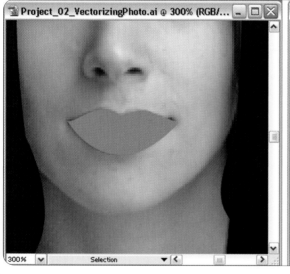

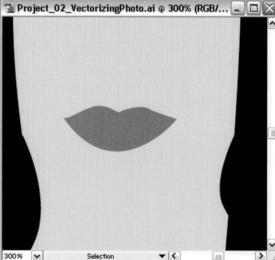

26. Now create another shape that encompasses the inner area of the lips where the teeth are.

27. Select both shapes and create a compound path from them by choosing Object ➤ Compound Path ➤ Make (*CTRL/CMD+8*). Name the resulting sub-layer LIPS and fill this shape with the following settings: R:192 G:101 B:84.

28. Create a sublayer below LIPS that contains a white shape for the teeth. In this example, I used the Rectangle tool. There's no need for any detail at this point as the teeth barely show through the lips.

Next, you need to create the nose. Many noses are alike. As you create this type of illustration you may notice that you can reuse certain features from other illustrations. The nose tends to be one of the features that I reuse often. You can create a few simple shapes that give the impression of a nose being in place but you won't need to spend a great deal of time on the detail.

29. Zoom in to see the eyes and the lips better.

30. Create a small crescent shape with the Pen tool inside one of the eyes. Fill this shape with the following settings: R:201 G:175 B:150.

31. Use the Reflect command (Object ➤ Transform ➤ Reflect) just as you did with the eye to create a duplicate of this shape for the other side of the nose.

33. Now create two small shapes with the Pen tool for the nostrils. Again, you don't want to draw too much attention to this area so don't create large shapes. Fill these shapes with the following settings: R:70 G:31 B:32.

32. Next, create a small shape at the bottom. If you zoom in on the original photograph, you can trace the bottom of the nose to create this shape. Fill this with R:156 G:107 B:87.

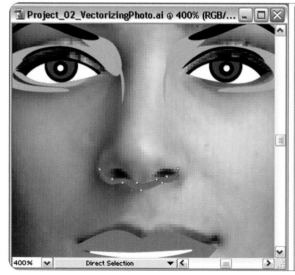

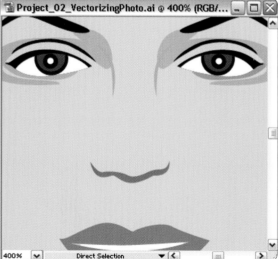

34. Finally, add a small oval shaped highlight using the Ellipse tool. Fill this shape with R:252 G:220 B:187.

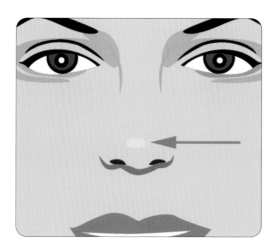

OK, if you've followed along so far your illustration should look similar to this reference image.

So far it looks nice but it's lacking key highlights and details that will really bring it alive.

35. First, let's start with the face. One thing you'll notice is that there is no way to tell where the bottom of the face (chin area) ends and the neck begins. This is simple to fix.

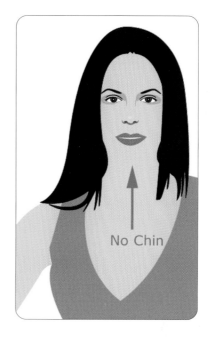

36. Within the HEAD layer, use the Pen tool to create a shape similar to this reference image. This shape should be on top of the other sublayers in HEAD. Fill this shape with R:201 G:175 B:150.

37. Duplicate the shape and fill it with R:214 G:162 B:104. Use the Selection tool or down arrow key to move the duplicate down.

38. Still within the HEAD layer, create two long ovals on each side of the face. Most of the two oval shapes should be hidden by the hair with just a small amount showing. Fill these shapes with R: 222 G:171 B:127.

Next, you're going to leave the hair alone for now and add some shadows and highlights on the skin. However, you'll return to it later.

39. Within the ARM layer, draw a path using the Pen tool in a shadow area that needs a slightly darker skin tone than the rest of the body. Fill this path with R:192 G:155 B:123 and be sure the stroke is set to None. Again, don't worry if this path extends beyond the shape of the body. You can use the Pathfinder palette to subtract this area.

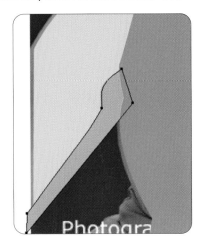

Next, use a technique similar to the one used for the eyes to remove the portion of that path that extends beyond the shape of the original arm.

40. Duplicate the sublayer containing the arms. Select the duplicate ARM sublayer as well as the shadow shape that you just created in step 39. Hold down the *ALT/OPTION* key and click the Intersect Shape Area button in the Pathfinder palette.

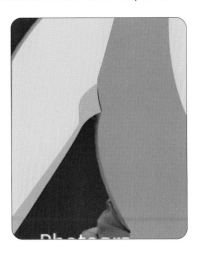

41. Repeat this process and add a highlight to the outside area of the arm. Fill this shape with R:252 G:220 B:187.

At this point, you may be left wondering "How do I determine what areas should be shadows and highlights?" For some of you, this may come easy and you can spot them right away. See reference image opposite for an example of what you may see when looking for shadows and highlights.

However, some of you may not be able to tell so quickly. If you're one of those people or if you would just like to speed along the process of creating the various tones within an illustration, follow the next few steps. However, please note that this technique requires the use of a paint program such as Adobe Photoshop. If you don't have access to this program (or another like it), just viewing the steps below may help you anyway.

42. Open your reference photo in Photoshop. Be sure you're opening the same size photo as the one you're working with in Illustrator.

43. Remove all of the color from your reference photo by choosing Image ➤ Adjustments ➤ Desaturate. If a window pops up asking you to delete all of the color data simply click OK.

44. Next, choose Image ➤ Adjustments ➤ Posterize. Enter 6 in the levels text box and click OK.

45. You should now have something similar to this reference image.

As you can see, you have reduced the image to only six colors. Now you can easily see where some highlights and shadows may be formed. If you don't have Photoshop, you can download a free trial at www.adobe.com to follow along with this project if you choose. Alternatively, if you have a good eye, you can try to envision the highlights and shadows and create them yourself. Here is a sample of how you would proceed.

Depending on your ability and desire to be detailed, you can either refer back to this image to create your shadows and highlights without tracing or you can import this photo into Illustrator and place it above your original reference template. Either way, follow the next few steps to create the shadow and highlights.

46. Open the HEAD layer. Create a new path in the chest area with the Pen tool based on the image modified in Photoshop. This path will serve as a highlight. Fill it with the following settings: R:252 G:220 B:187.

This shape doesn't have to be perfect. Just following the general shapes and locations of the highlights and shadows will do fine. There's no need to spend too much time tracing the exact shape.

47. Repeat the process of creating the highlights and shadows throughout the chest area. I have filled the shadows with R:201 G:175 B:150. Also, since the SHIRT and HAIR layers are above the HEAD layer there is no need to worry about paths extending beyond the boundaries of the chest area.

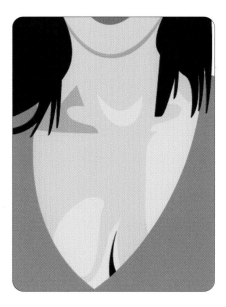

48. The folds on the shirt, which are just highlights and shadows, are created in the same way.

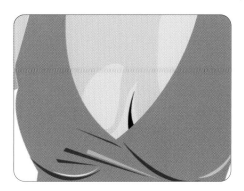

Finally, all that remains is the hair. In order to make the hair appear more realistic, you need to add some highlights to it.

49. Open the HAIR layer. Create new sublayers above the basic hair shape to serve as highlights. Fill these shapes with R:141 G:103 B:27. Be sure to try to conform to the general curve of the hair when you create the highlights. If you take some time during this step, it will really pay off in the end.

At last! The final illustration.

Summary

Hopefully, you now realize just how powerful this technique is. While it may seem simple, vectorizing photographs can be a difficult task to master. It requires a strong sense of composition. You need to be able to look at a photograph and determine which details are necessary to keep and which can be discarded in the transition from photo to vector. Even though you may trace much of your work, it really is an art form. Also, keep in mind that this effect isn't limited to photographs of people. Photographs of scenery, buildings, cars, and just about any other objects you can think of are good candidates. So, in the spirit of what I've said many times throughout this book, get creative. Look at the world around you. Take pictures with your camera and load them into Illustrator. Vectorize certain objects from one photograph and merge them with objects from other photographs. The sky's the limit, so enjoy and have fun.

Issue:

Project 3

RETRO EFFECTS

Retro is in

Retro is in! Just look around you. Styles that were popular in the mid to late twentieth century are now popular again. For this project, you're going to take part in a small role-playing game. You need to create a magazine cover for *Illustrator* magazine. The challenge: This cover must convey the theme of the proposed issue, entitled "A Tour Through the Decades." Conveniently enough, I'm your manager for this project and I've decided that I'd like to explore the retro styles that were popular a few decades ago and are now popular again.

OK, enough role-playing. Hopefully you get the picture. Throughout this chapter, you'll deconstruct several popular styles and techniques used in creating retro illustrations.

1. First, open `Project_03_MagazineCoverStart.ai`. This file contains the base of the project. The magazine editor has already placed key elements such as the title and copy text that explains what's in this issue. You'll notice a layer named COPY and several hidden sublayers within it. That's fine, you'll come back to them later.

2. Next, you'll notice a few other hidden layers named GROOVY GUY1, GROOVY GUY2, and GROOVY GUY3.

I've already created the focus shapes for this illustration to save you some time. However, this is a simple process of drawing a silhouette shape of a person. If you can't draw one, then trace one. Inspiration for this is available all over the Web. A simple Google search for "disco" will yield plenty of results. However, keep in mind that what you see may be copyrighted work. Be sure to only use your findings as a reference to help you tune your skills.

3. Unhide the three GROOVY GUY layers so you can see where they are positioned in the illustration. However, be sure to leave them locked at this point.

A key task in any illustration is to create a color palette. It's especially important in this illustration as not all colors work for retro-style illustrations. I've already created a color palette for you to use in this project. Again, the Web, old books, and magazines are a wonderful resource for this task.

4. Select Window ➤ Swatches to display the Swatches palette.

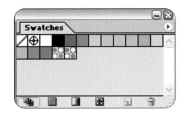

5. Note the colors within this palette. If you briefly hover over a swatch you'll notice that each has a name (GREEN1, GREEN2, and so on). This is something new for this project. Since you'll be using a fixed palette of colors and referring to them often this seemed like the easiest way. Thus, I'll refer to colors by their name throughout this project to make it easier to follow along.

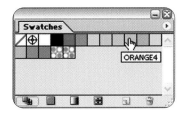

The next step is to create background shapes to add some color to the illustration. Retro style shapes often aren't symmetrical. Instead of perfect squares or rectangles, you'll notice many times that the shapes used are slightly skewed.

6. Create a new layer above BACKGROUND named SHAPES.

7. Using the Pen tool, create a shape similar to this reference image. Fill this shape with the ORANGE5 color in the Swatches palette.

8. Next, create another shape on top of the shape just created. Fill this shape with the ORANGE2 color.

9. Open the Transparency palette and change the Blend mode to Multiply. This will allow you to view part of the bottom rectangle through the top rectangle.

10. Next, create a few circles throughout the illustration. I've created four. From left to right I've filled these circles with ORANGE5, RED2, YELLOW1, and GREEN1.

11. Unlock and expand the COPY layer so you can view the sublayers within. As mentioned previously, several sublayers are hidden. Go ahead and unhide all sublayers within COPY at this time.

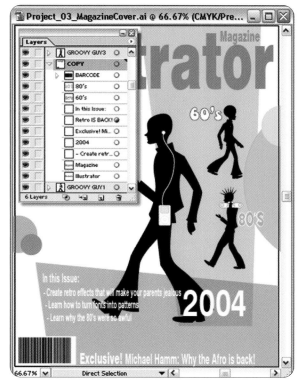

Great, now the cover is beginning to take on some life. Next, let's add more text.

12. Using the Text tool, type the words Retro IS BACK! just under the 2004 text. I set the font to Keep On Truckin, which was used in past exercises (download at www.fontdiner.com).

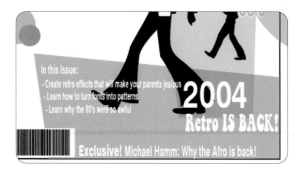

13. Select the text and choose Object ➤ Warp ➤ Arc. Enter 17 for the Bend setting. Check the Horizontal radio button and enter 38% in the Horizontal check box. Click OK.

The next group of steps will walk you through creating various retro-style shapes. Use the familar resources as I mentioned earlier when you search for inspiration for this task (for example, the Web and old magazines).

14. First, create a new layer named RINGS above all three GROOVY GUY layers.

15. Select the Ellipse tool and click the Artboard. Enter 30 pt for the Width setting and 65 pt for the Height setting. Set the fill color of this oval to None and the stroke to GREEN3. Also, set the stroke Width setting to 4 pt.

16. With the oval selected, choose Effect ➤ Distort & Transform ➤ Transform. Enter the following settings and click OK.

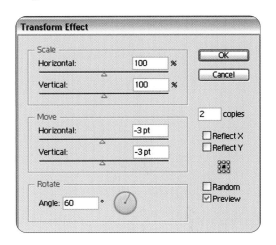

17. To complete this shape, add a few randomly placed circles along the outlines of the ovals.

Next, you'll create another popular retro shape.

18. Create a new layer named STAR. Select the Line Segment tool. Click the Artboard and enter 80 pt for the Length setting and 80 degrees for the Angle setting. Click OK.

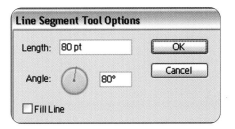

19. Set the fill color of this line to None and the stroke to RED3. Also, set the stroke Width setting to 4 pt.

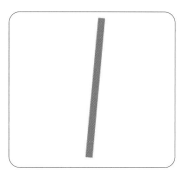

20. Create two more lines in the same way.

21. Select the Ellipse tool and create a circle 20 pt in width and height. Position this circle at the end of one of the lines.

22. Duplicate the circle by selecting it and holding down the *ALT/OPTION* key. Then drag it to the end of another line.

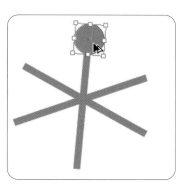

After you hold down the ALT/OPTION key and position your cursor over the circle, you should see a double arrow cursor. This lets you know that the circle will indeed be duplicated if you drag.

23. Repeat this process so a circle is placed at the end of each line.

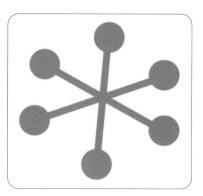

Next, retro illustrations always seem to use some sort of twinkling star, so let's make one.

24. Create a new layer named STAR 2. Create an oval 20 pt in width and 60 pt in height. Fill this oval with the ORANGE5 color.

25. Select the oval shape and choose Effect ➤ Distort & Transform ➤ Pucker & Bloat. Enter –80 in the text box and click OK.

26. Create a small square approximately 25 pt in width and height. Apply a Pucker & Bloat effect to it with a setting of –80 as well.

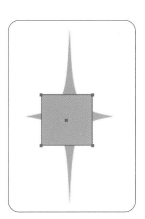

Finally, who can forget the flower shapes that seemed all too popular?

27. Create a new layer named FLOWER.

28. Select the Polygon tool. Click the Artboard and enter 35 pt for the Radius setting and set the number of sides to 6. Click OK. Fill this shape with ORANGE3.

29. Select the Polygon and apply the Pucker & Bloat effect to it. This time set the Percent setting to 90%. Click OK. Instant flower!

30. Next, simply create a small circle in the center of the flower. Fill this circle with YELLOW2.

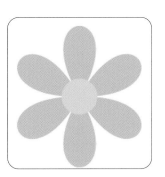

31. Now that all of your shapes are complete, duplicate and spread them around the magazine cover.
Feel free to change the colors, shapes, and sizes of
any of them as well.

In this last part of this project, you'll be introduced to
one of my favorite retro fonts: '60s Chic. This font is free
and can be downloaded at http://www.bvfonts.com.
However, please be sure to abide by the owner's
licensing agreement.

32. Once installed, select the 60's Chic font. Type the letter S. Use a font size of about 300 pt. Set the fill color to ORANGE2 and the stroke to None.

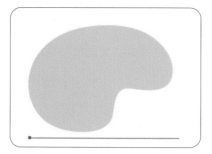

33. Select the S and choose Type ➤ Create Outlines (*CTRL/CMD+SHIFT+O*).

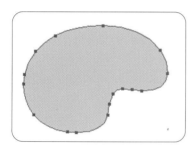

34. Do the same for the letter T but fill this shape with RED2. Set this font size to around 320 pt and position this shape just above the S shape that you created in the previous step.

35. Duplicate the shape that was once an S. Fill the top shape with an orange to white gradient. Do not deselect it yet though.

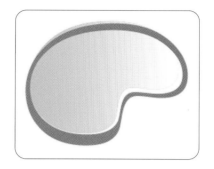

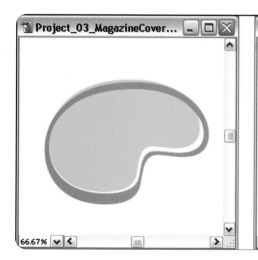

36. Choose Effect ➤ Pixelate ➤ Color Halftone. Enter the following settings:

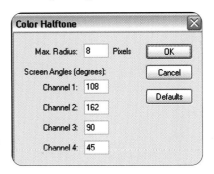

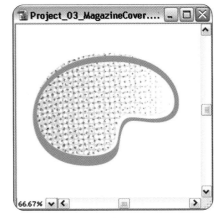

37. Now use the Transparency palette to reduce the opacity of this shape to 40%. You should have something similar to this reference image.

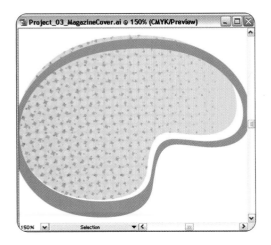

38. Next, type the letter N using the '60s Chic font. Set the font size to 24 pt. Set the fill to ORANGE5 and the stroke to None. Reduce this text to outlines (*CTRL/CMD+SHIFT+O*) just as you did in the previous steps.

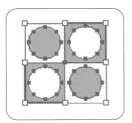

39. Select what used to be the N. Drag this shape over to the Swatches palette to define it as a pattern. Name it RETRO CIRCLES.

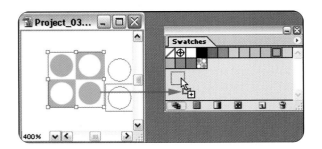

40. Unlock and expand the GROOVY GUY1 layer so that you can view the sublayers within.

41. Select the silhouette's SHIRT sublayer. Change the fill from black to the newly defined RETRO CIRCLES pattern by clicking the swatch in the Swatches palette.

Finally, all that remains is to add text that promotes the theme of this issue of the magazine.

42. Once again, I used Keep On Truckin as the font of choice to create two text objects. One for the word "Illustrator" (set at 60 pt) and one for the remaining words (set at 48 pt). For the text object, use the Free Transform tool (*E*) to rotate it slightly.

43. Set the stroke for this text using the multistroked text effect that was previously discussed in Chapter 2.

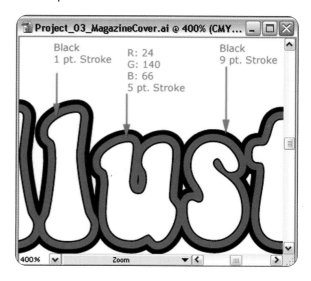

44. Finally, apply another Arc warp effect to the type and position it in place.

Whew! If you've followed along, your magazine cover should now be complete.

You could always modify the colors as well to produce
an entirely difference look.

Summary

Wow! You made it. I hope you've had as much fun with the techniques and effects in this book as I've had creating them. Illustrator is a wonderful tool and its popularity seems to be growing with each new version. friends of ED and I have gone to great lengths to bring you some of the most wanted Illustrator techniques and effects. However, I encourage you to go beyond this book. Use it as a resource and a stepping stone toward creating your own style of illustration. If I can give you any advice at this point it would be to practice. Deconstruct every illustration you can get your hands on. Learn from others' work. Don't just look at what they've done and how they've done it. Instead, ask yourself why a certain illustration looks good or bad. Then take what you've learned in this book and use it. I cannot emphasize this enough. It isn't adequate to merely learn the techniques. You must practice using those techniques within your own illustrations.

Also, don't forget to find and use the vast resources available to you. My website (www.ExtremeIllustrator.com) as well as the technical editor's, Michael Hamm (www.Ergodraw.com), are two great resources. Plus, friends of ED is excellent when it comes to support. Visit their forums at www.friendsofed.com/forums. I'll be checking the forum often to answer any questions that you may have.

Finally, have fun. Often you can get caught up in the vast amount of information, software versions, and tools at your fingertips. Adobe Illustrator CS is meant to make your life as an illustrator easier. Remember that and enjoy it. Good luck!

Index